JUSTICE LEAGUE

A Midsummer's Nightmare

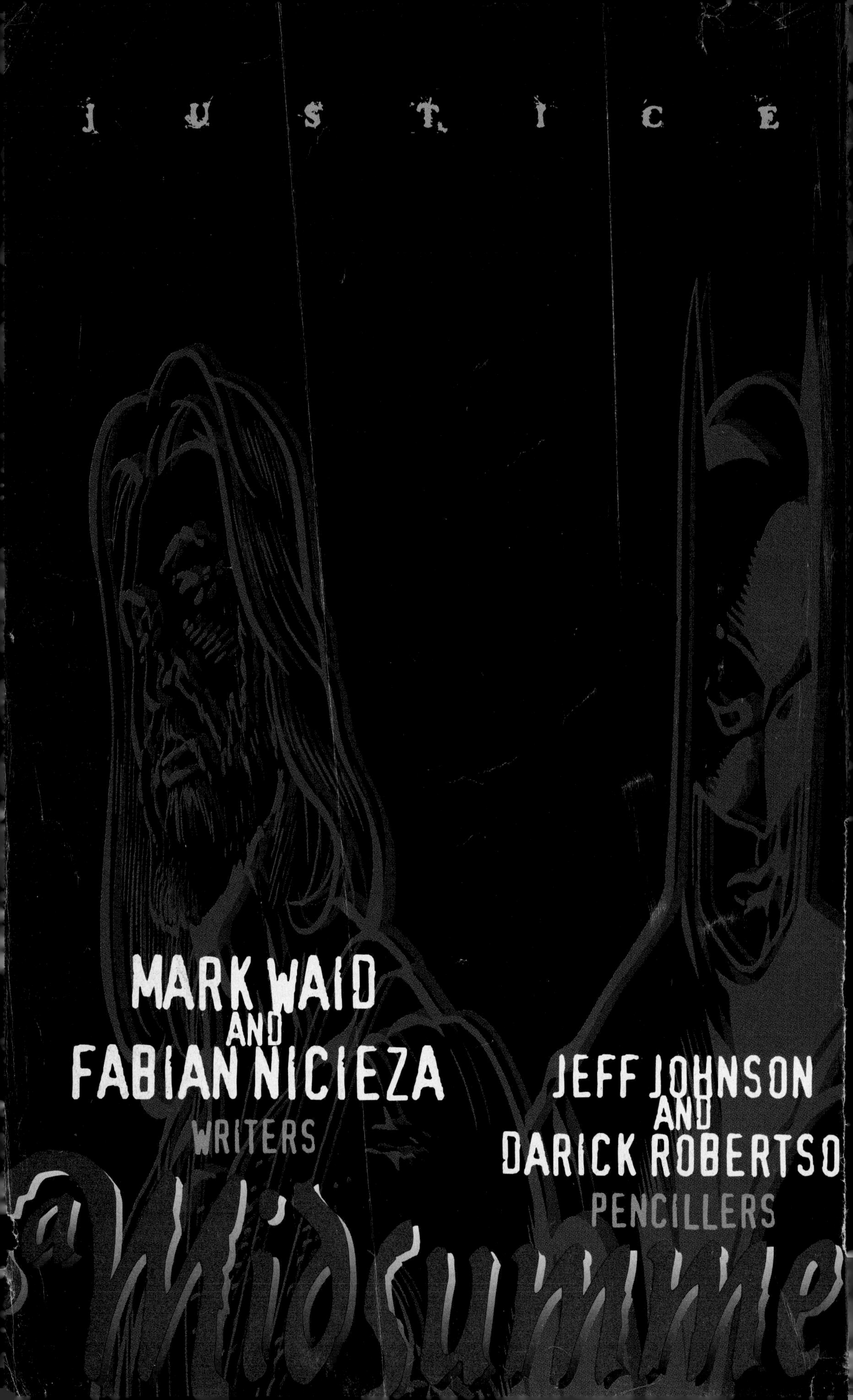
JUSTICE
MARK WAID
AND
FABIAN NICIEZA
WRITERS
JEFF JOHNSON
AND
DARICK ROBERTSO
PENCILLERS

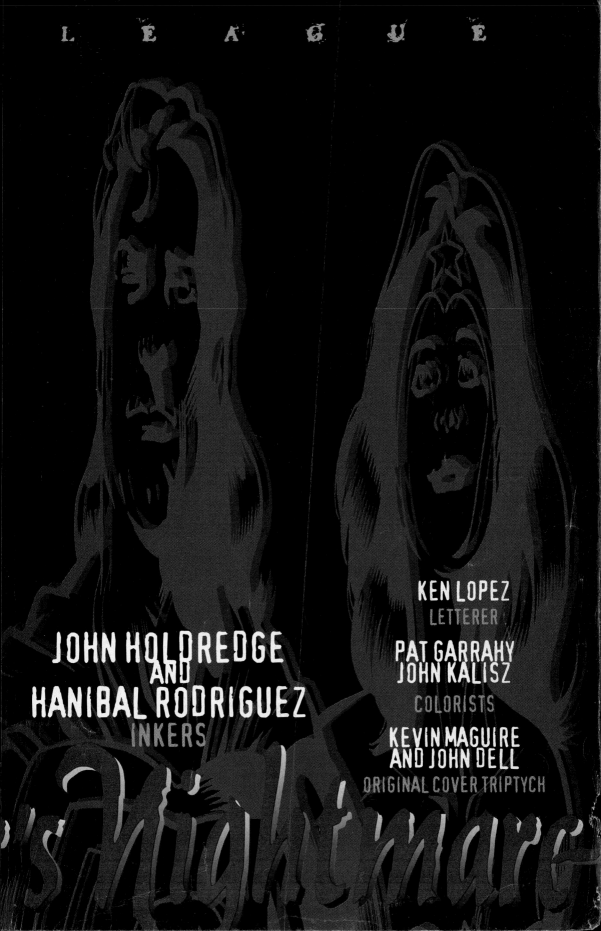

LEAGUE

JOHN HOLDREDGE
AND
HANIBAL RODRIGUEZ
INKERS

KEN LOPEZ
LETTERER

PAT GARRAHY
JOHN KALISZ
COLORISTS

KEVIN MAGUIRE
AND JOHN DELL
ORIGINAL COVER TRIPTYCH

JUSTICE LEAGUE: A MIDSUMMER'S NIGHTMARE
Published by DC Comics. Cover, introduction and
compilation copyright © 1996 DC Comics.
All Rights Reserved.

Originally published in single magazine form as
JUSTICE LEAGUE: A MIDSUMMER'S
NIGHTMARE 1-3. Copyright © 1996 DC Comics.
All Rights Reserved. All characters, their
distinctive likenesses and related indicia
featured in this publication are
trademarks of DC Comics.
The stories, characters, and incidents featured in this
publication are entirely fictional.

DC Comics, 1700 Broadway,
New York, NY 10019
A division of Warner Bros. - A Time Warner
Entertainment Company
Printed in Canada. Third Printing.
ISBN: 1-56389-338-X
Cover illustration by Kevin Maguire
and John Dell.
Cover color art by Pat Garrahy
Cover color separations by Digital Chameleon

intro

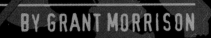

BY GRANT MORRISON

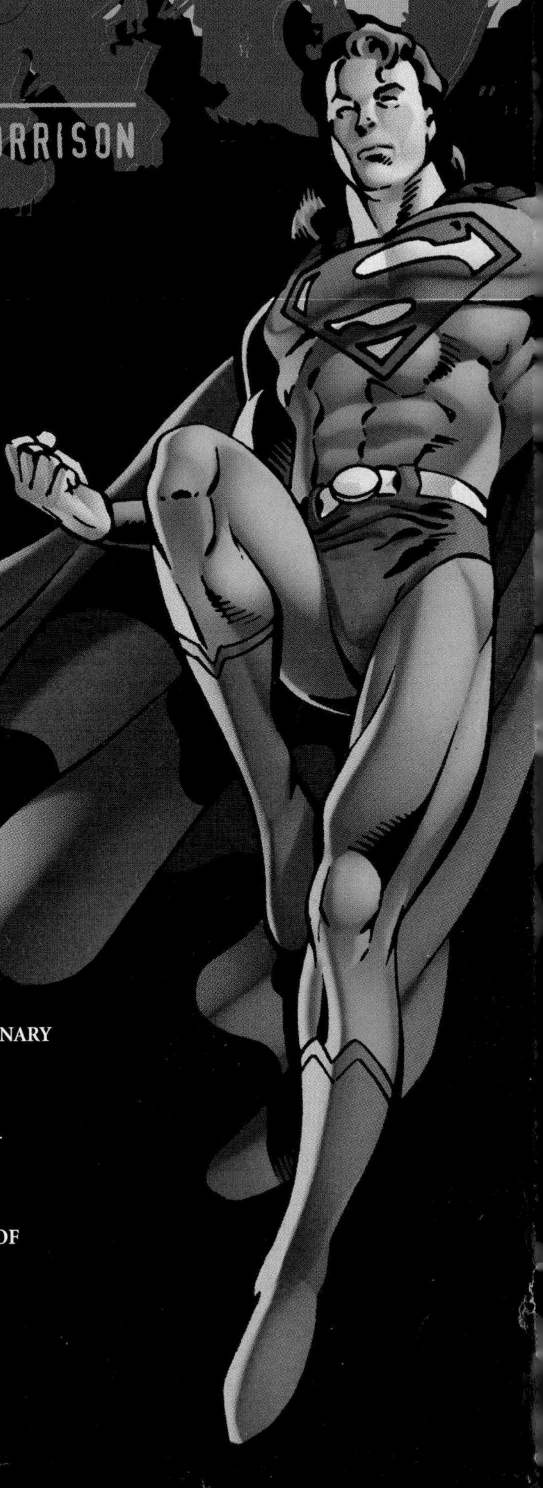

HEN FUTURE HISTORIES OF THE SUPER-HERO GENRE ARE WRITTEN, I HAVE A FEELING THAT 1996 WILL BE SEEN AS A WATERSHED YEAR. FORTY YEARS PREVIOUSLY, IN THE PAGES OF DC'S SHOWCASE TITLE, A REVAMPED VERSION OF THE GOLDEN AGE FLASH CHARACTER INAUGURATED WHAT CAME TO BE KNOWN AS THE SILVER AGE OF COMICS AND FIRED A NEW APPETITE FOR THE OUTLANDISH EXPLOITS OF SCIENCE-FICTION SUPERMEN WITH EXTRAORDINARY ABILITIES. THE ORIGINAL JUSTICE LEAGUE OF AMERICA IN 1960 GREW OUT OF THAT FORWARD-LOOKING, INSPIRATIONAL SENSIBILITY AND PAVED THE WAY FOR A VERITABLE *MARDI GRAS* OF COLORFUL COSTUMES, BIZARRE POWERS AND BREATHTAKINGLY IMAGINATIVE ADVENTURES.

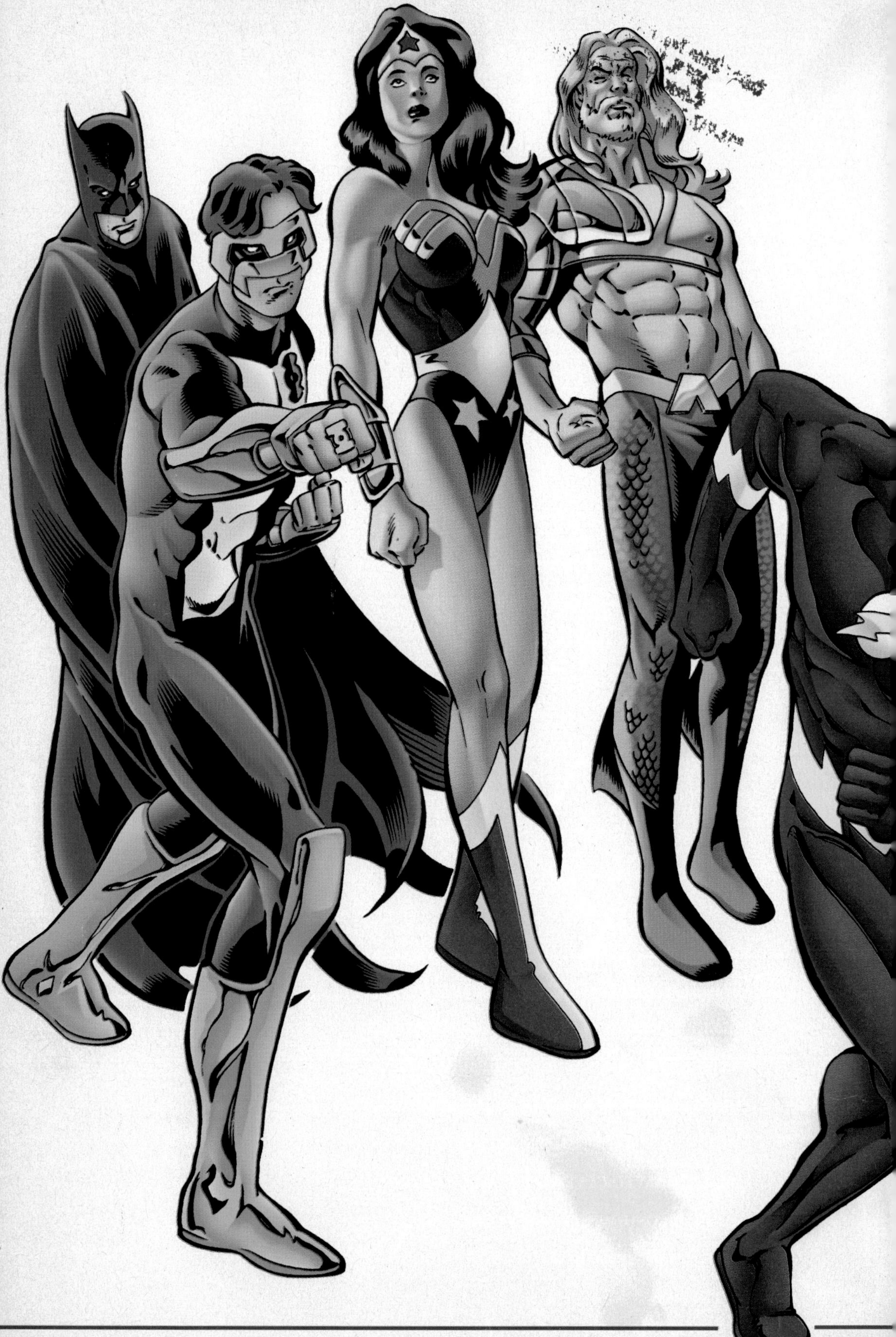

The Silver Age was, of course, superseded in its turn by what, in hindsight, can only be called the "Dark Age" of super-heroes, when optimism couldn't cut the mustard and costumed characters were unmasked as creatures with flaws and problems just like the rest of us. It was good while it lasted and yielded at least two authentic masterpieces in Miller's DARK KNIGHT RETURNS and Moore and Gibbons's WATCHMEN, but what began as an era of bold experimentation and adult themes soon grew tired and repetitive, as the decade from 1986 became characterized by a relentless tide of unsmiling, uptight mental cases in trench coats. The new "heroes" were deranged psychos, mother-fixated perverts and cold-eye killers, barely distinguishable from the villains they so callously dispatched with a dazzling array of brutal weaponry. There was a growing feeling among readers and creators alike that something had been lost and, given the speed at which culture and technology is currently accelerating, it was hardly surprising that the Dark Age, too, would find itself outmoded with ruthless rapidity. Now it's 1996 and here we stand, on the cusp of the next transforma-tion, the next explosion.

History lessons aside, however, what I'm really here to say, I suppose, is that you now hold in your hands what will, I'm sure, come to be seen as one of the seminal texts of the current super-hero renaissance. This year has seen the publication of a number of projects that share a common desire to restore some sense of nobility and grandeur to the super-hero concept and I, for one, am relieved and gratified to see the circle finally turn away from the darkness and into the light.

Almost single-handedly, über-scribe Mark Waid—in books like FLASH, IMPULSE and *Captain America*—has rescued the super-heroes finally from the Ghetto of Grim 'n' Gritty. His recent best-selling collaboration with Alex Ross in KINGDOM COME firmly established the new *zeitgeist* with epic panache. Now, in JUSTICE LEAGUE: A MIDSUMMER'S NIGHTMARE, he and Fabian Nicieza—undoubtedly one of the best and most thoughtful writers to have emerged from Marvel Comics in recent years—recreate the Justice League as a pantheon of iconic figures for the twenty-first century. The World's Greatest Super-Heroes.

As in KINGDOM COME, there's a fresh and powerful sense of renewed vigor and positivity here. Waid and Nicieza—admirably aided by Jeff Johnson, Darick Robertson, Jon Holdredge and Hanibal Rodriguez—understand exactly what makes each of the icon characters tick and they go about establishing the new team dynamic with admirable

brevity and clarity. The names are the same but these are no longer the bland, untroubled characters of the Silver Age. The new Justice League has to justify its existence in a more sophisticated and suspicious world. And, as in KINGDOM COME, the emphasis on heroism and hope is tinged with a bracing hint of end-of-the-world paranoia. We can no longer blindly accept the super-people as our saviors. Their very presence in the world raises moral and ethical questions which MIDSUMMER'S NIGHTMARE attempts to explore.

It's been an exciting year for mainstream comics, and as the last decade's dour "realism" begins to mutate into something strange and magical, JUSTICE LEAGUE: A MIDSUMMER'S NIGHTMARE stands as a boundary marker and offers a glimpse of the possibilities ahead.

Our heroes are back, no doubt about that. It's up to us now to decide whether or not we want them.

Grant Morrison
Glasgow
August '96

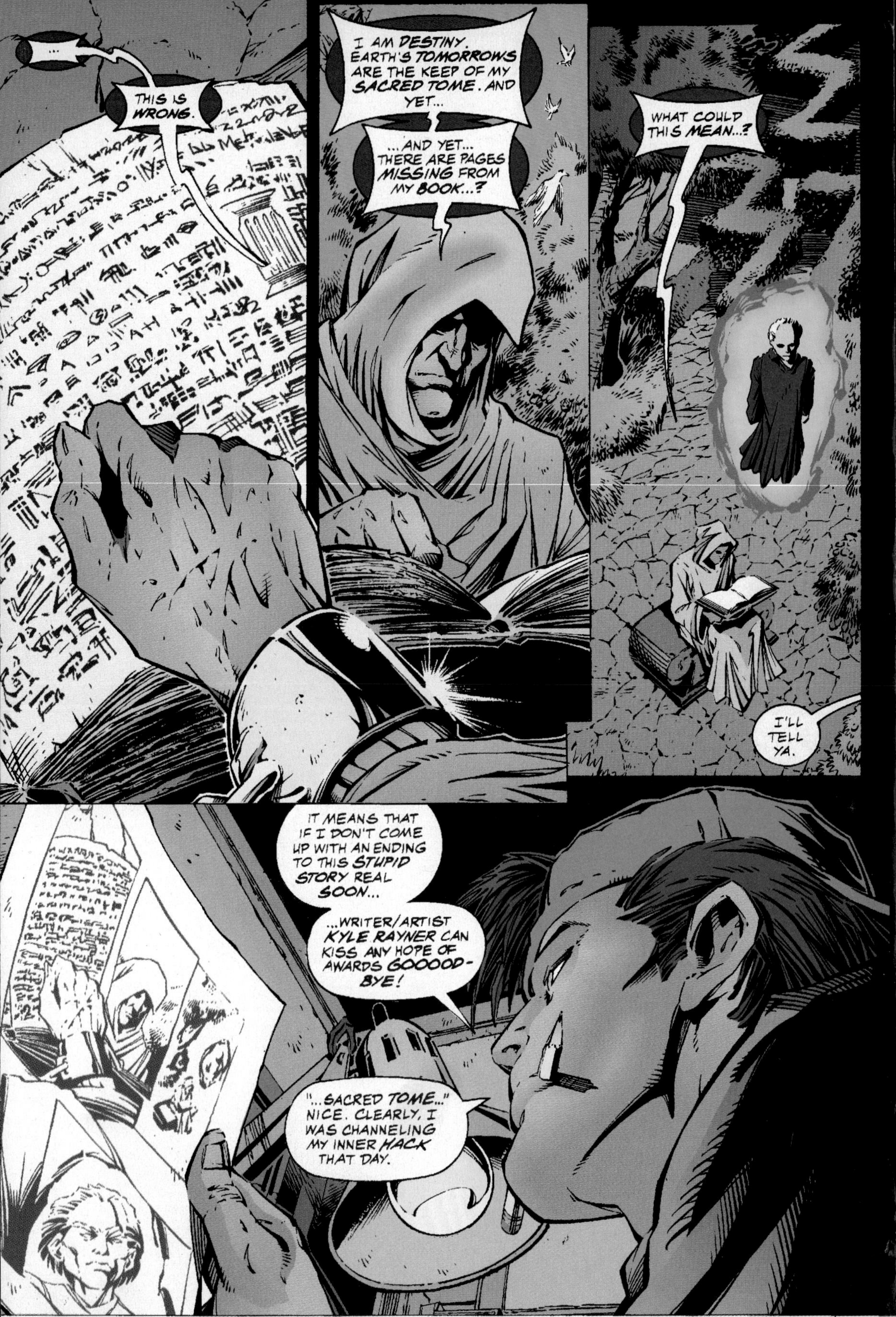
...
THIS IS WRONG.
I AM DESTINY. EARTH'S TOMORROWS ARE THE KEEP OF MY SACRED TOME. AND YET...
...AND YET... THERE ARE PAGES MISSING FROM MY BOOK...?
WHAT COULD THIS MEAN...?
I'LL TELL YA.
IT MEANS THAT IF I DON'T COME UP WITH AN ENDING TO THIS STUPID STORY REAL SOON...
...WRITER/ARTIST KYLE RAYNER CAN KISS ANY HOPE OF AWARDS GOOOOD-BYE!
"...SACRED TOME..." NICE. CLEARLY, I WAS CHANNELING MY INNER HACK THAT DAY.

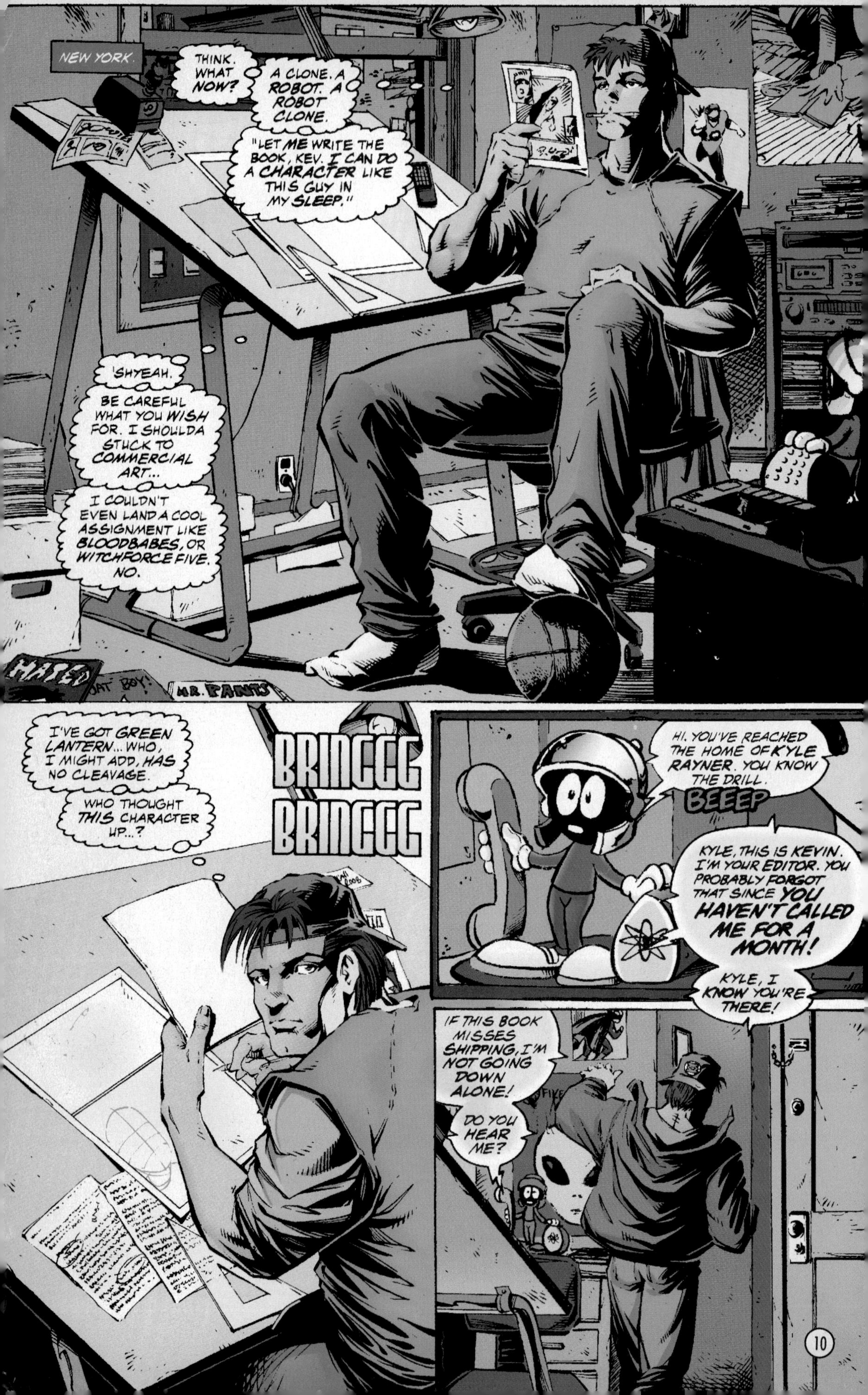
NEW YORK.
THINK. WHAT NOW?
A CLONE. A ROBOT. A ROBOT CLONE.
"LET ME WRITE THE BOOK, KEV. I CAN DO A CHARACTER LIKE THIS GUY IN MY SLEEP."
'SHYEAH.
BE CAREFUL WHAT YOU WISH FOR. I SHOULDA STUCK TO COMMERCIAL ART...
I COULDN'T EVEN LAND A COOL ASSIGNMENT LIKE BLOODBABES, OR WITCHFORCE FIVE. NO.
HATED
MR. PANTS
I'VE GOT GREEN LANTERN... WHO, I MIGHT ADD, HAS NO CLEAVAGE.
WHO THOUGHT THIS CHARACTER UP...?
BRINGGG
BRINGGG
HI. YOU'VE REACHED THE HOME OF KYLE RAYNER. YOU KNOW THE DRILL.
BEEEP
KYLE, THIS IS KEVIN. I'M YOUR EDITOR. YOU PROBABLY FORGOT THAT SINCE YOU HAVEN'T CALLED ME FOR A MONTH!
KYLE, I KNOW YOU'RE THERE!
IF THIS BOOK MISSES SHIPPING, I'M NOT GOING DOWN ALONE!
DO YOU HEAR ME?

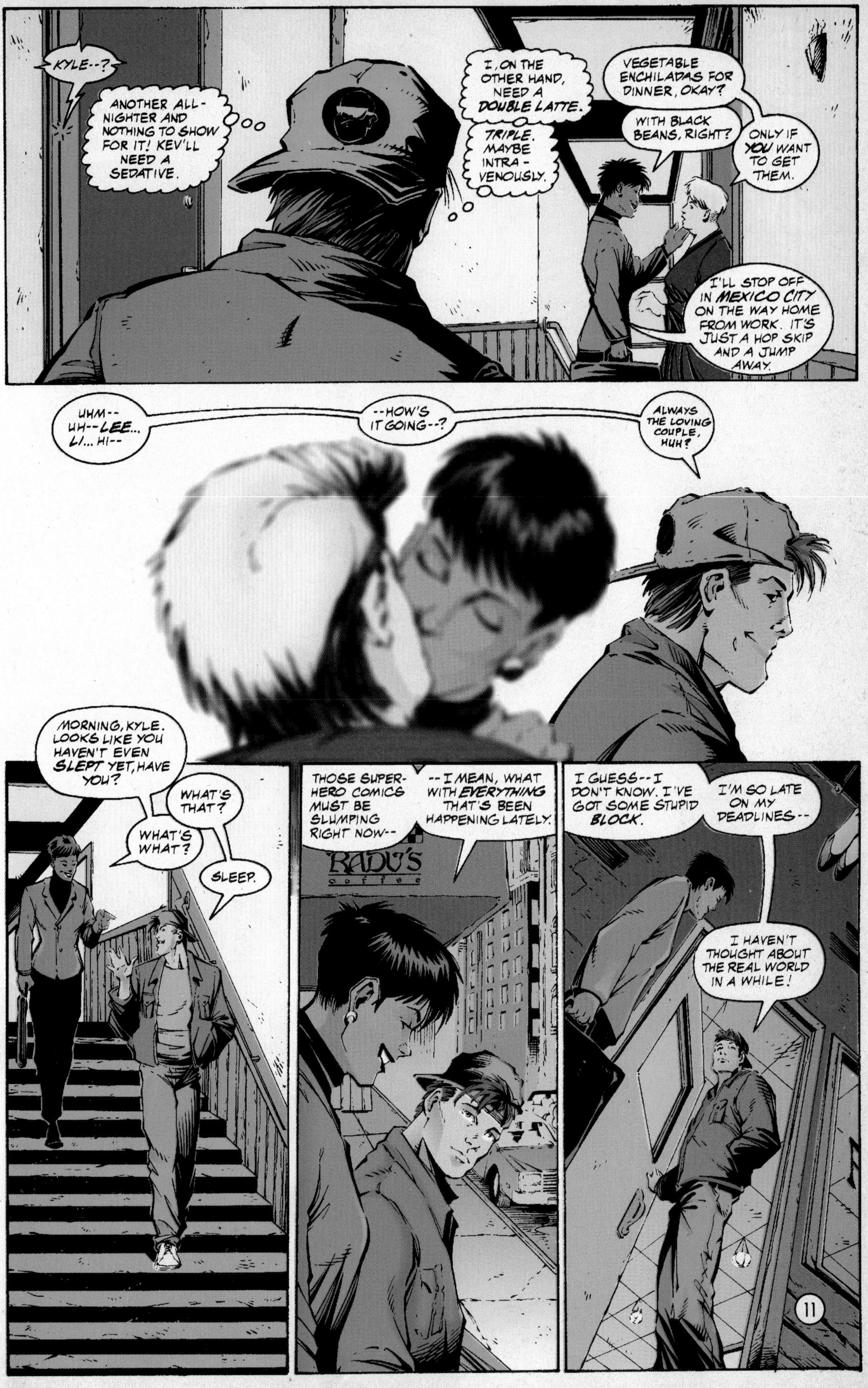
KYLE--?
ANOTHER ALL-NIGHTER AND NOTHING TO SHOW FOR IT! KEV'LL NEED A SEDATIVE.
I, ON THE OTHER HAND, NEED A DOUBLE LATTE.
TRIPLE. MAYBE INTRA-VENOUSLY.
VEGETABLE ENCHILADAS FOR DINNER, OKAY?
WITH BLACK BEANS, RIGHT?
ONLY IF YOU WANT TO GET THEM.
I'LL STOP OFF IN MEXICO CITY ON THE WAY HOME FROM WORK. IT'S JUST A HOP SKIP AND A JUMP AWAY.
UHM-- UH--LEE... LI... HI--
--HOW'S IT GOING--?
ALWAYS THE LOVING COUPLE, HUH?
MORNING, KYLE. LOOKS LIKE YOU HAVEN'T EVEN SLEPT YET, HAVE YOU?
WHAT'S THAT?
WHAT'S WHAT?
SLEEP.
THOSE SUPER-HERO COMICS MUST BE SLUMPING RIGHT NOW--
--I MEAN, WHAT WITH EVERYTHING THAT'S BEEN HAPPENING LATELY.
RADU'S coffee
I GUESS--I DON'T KNOW. I'VE GOT SOME STUPID BLOCK.
I'M SO LATE ON MY DEADLINES--
I HAVEN'T THOUGHT ABOUT THE REAL WORLD IN A WHILE!

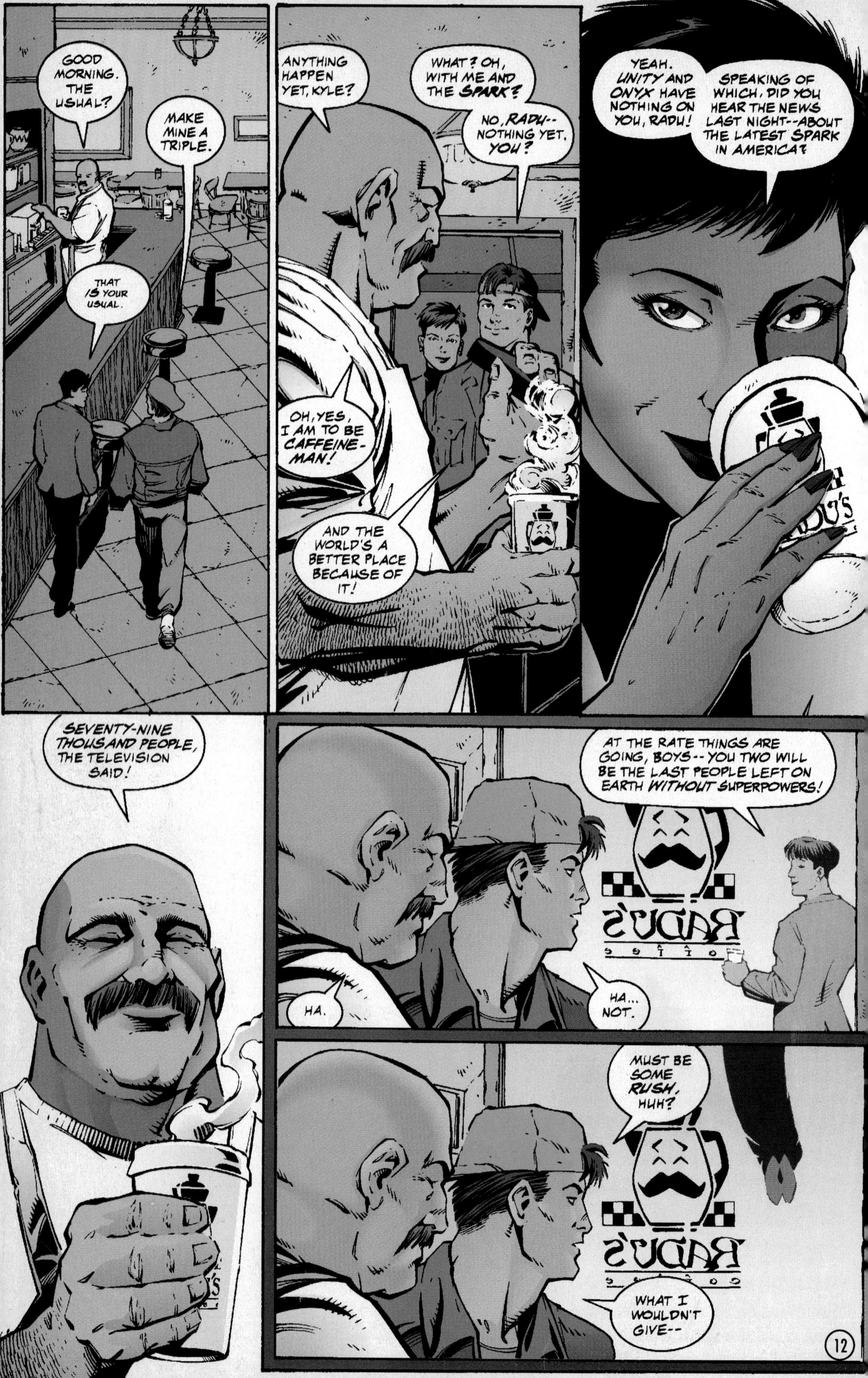
GOOD MORNING. THE USUAL?
MAKE MINE A TRIPLE.
THAT IS YOUR USUAL.
ANYTHING HAPPEN YET, KYLE?
WHAT? OH, WITH ME AND THE SPARK?
NO, RADU-- NOTHING YET. YOU?
OH, YES, I AM TO BE CAFFEINE-MAN!
AND THE WORLD'S A BETTER PLACE BECAUSE OF IT!
YEAH. UNITY AND ONYX HAVE NOTHING ON YOU, RADU!
SPEAKING OF WHICH, DID YOU HEAR THE NEWS LAST NIGHT--ABOUT THE LATEST SPARK IN AMERICA?
SEVENTY-NINE THOUSAND PEOPLE, THE TELEVISION SAID!
AT THE RATE THINGS ARE GOING, BOYS--YOU TWO WILL BE THE LAST PEOPLE LEFT ON EARTH WITHOUT SUPERPOWERS!
RADU'S
HA.
HA... NOT.
MUST BE SOME RUSH, HUH?
RADU'S
WHAT I WOULDN'T GIVE--
12

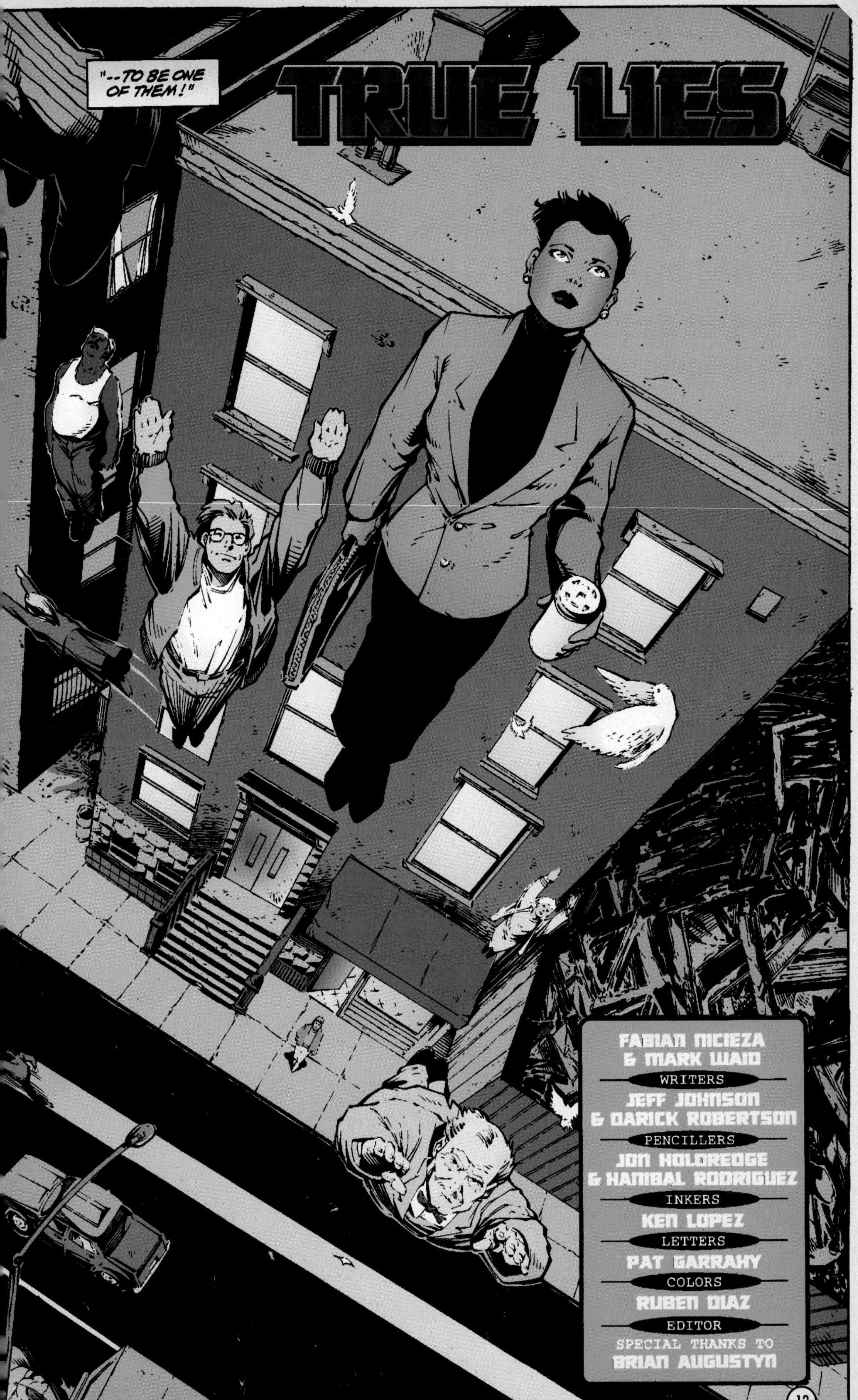
"--TO BE ONE OF THEM!"
TRUE LIES
FABIAN NICIEZA & MARK WAID
WRITERS
JEFF JOHNSON & DARICK ROBERTSON
PENCILLERS
JON HOLDREDGE & HANIBAL RODRIGUEZ
INKERS
KEN LOPEZ
LETTERS
PAT GARRAHY
COLORS
RUBEN DIAZ
EDITOR
SPECIAL THANKS TO
BRIAN AUGUSTYN

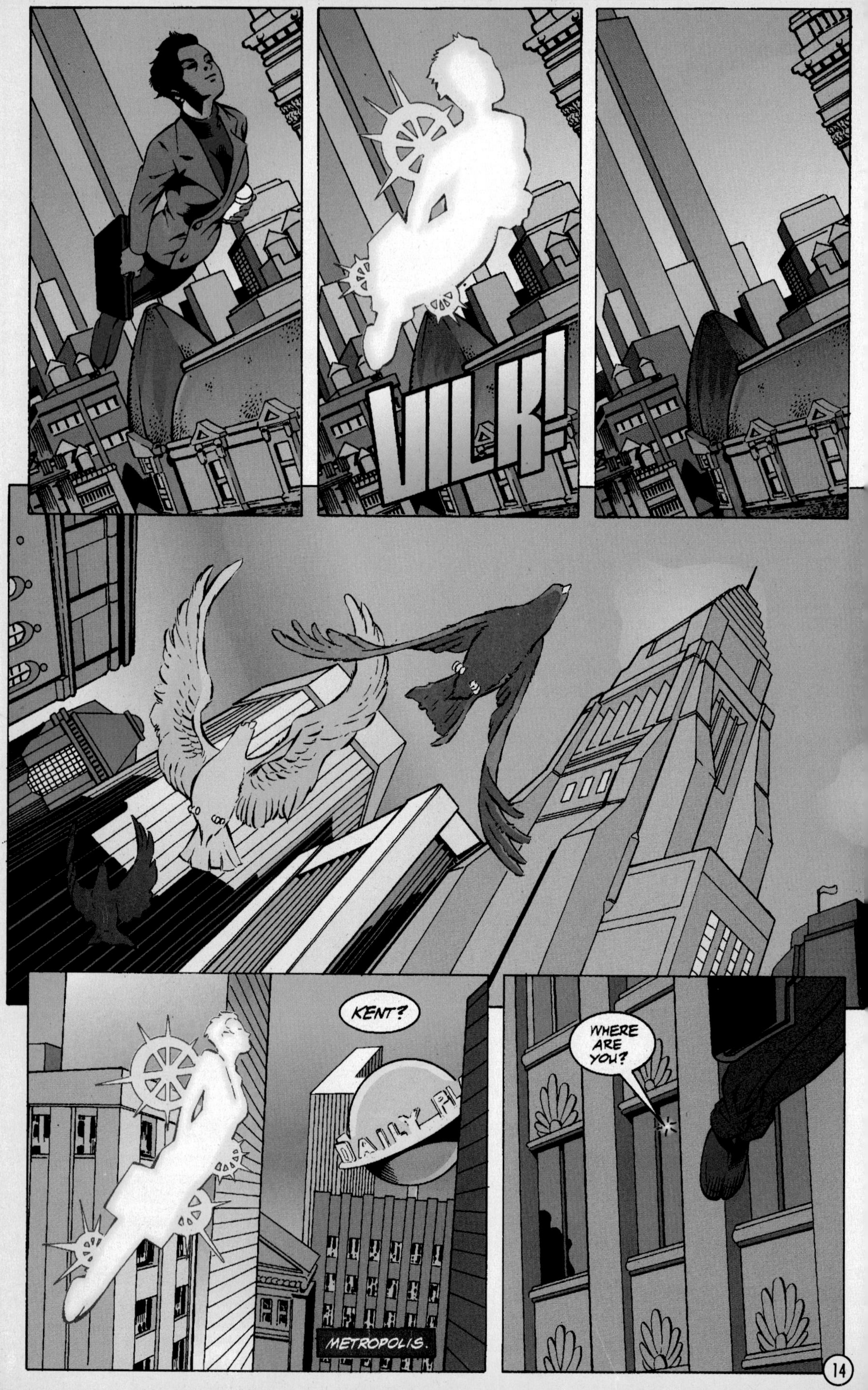
VILK!
KENT?
METROPOLIS.
WHERE ARE YOU?

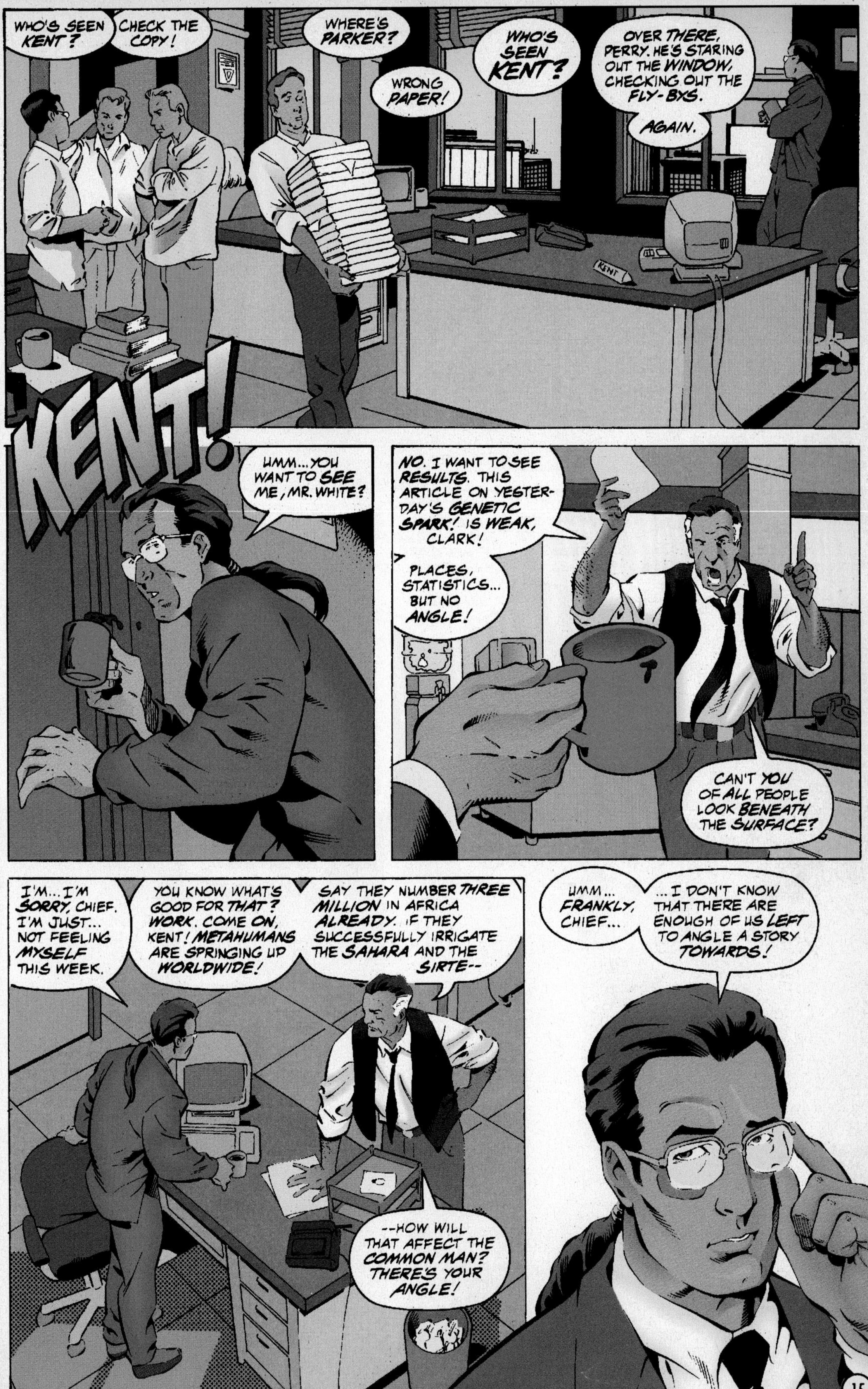
WHO'S SEEN KENT?
CHECK THE COPY!
WHERE'S PARKER?
WRONG PAPER!
WHO'S SEEN KENT?
OVER THERE, PERRY. HE'S STARING OUT THE WINDOW, CHECKING OUT THE FLY-BYS.
AGAIN.
KENT
KENT!
UMM...YOU WANT TO SEE ME, MR. WHITE?
NO. I WANT TO SEE RESULTS. THIS ARTICLE ON YESTERDAY'S GENETIC SPARK! IS WEAK, CLARK!
PLACES, STATISTICS... BUT NO ANGLE!
CAN'T YOU OF ALL PEOPLE LOOK BENEATH THE SURFACE?
I'M... I'M SORRY, CHIEF. I'M JUST... NOT FEELING MYSELF THIS WEEK.
YOU KNOW WHAT'S GOOD FOR THAT? WORK. COME ON, KENT! METAHUMANS ARE SPRINGING UP WORLDWIDE!
SAY THEY NUMBER THREE MILLION IN AFRICA ALREADY. IF THEY SUCCESSFULLY IRRIGATE THE SAHARA AND THE SIRTE--
--HOW WILL THAT AFFECT THE COMMON MAN? THERE'S YOUR ANGLE!
UMM... FRANKLY, CHIEF...
...I DON'T KNOW THAT THERE ARE ENOUGH OF US LEFT TO ANGLE A STORY TOWARDS!

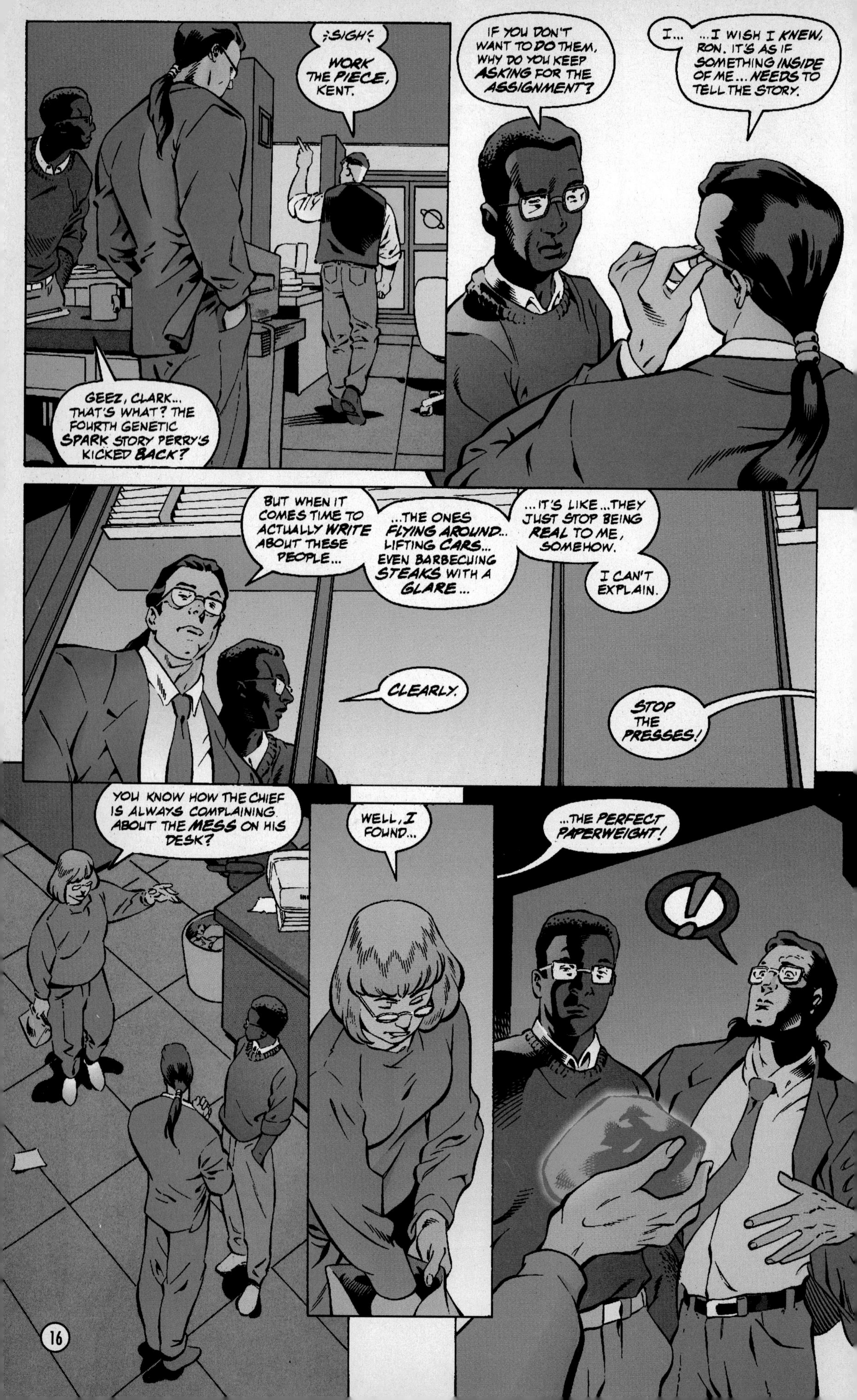
;SIGH;
WORK THE PIECE, KENT.
GEEZ, CLARK... THAT'S WHAT? THE FOURTH GENETIC SPARK STORY PERRY'S KICKED BACK?
IF YOU DON'T WANT TO DO THEM, WHY DO YOU KEEP ASKING FOR THE ASSIGNMENT?
I...
...I WISH I KNEW, RON. IT'S AS IF SOMETHING INSIDE OF ME... NEEDS TO TELL THE STORY.
BUT WHEN IT COMES TIME TO ACTUALLY WRITE ABOUT THESE PEOPLE...
...THE ONES FLYING AROUND... LIFTING CARS... EVEN BARBECUING STEAKS WITH A GLARE...
...IT'S LIKE...THEY JUST STOP BEING REAL TO ME, SOMEHOW.
I CAN'T EXPLAIN.
CLEARLY.
STOP THE PRESSES!
YOU KNOW HOW THE CHIEF IS ALWAYS COMPLAINING ABOUT THE MESS ON HIS DESK?
WELL, I FOUND...
...THE PERFECT PAPERWEIGHT!
!

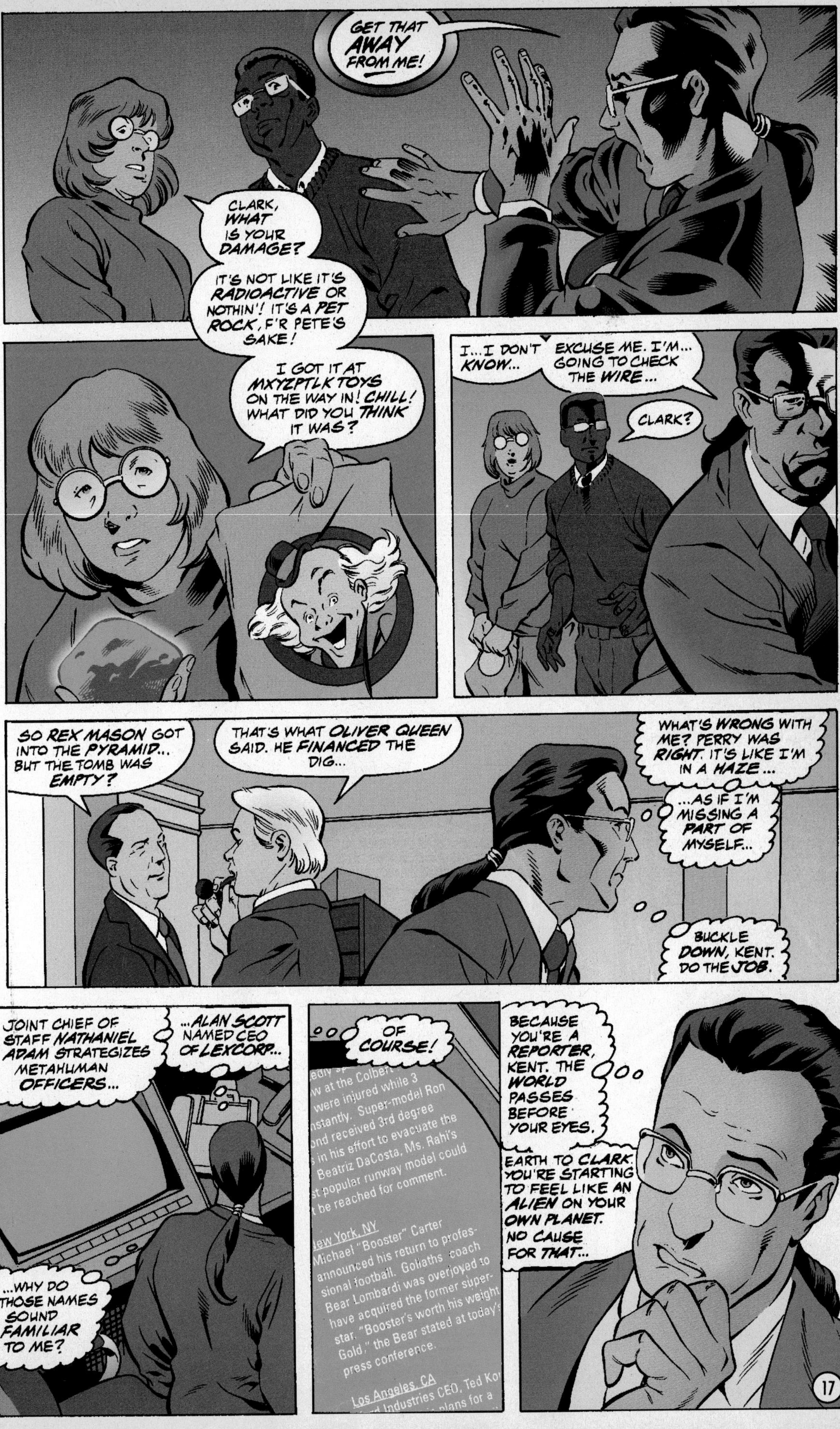

GET THAT AWAY FROM ME!
CLARK, WHAT IS YOUR DAMAGE?
IT'S NOT LIKE IT'S RADIOACTIVE OR NOTHIN'! IT'S A PET ROCK, F'R PETE'S SAKE!
I GOT IT AT MXYZPTLK TOYS ON THE WAY IN! CHILL! WHAT DID YOU THINK IT WAS?
I...I DON'T KNOW...
EXCUSE ME. I'M... GOING TO CHECK THE WIRE...
CLARK?
SO REX MASON GOT INTO THE PYRAMID... BUT THE TOMB WAS EMPTY?
THAT'S WHAT OLIVER QUEEN SAID. HE FINANCED THE DIG...
WHAT'S WRONG WITH ME? PERRY WAS RIGHT. IT'S LIKE I'M IN A HAZE...
...AS IF I'M MISSING A PART OF MYSELF...
BUCKLE DOWN, KENT. DO THE JOB.
JOINT CHIEF OF STAFF NATHANIEL ADAM STRATEGIZES METAHUMAN OFFICERS...
...ALAN SCOTT NAMED CEO OF LEXCORP...
...WHY DO THOSE NAMES SOUND FAMILIAR TO ME?
OF COURSE!
w at the Colbert
were injured while 3
nstantly. Super-model Ron
ond received 3rd degree
in his effort to evacuate the
Beatriz DaCosta, Ms. Rahi's
st popular runway model could
t be reached for comment.
New York, NY
Michael "Booster" Carter
announced his return to profes-
sional football. Goliaths coach
Bear Lombardi was overjoyed to
have acquired the former super-
star. "Booster's worth his weight
Gold," the Bear stated at today's
press conference.
Los Angeles, CA
Industries CEO, Ted Ko
plans for a
BECAUSE YOU'RE A REPORTER, KENT. THE WORLD PASSES BEFORE YOUR EYES.
EARTH TO CLARK. YOU'RE STARTING TO FEEL LIKE AN ALIEN ON YOUR OWN PLANET. NO CAUSE FOR THAT...

Gotham Gazette

KNIGHTS WIN BIG

Jones Pitches Shutout

Kollns With 4 RBI's

Gotham Gazette

WAYNE GOBBLES SCOTT

BILLION DOLLAR MERGER ANNOUNCED

Global Telecommunications
Called Key to Deal

HARD TO BELIEVE, ISN'T IT, *BRUCE*?

IT IS. RATHER NIGHTMARISH, IN FACT.

I MEAN, PEOPLE ALL OVER THE PLANET SUDDENLY GETTING EXTRAORDINARY ABILITIES--

--AND ALL THE GAZETTE CARES ABOUT IS *RUINING* YOUR PUBLIC IMAGE ON THIS DEAL.

WHM--THEN WHAT WERE *YOU* TALKING ABOUT?

HMM.

I HADN'T EVEN NOTICED, *LUCIUS*. DEALING WITH *TRIVIAL* DETAILS IS SOMETHING I DEFER TO *YOU*.

THIS. MORE IMPORTANT THAN A "Q" RATING, WOULDN'T YOU SAY?

Husband And Wife Slain By Bloomers As S.. Watches

TERRIBLE. YOU'D THINK THERE'D BE *LESS* TROUBLE ON THE STREETS NOW...

HAVE CUNNINGHAM CUT THE BOY A *CHECK*.

MAKE SURE HE *NEVER* WANTS FOR ANYTHING. SLEEPS IN PEACE TO OLD AGE.

AGAIN? BRUCE...YOU CAN'T BE SOME KIND OF BENEVOLENT *GUARDIAN* TO *EVERYBODY* IN THIS CITY!

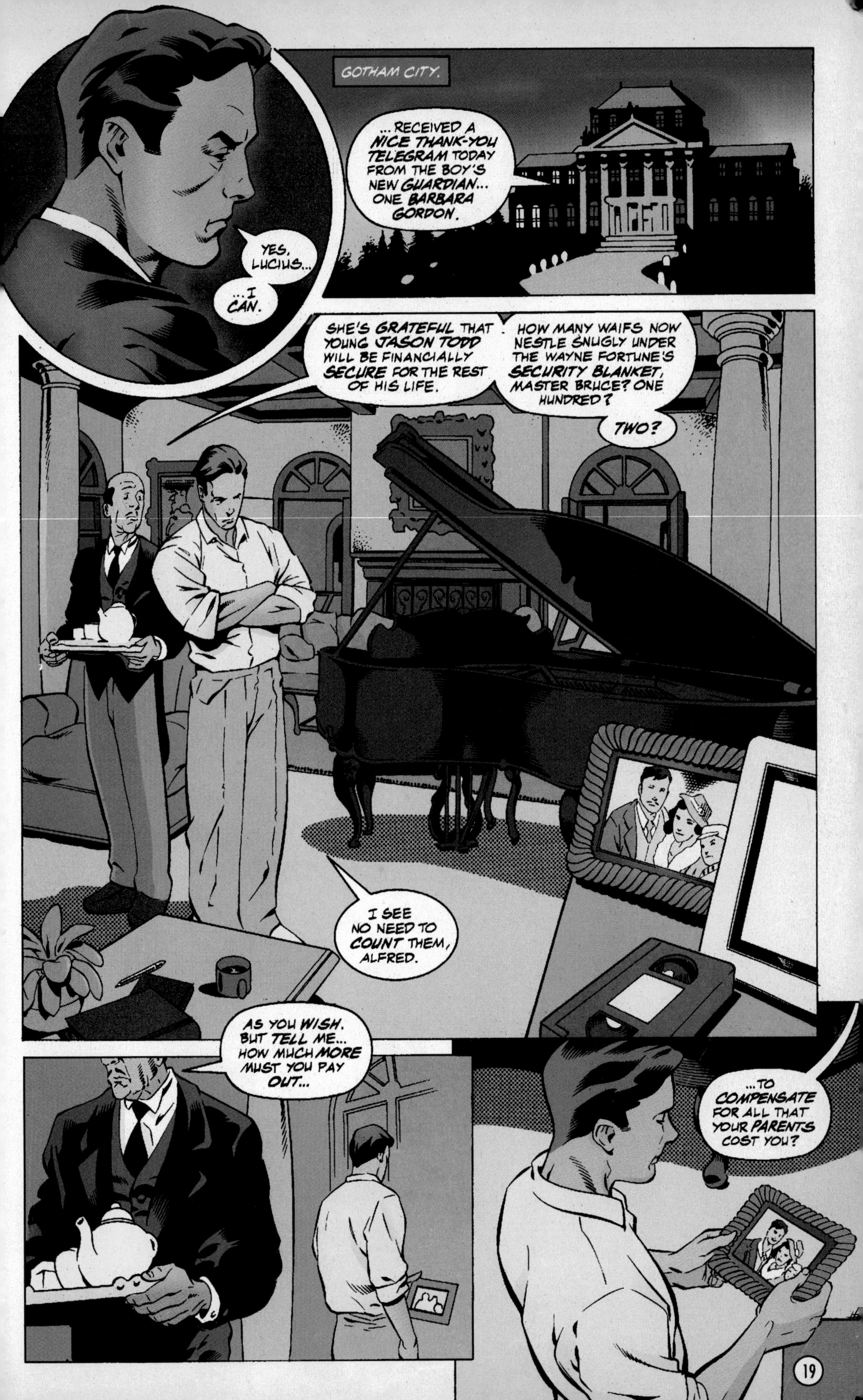
GOTHAM CITY.
...RECEIVED A NICE THANK-YOU TELEGRAM TODAY FROM THE BOY'S NEW GUARDIAN... ONE BARBARA GORDON.
YES, LUCIUS...
...I CAN.
SHE'S GRATEFUL THAT YOUNG JASON TODD WILL BE FINANCIALLY SECURE FOR THE REST OF HIS LIFE.
HOW MANY WAIFS NOW NESTLE SNUGLY UNDER THE WAYNE FORTUNE'S SECURITY BLANKET, MASTER BRUCE? ONE HUNDRED?
TWO?
I SEE NO NEED TO COUNT THEM, ALFRED.
AS YOU WISH. BUT TELL ME... HOW MUCH MORE MUST YOU PAY OUT...
...TO COMPENSATE FOR ALL THAT YOUR PARENTS COST YOU?

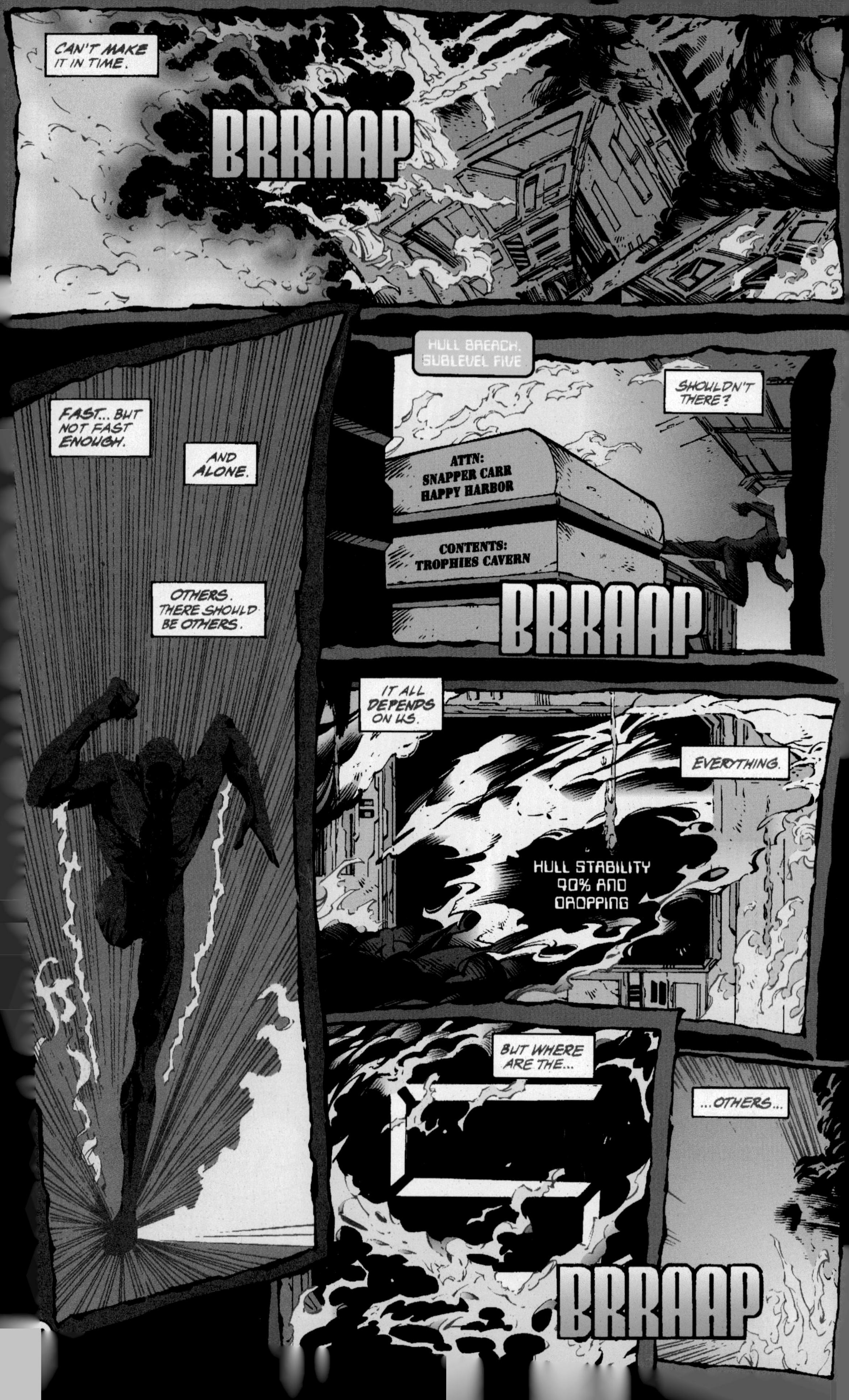
CAN'T MAKE IT IN TIME.
BRRAAP
FAST... BUT NOT FAST ENOUGH.
AND ALONE.
OTHERS. THERE SHOULD BE OTHERS.
HULL BREACH. SUBLEVEL FIVE
SHOULDN'T THERE?
ATTN: SNAPPER CARR HAPPY HARBOR
CONTENTS: TROPHIES CAVERN
BRRAAP
IT ALL DEPENDS ON US.
EVERYTHING.
HULL STABILITY 90% AND DROPPING
BUT WHERE ARE THE...
...OTHERS...
BRRAAP

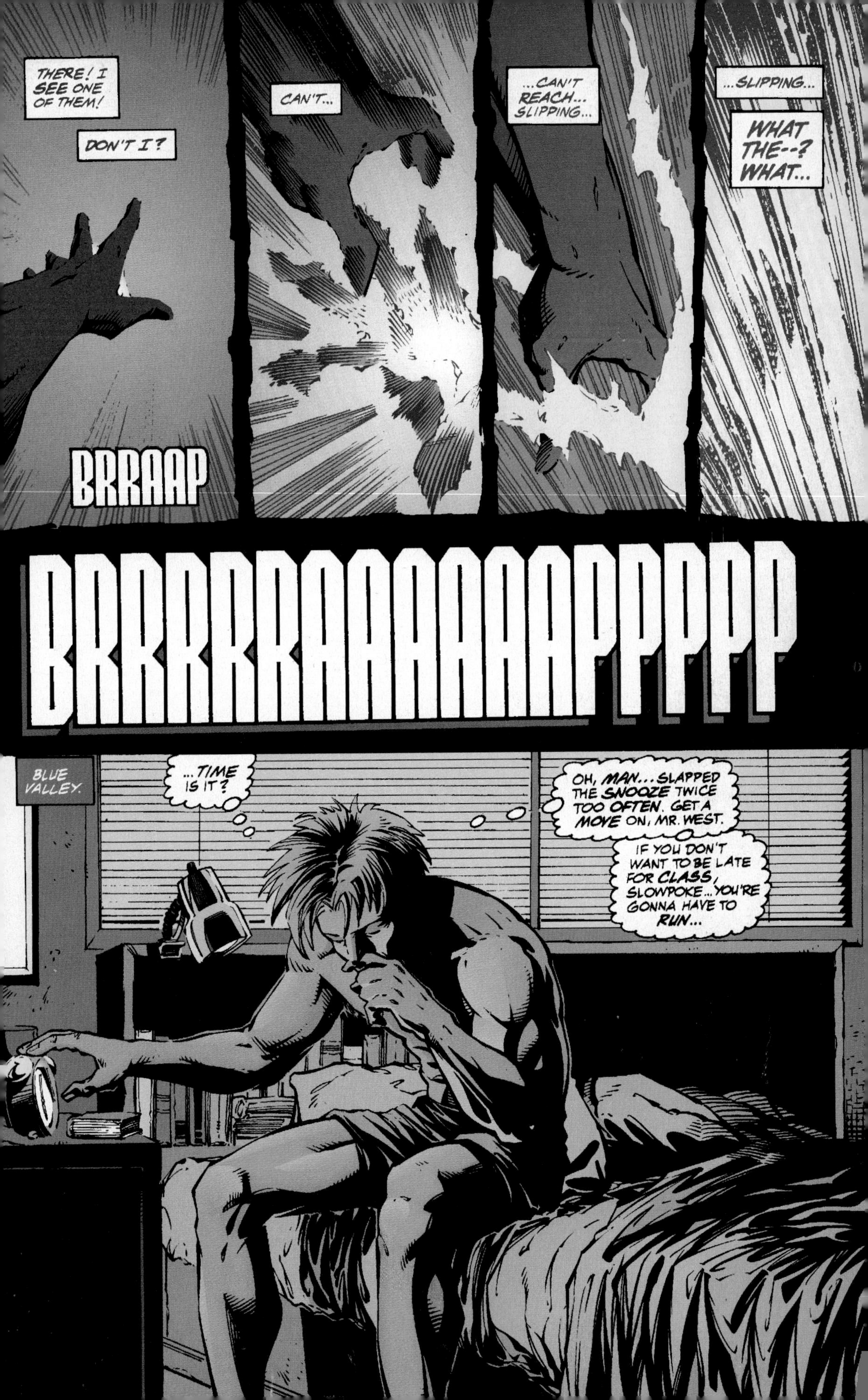
THERE! I SEE ONE OF THEM!
DON'T I?
BRRAAP
CAN'T...
...CAN'T REACH... SLIPPING...
...SLIPPING...
WHAT THE--? WHAT...
BRRRRAAAAAAAAPPPPP
BLUE VALLEY.
...TIME IS IT?
OH, MAN... SLAPPED THE SNOOZE TWICE TOO OFTEN. GET A MOVE ON, MR. WEST.
IF YOU DON'T WANT TO BE LATE FOR CLASS, SLOWPOKE... YOU'RE GONNA HAVE TO RUN...

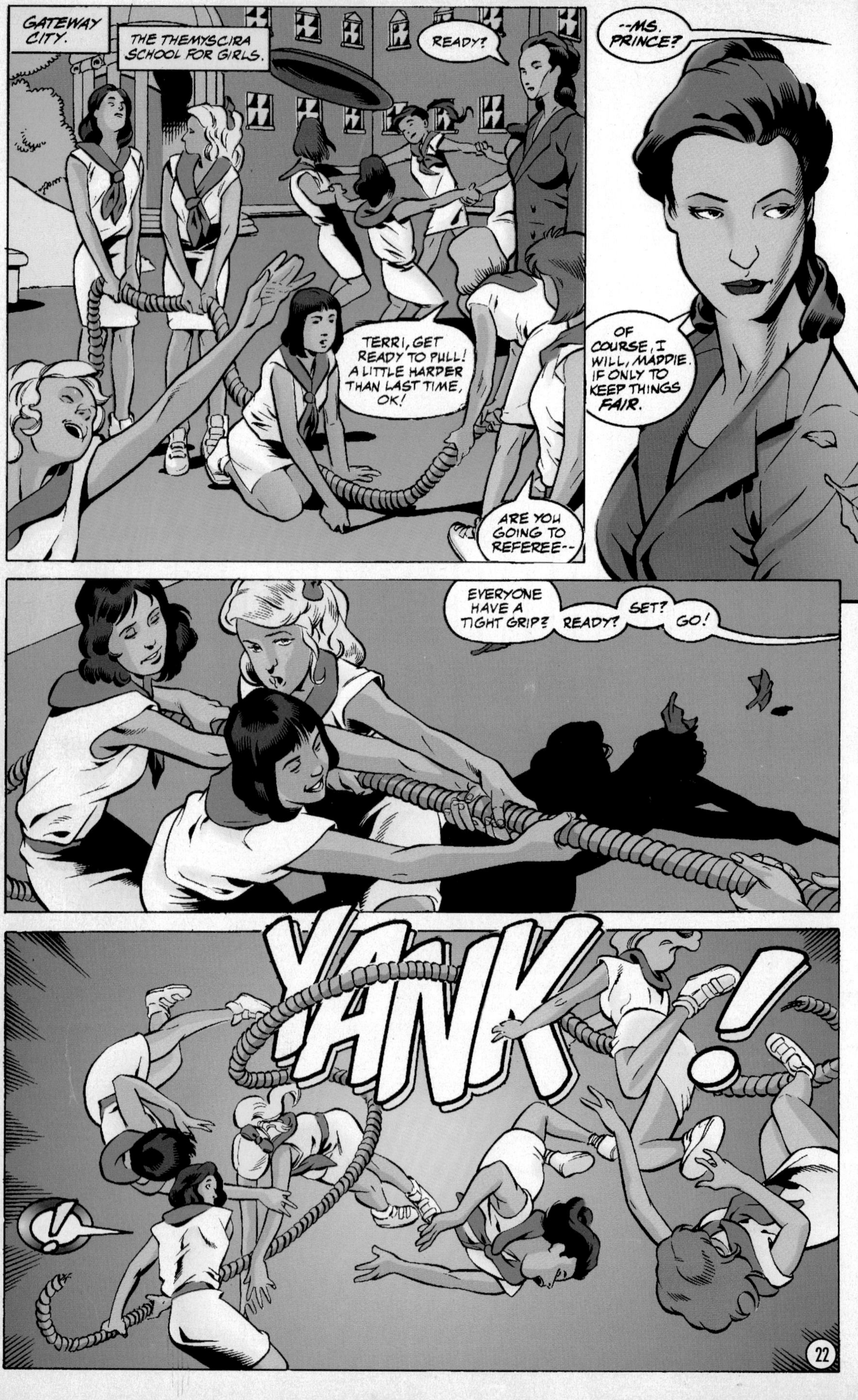
GATEWAY CITY.
THE THEMYSCIRA SCHOOL FOR GIRLS.
READY?
TERRI, GET READY TO PULL! A LITTLE HARDER THAN LAST TIME, OK!
ARE YOU GOING TO REFEREE--
--MS. PRINCE?
OF COURSE, I WILL, MADDIE. IF ONLY TO KEEP THINGS FAIR.
EVERYONE HAVE A TIGHT GRIP?
READY?
SET?
GO!
YANK!

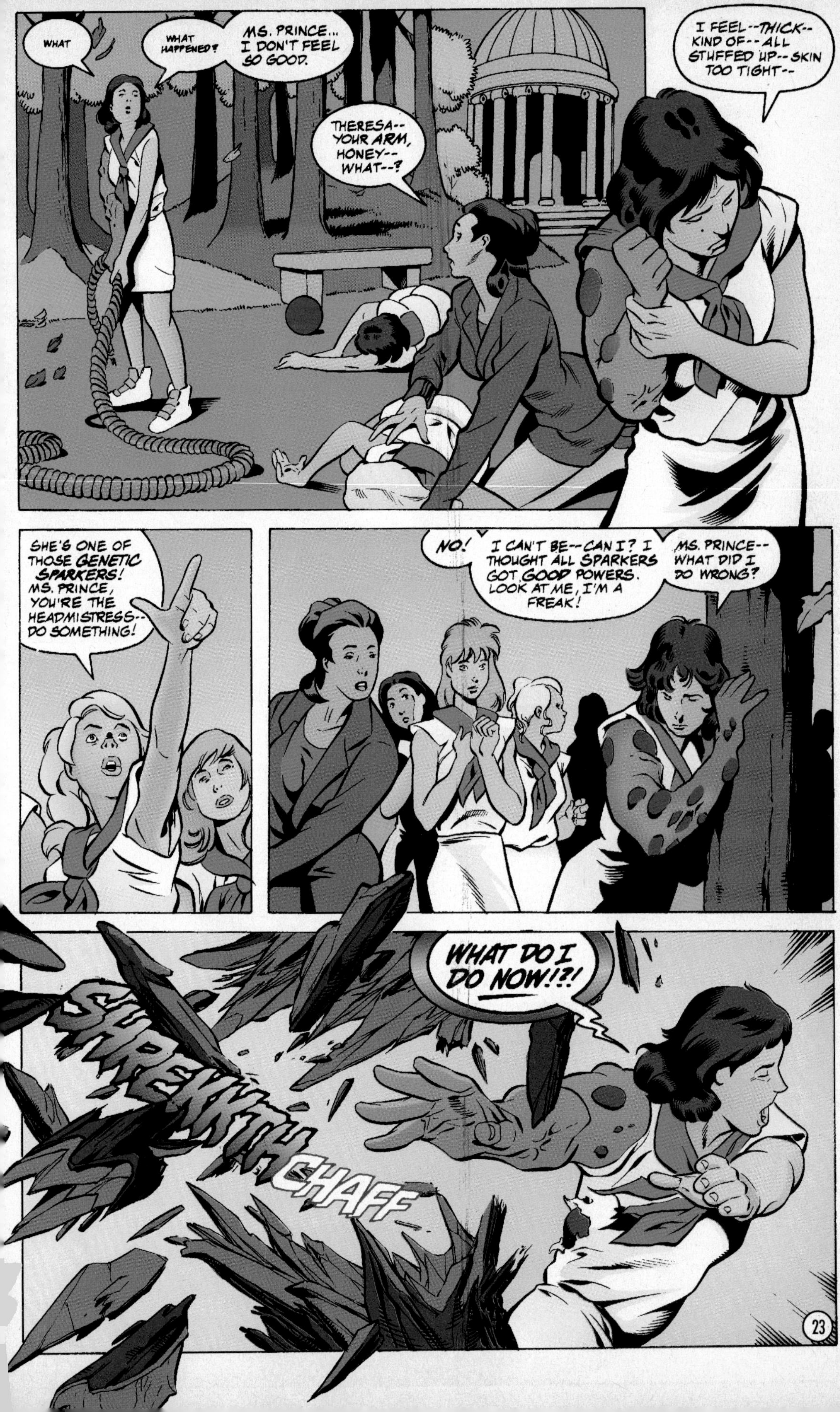
WHAT
WHAT HAPPENED?
MS. PRINCE... I DON'T FEEL SO GOOD.
THERESA-- YOUR ARM, HONEY-- WHAT--?
I FEEL--THICK-- KIND OF--ALL STUFFED UP--SKIN TOO TIGHT--
SHE'S ONE OF THOSE GENETIC SPARKERS! MS. PRINCE, YOU'RE THE HEADMISTRESS-- DO SOMETHING!
NO!
I CAN'T BE--CAN I? I THOUGHT ALL SPARKERS GOT GOOD POWERS. LOOK AT ME, I'M A FREAK!
MS. PRINCE-- WHAT DID I DO WRONG?
WHAT DO I DO NOW!?!
SHREKKTH
CHAFF

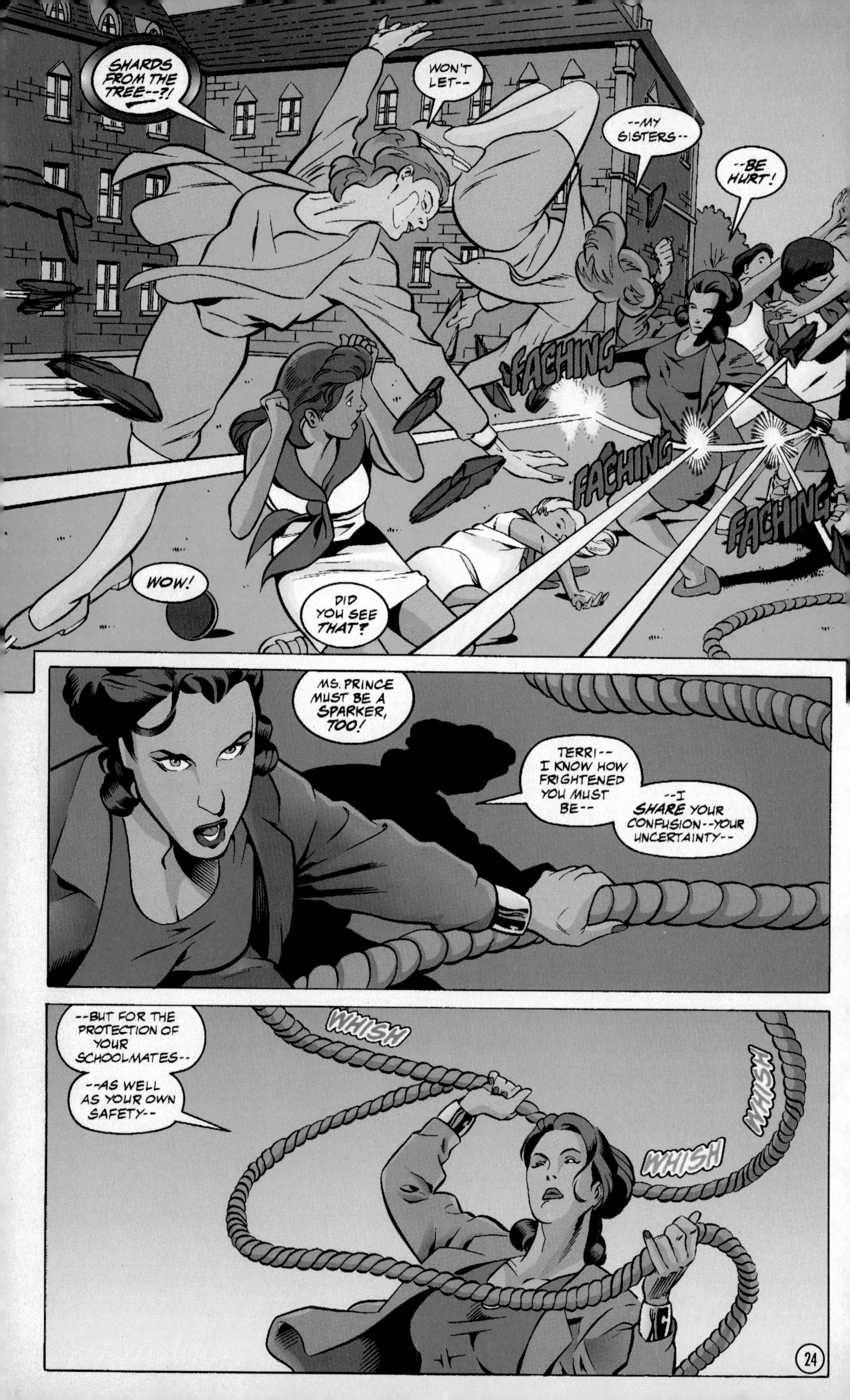
SHARDS FROM THE TREE--?!
WON'T LET--
--MY SISTERS--
--BE HURT!
FACHING
FACHING
FACHING
WOW!
DID YOU SEE THAT?
MS. PRINCE MUST BE A SPARKER, TOO!
TERRI-- I KNOW HOW FRIGHTENED YOU MUST BE--
--I SHARE YOUR CONFUSION--YOUR UNCERTAINTY--
--BUT FOR THE PROTECTION OF YOUR SCHOOLMATES--
--AS WELL AS YOUR OWN SAFETY--
WHISH
WHISH
WHISH

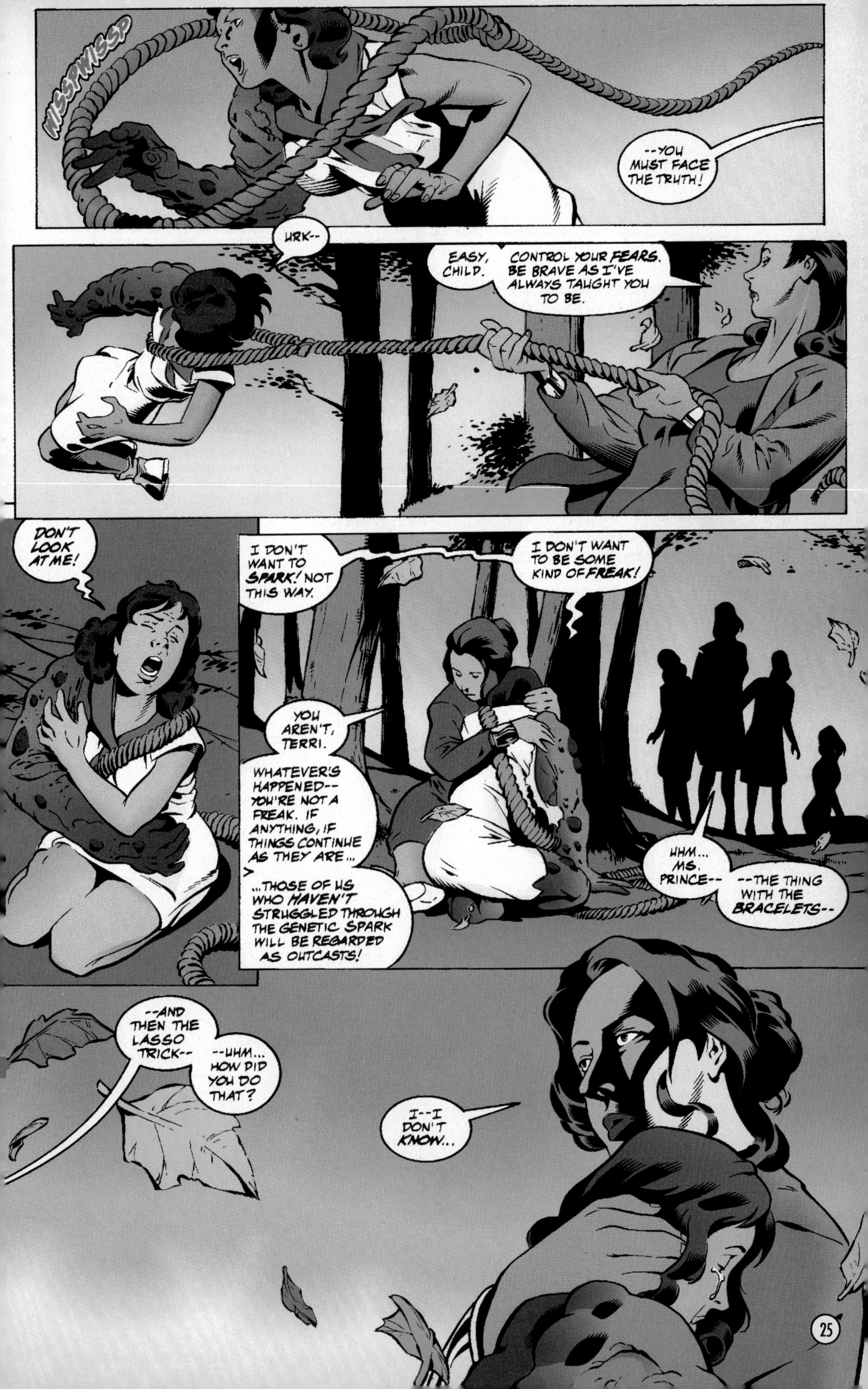
WISSPWISSP
--YOU MUST FACE THE TRUTH!
URK--
EASY, CHILD.
CONTROL YOUR FEARS. BE BRAVE AS I'VE ALWAYS TAUGHT YOU TO BE.
DON'T LOOK AT ME!
I DON'T WANT TO SPARK! NOT THIS WAY.
I DON'T WANT TO BE SOME KIND OF FREAK!
YOU AREN'T, TERRI.
WHATEVER'S HAPPENED-- YOU'RE NOT A FREAK. IF ANYTHING, IF THINGS CONTINUE AS THEY ARE...
...THOSE OF US WHO HAVEN'T STRUGGLED THROUGH THE GENETIC SPARK WILL BE REGARDED AS OUTCASTS!
UHM... MS. PRINCE--
--THE THING WITH THE BRACELETS--
--AND THEN THE LASSO TRICK--
--UHM... HOW DID YOU DO THAT?
I--I DON'T KNOW...

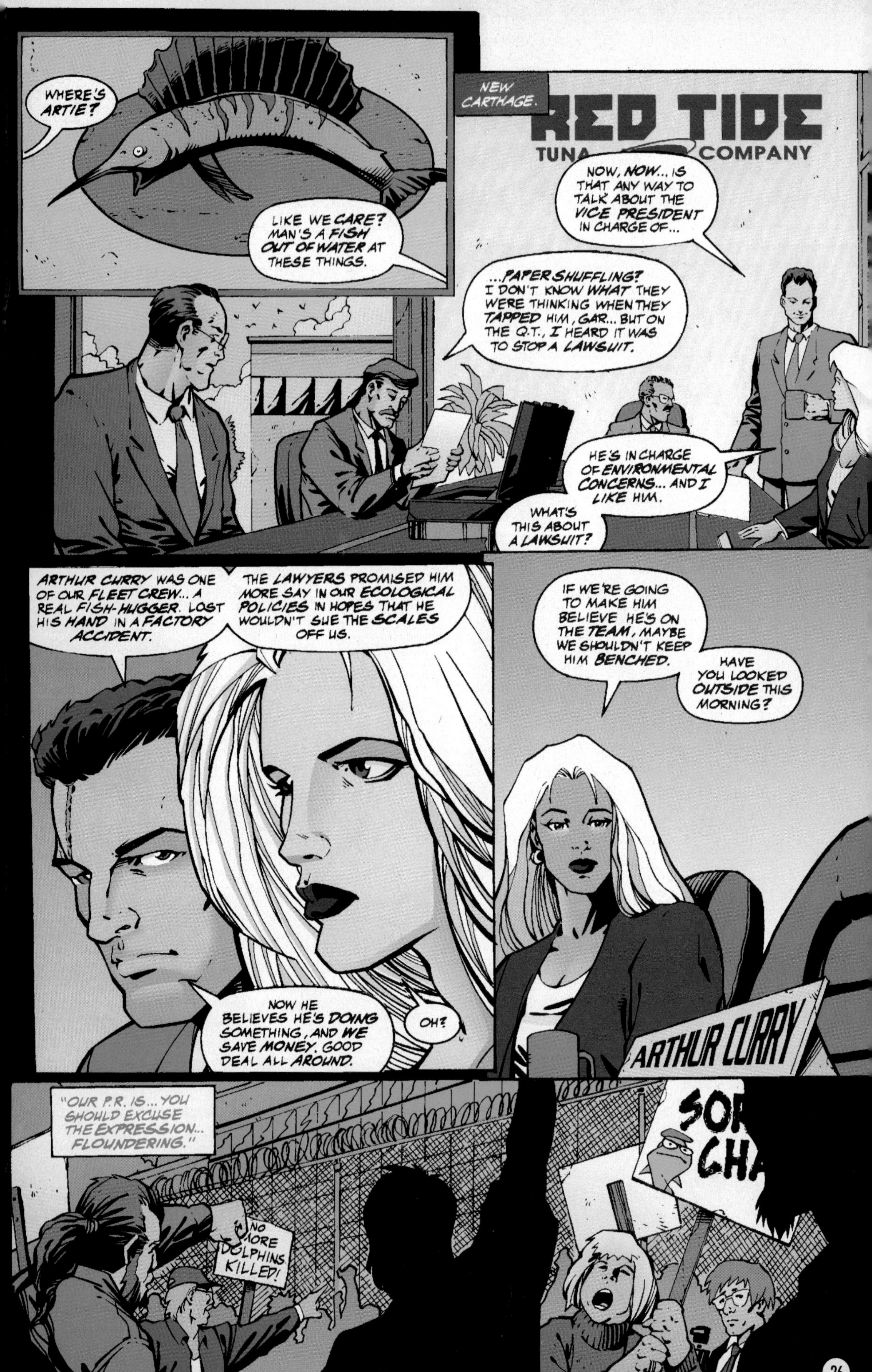
WHERE'S ARTIE?
LIKE WE CARE? MAN'S A FISH OUT OF WATER AT THESE THINGS.
NEW CARTHAGE.
RED TIDE
TUNA COMPANY
NOW, NOW... IS THAT ANY WAY TO TALK ABOUT THE VICE PRESIDENT IN CHARGE OF...
...PAPER SHUFFLING? I DON'T KNOW WHAT THEY WERE THINKING WHEN THEY TAPPED HIM, GAR... BUT ON THE Q.T., I HEARD IT WAS TO STOP A LAWSUIT.
HE'S IN CHARGE OF ENVIRONMENTAL CONCERNS... AND I LIKE HIM.
WHAT'S THIS ABOUT A LAWSUIT?
ARTHUR CURRY WAS ONE OF OUR FLEET CREW... A REAL FISH-HUGGER. LOST HIS HAND IN A FACTORY ACCIDENT.
THE LAWYERS PROMISED HIM MORE SAY IN OUR ECOLOGICAL POLICIES IN HOPES THAT HE WOULDN'T SUE THE SCALES OFF US.
NOW HE BELIEVES HE'S DOING SOMETHING, AND WE SAVE MONEY. GOOD DEAL ALL AROUND.
OH?
IF WE'RE GOING TO MAKE HIM BELIEVE HE'S ON THE TEAM, MAYBE WE SHOULDN'T KEEP HIM BENCHED.
HAVE YOU LOOKED OUTSIDE THIS MORNING?
ARTHUR CURRY
"OUR P.R. IS... YOU SHOULD EXCUSE THE EXPRESSION... FLOUNDERING."
NO MORE DOLPHINS KILLED!

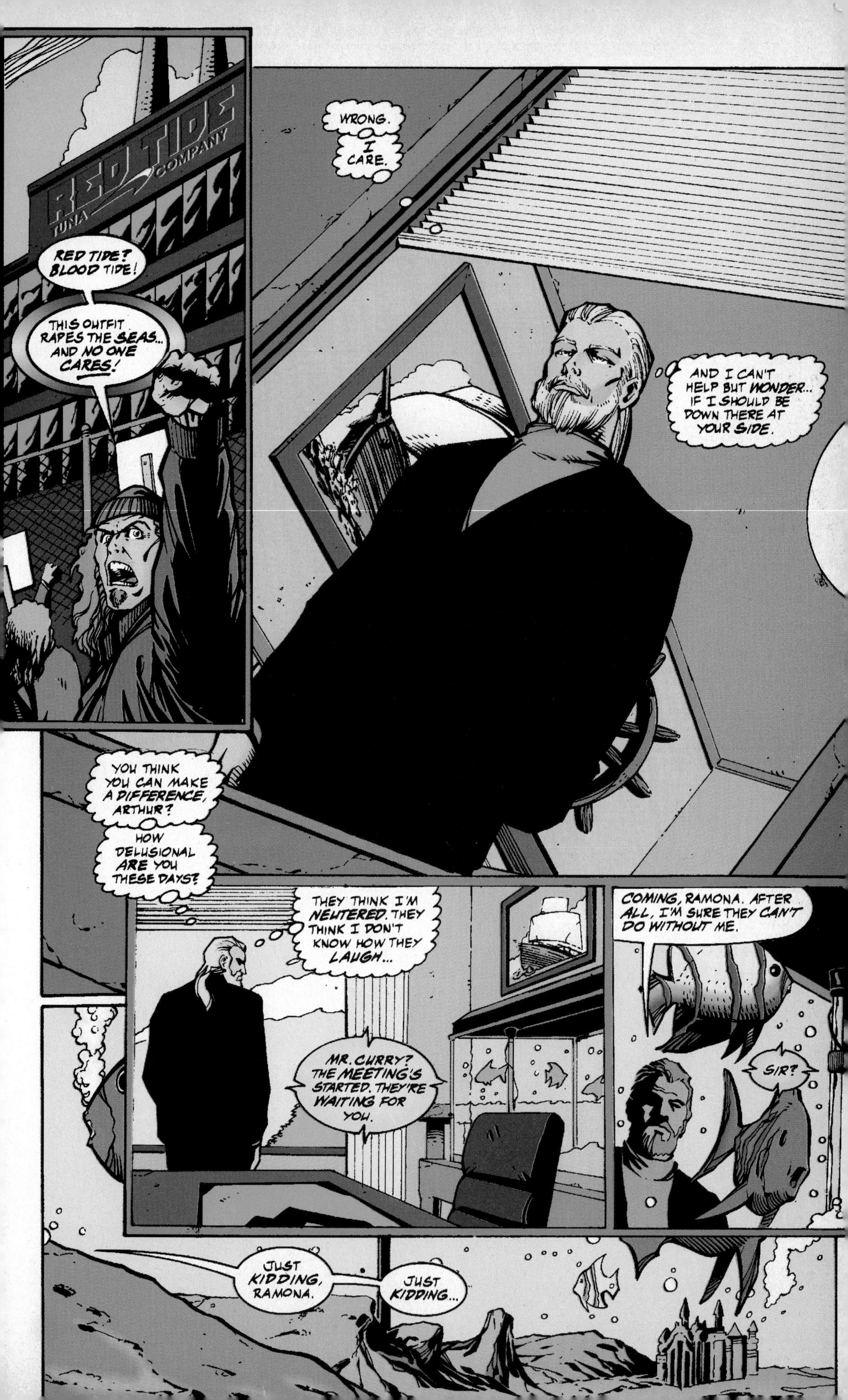
RED TIDE TUNA COMPANY
RED TIDE? BLOOD TIDE!
THIS OUTFIT RAPES THE SEAS... AND NO ONE CARES!
WRONG.
I CARE.
AND I CAN'T HELP BUT WONDER... IF I SHOULD BE DOWN THERE AT YOUR SIDE.
YOU THINK YOU CAN MAKE A DIFFERENCE, ARTHUR?
HOW DELUSIONAL ARE YOU THESE DAYS?
THEY THINK I'M NEUTERED. THEY THINK I DON'T KNOW HOW THEY LAUGH...
MR. CURRY? THE MEETING'S STARTED. THEY'RE WAITING FOR YOU.
COMING, RAMONA. AFTER ALL, I'M SURE THEY CAN'T DO WITHOUT ME.
SIR?
JUST KIDDING, RAMONA.
JUST KIDDING...

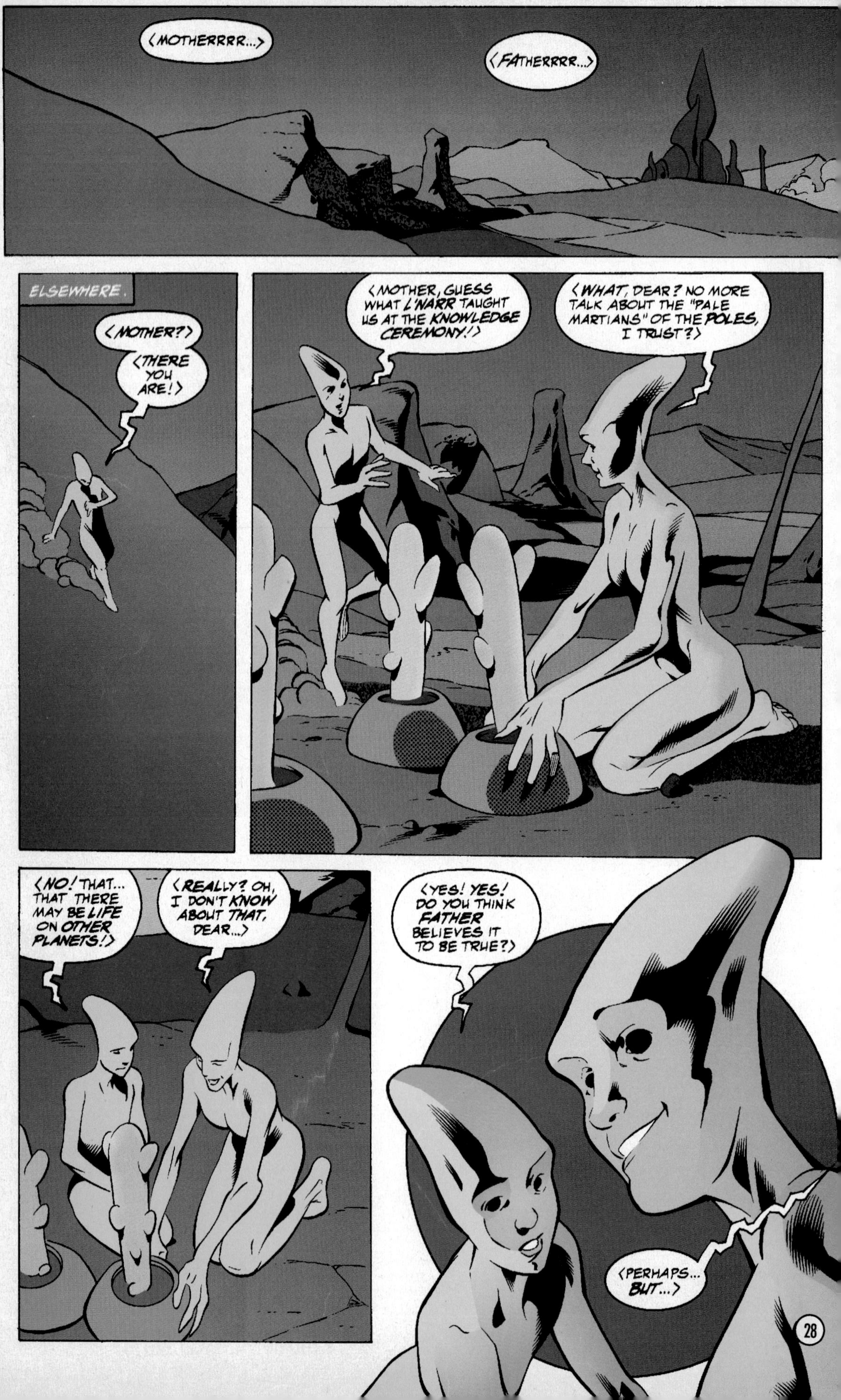

⟨MOTHERRRR...⟩
⟨FATHERRRR...⟩
ELSEWHERE.
⟨MOTHER?⟩
⟨THERE YOU ARE!⟩
⟨MOTHER, GUESS WHAT L'NARR TAUGHT US AT THE KNOWLEDGE CEREMONY!⟩
⟨WHAT, DEAR? NO MORE TALK ABOUT THE "PALE MARTIANS" OF THE POLES, I TRUST?⟩
⟨NO! THAT... THAT THERE MAY BE LIFE ON OTHER PLANETS!⟩
⟨REALLY? OH, I DON'T KNOW ABOUT THAT, DEAR...⟩
⟨YES! YES! DO YOU THINK FATHER BELIEVES IT TO BE TRUE?⟩
⟨PERHAPS... BUT...⟩

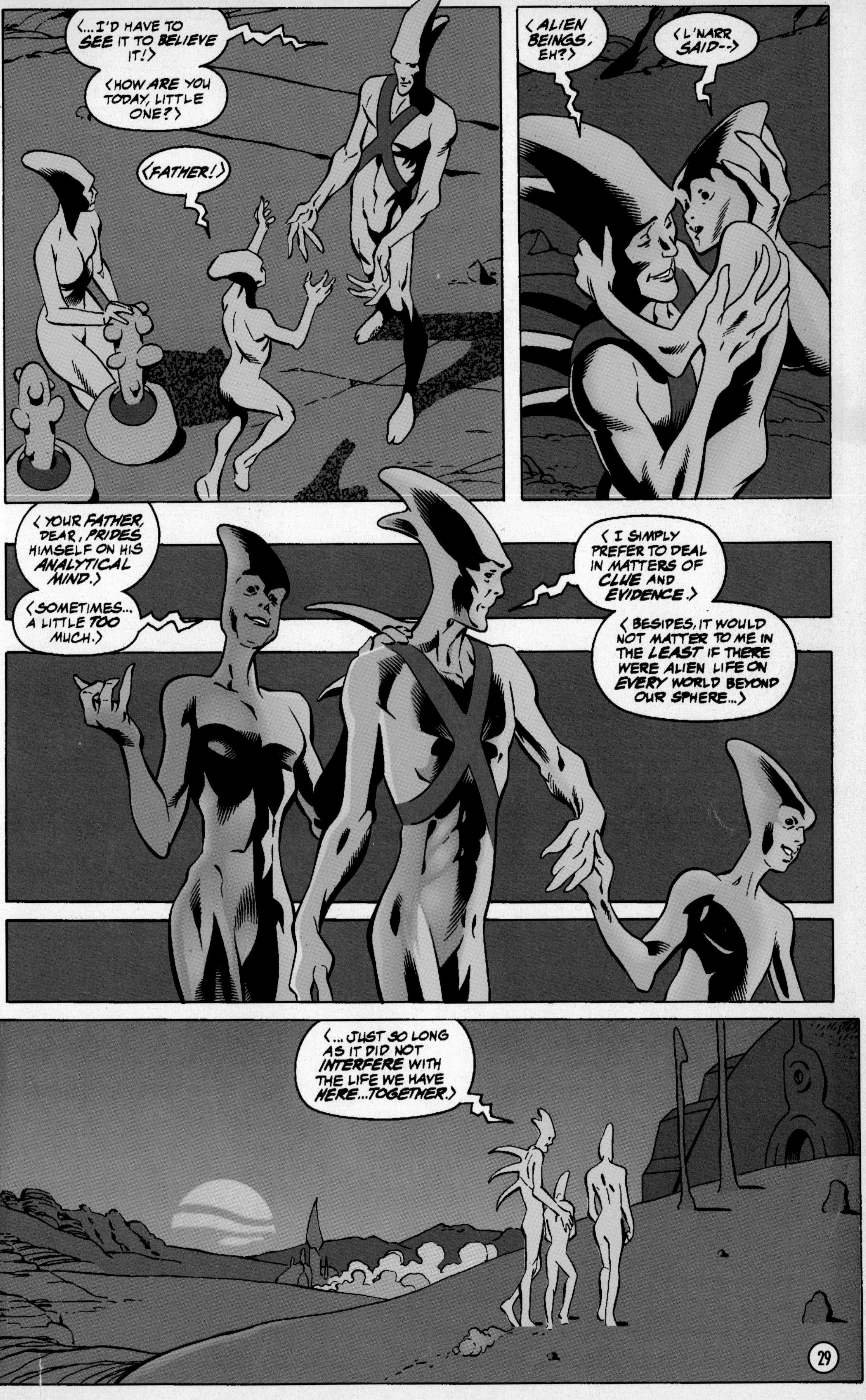
⟨...I'D HAVE TO SEE IT TO BELIEVE IT!⟩
⟨HOW ARE YOU TODAY, LITTLE ONE?⟩
⟨FATHER!⟩
⟨ALIEN BEINGS, EH?⟩
⟨L'NARR SAID--⟩
⟨YOUR FATHER, DEAR, PRIDES HIMSELF ON HIS ANALYTICAL MIND.⟩
⟨SOMETIMES... A LITTLE TOO MUCH.⟩
⟨I SIMPLY PREFER TO DEAL IN MATTERS OF CLUE AND EVIDENCE.⟩
⟨BESIDES, IT WOULD NOT MATTER TO ME IN THE LEAST IF THERE WERE ALIEN LIFE ON EVERY WORLD BEYOND OUR SPHERE...⟩
⟨...JUST SO LONG AS IT DID NOT INTERFERE WITH THE LIFE WE HAVE HERE...TOGETHER.⟩

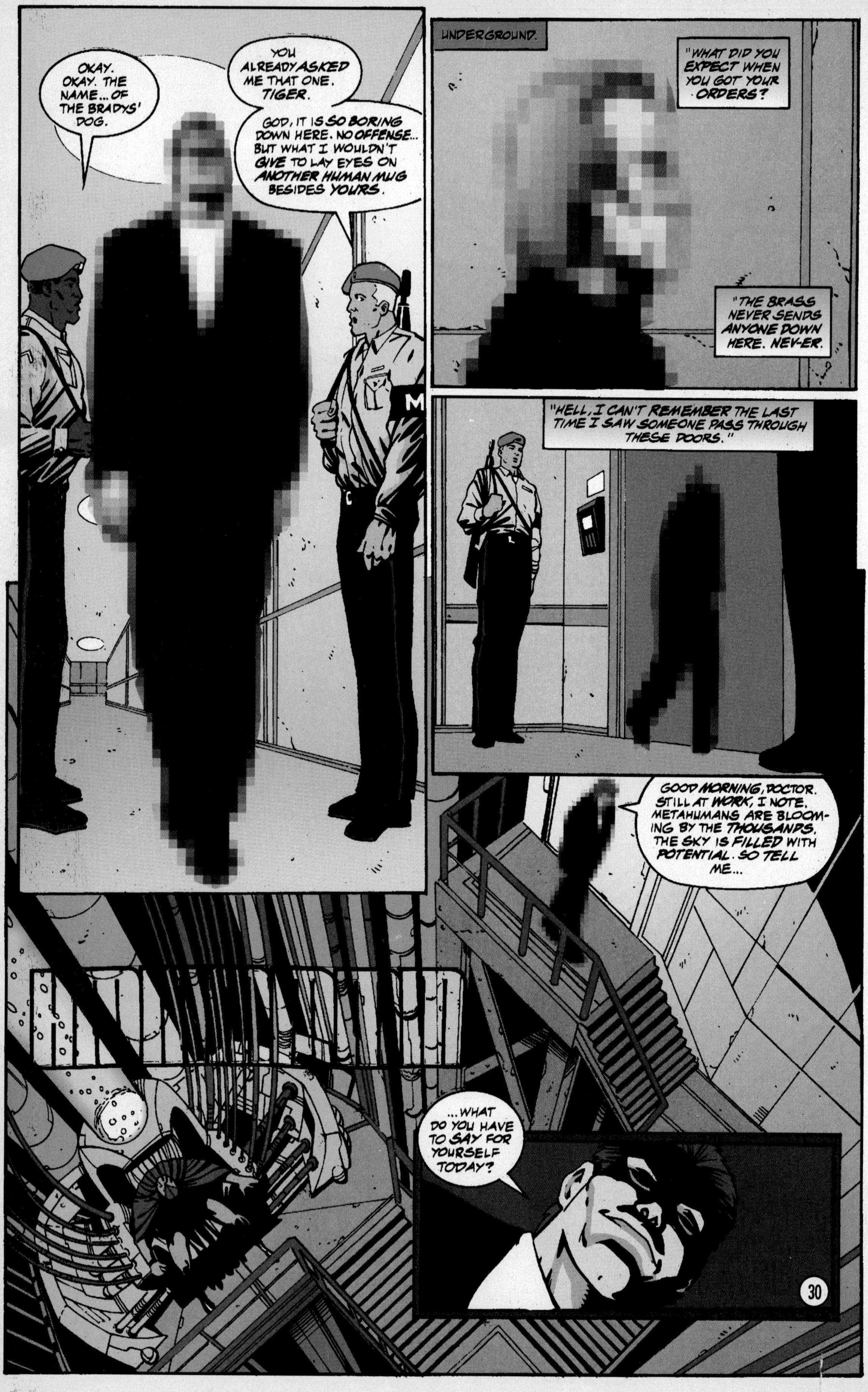

OKAY. OKAY. THE NAME... OF THE BRADYS' DOG.
YOU ALREADY ASKED ME THAT ONE. TIGER.
GOD, IT IS SO BORING DOWN HERE. NO OFFENSE... BUT WHAT I WOULDN'T GIVE TO LAY EYES ON ANOTHER HUMAN MUG BESIDES YOURS.
UNDERGROUND.
"WHAT DID YOU EXPECT WHEN YOU GOT YOUR ORDERS?
"THE BRASS NEVER SENDS ANYONE DOWN HERE. NEV-ER.
"HELL, I CAN'T REMEMBER THE LAST TIME I SAW SOMEONE PASS THROUGH THESE DOORS."
GOOD MORNING, DOCTOR. STILL AT WORK, I NOTE. METAHUMANS ARE BLOOMING BY THE THOUSANDS, THE SKY IS FILLED WITH POTENTIAL. SO TELL ME...
...WHAT DO YOU HAVE TO SAY FOR YOURSELF TODAY?

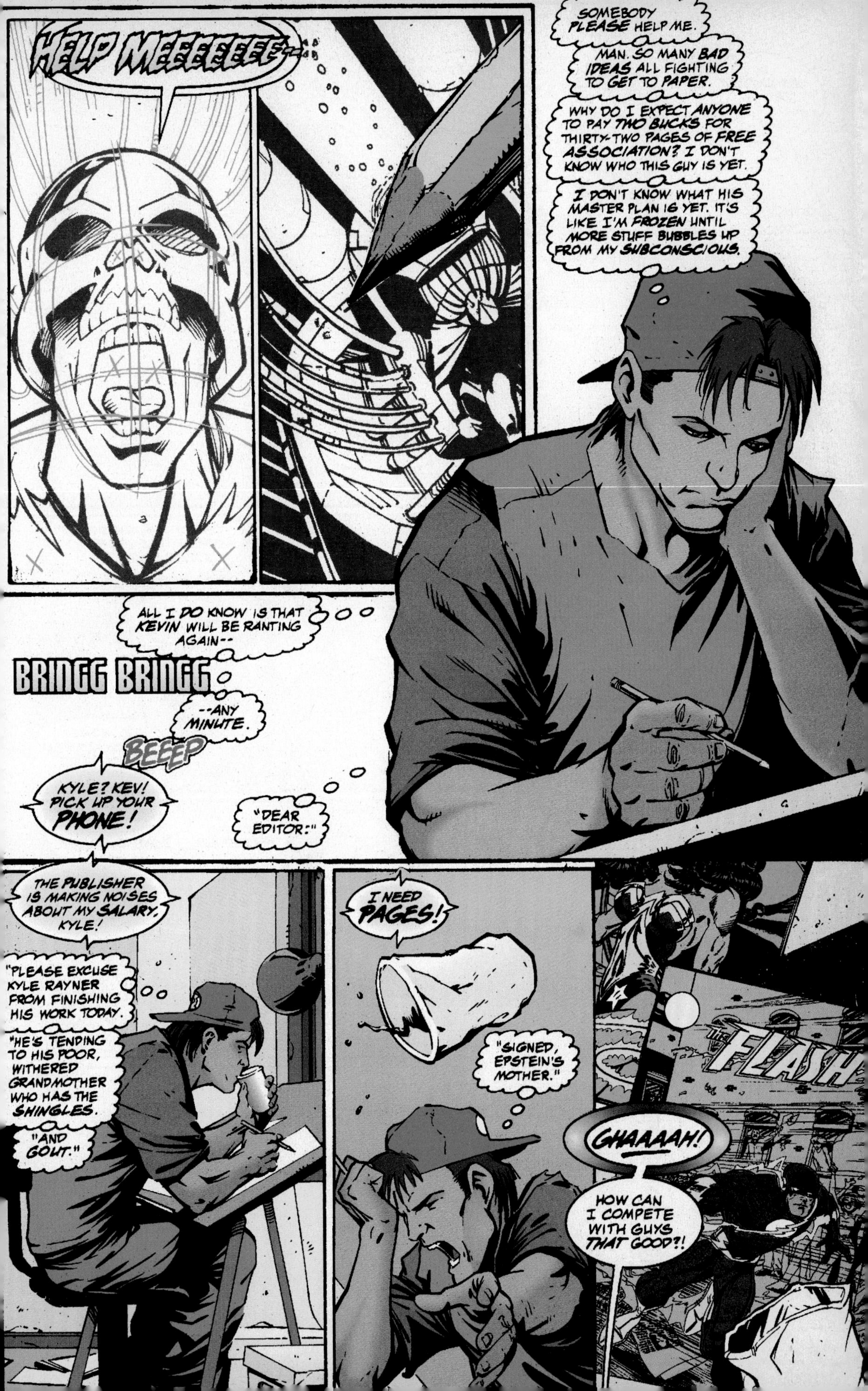
HELP MEEEEEEE--
SOMEBODY PLEASE HELP ME.
MAN. SO MANY BAD IDEAS ALL FIGHTING TO GET TO PAPER.
WHY DO I EXPECT ANYONE TO PAY TWO BUCKS FOR THIRTY-TWO PAGES OF FREE ASSOCIATION? I DON'T KNOW WHO THIS GUY IS YET.
I DON'T KNOW WHAT HIS MASTER PLAN IS YET. IT'S LIKE I'M FROZEN UNTIL MORE STUFF BUBBLES UP FROM MY SUBCONSCIOUS.
ALL I DO KNOW IS THAT KEVIN WILL BE RANTING AGAIN--
BRINGG BRINGG
--ANY MINUTE.
BEEEP
KYLE? KEV! PICK UP YOUR PHONE!
"DEAR EDITOR:"
THE PUBLISHER IS MAKING NOISES ABOUT MY SALARY, KYLE!
"PLEASE EXCUSE KYLE RAYNER FROM FINISHING HIS WORK TODAY.
"HE'S TENDING TO HIS POOR, WITHERED GRANDMOTHER WHO HAS THE SHINGLES.
"AND GOUT."
I NEED PAGES!
"SIGNED, EPSTEIN'S MOTHER."
FLASH
GHAAAAH!
HOW CAN I COMPETE WITH GUYS THAT GOOD?!

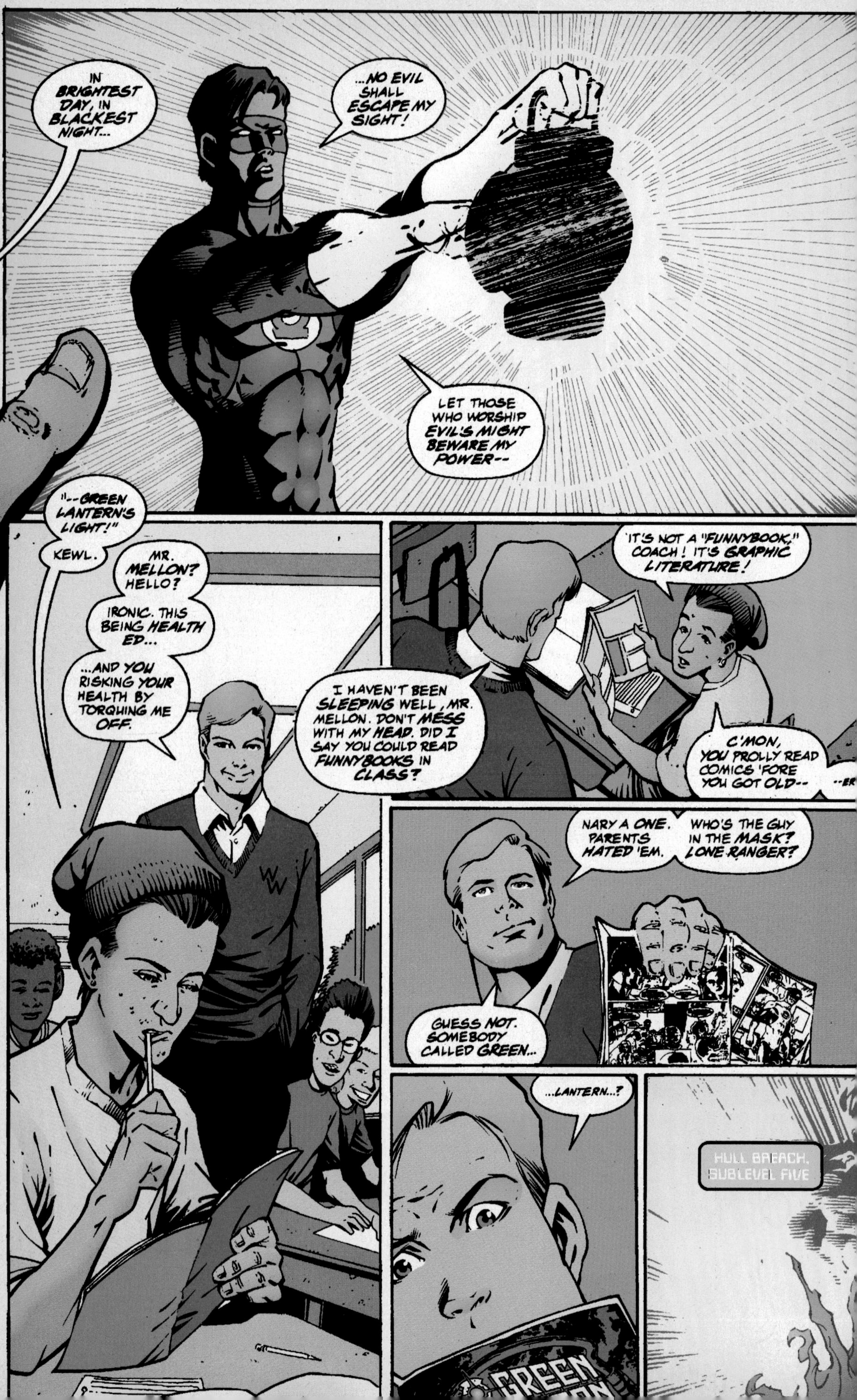
IN BRIGHTEST DAY, IN BLACKEST NIGHT...
...NO EVIL SHALL ESCAPE MY SIGHT!
LET THOSE WHO WORSHIP EVIL'S MIGHT BEWARE MY POWER--
"--GREEN LANTERN'S LIGHT!"
KEWL.
MR. MELLON? HELLO?
IRONIC. THIS BEING HEALTH ED...
...AND YOU RISKING YOUR HEALTH BY TORQUING ME OFF.
I HAVEN'T BEEN SLEEPING WELL, MR. MELLON. DON'T MESS WITH MY HEAD. DID I SAY YOU COULD READ FUNNYBOOKS IN CLASS?
IT'S NOT A "FUNNYBOOK," COACH! IT'S GRAPHIC LITERATURE!
C'MON, YOU PROLLY READ COMICS 'FORE YOU GOT OLD--
NARY A ONE. PARENTS HATED 'EM.
WHO'S THE GUY IN THE MASK? LONE RANGER?
GUESS NOT. SOMEBODY CALLED GREEN...
...LANTERN...?
HULL BREACH, SUBLEVEL FIVE

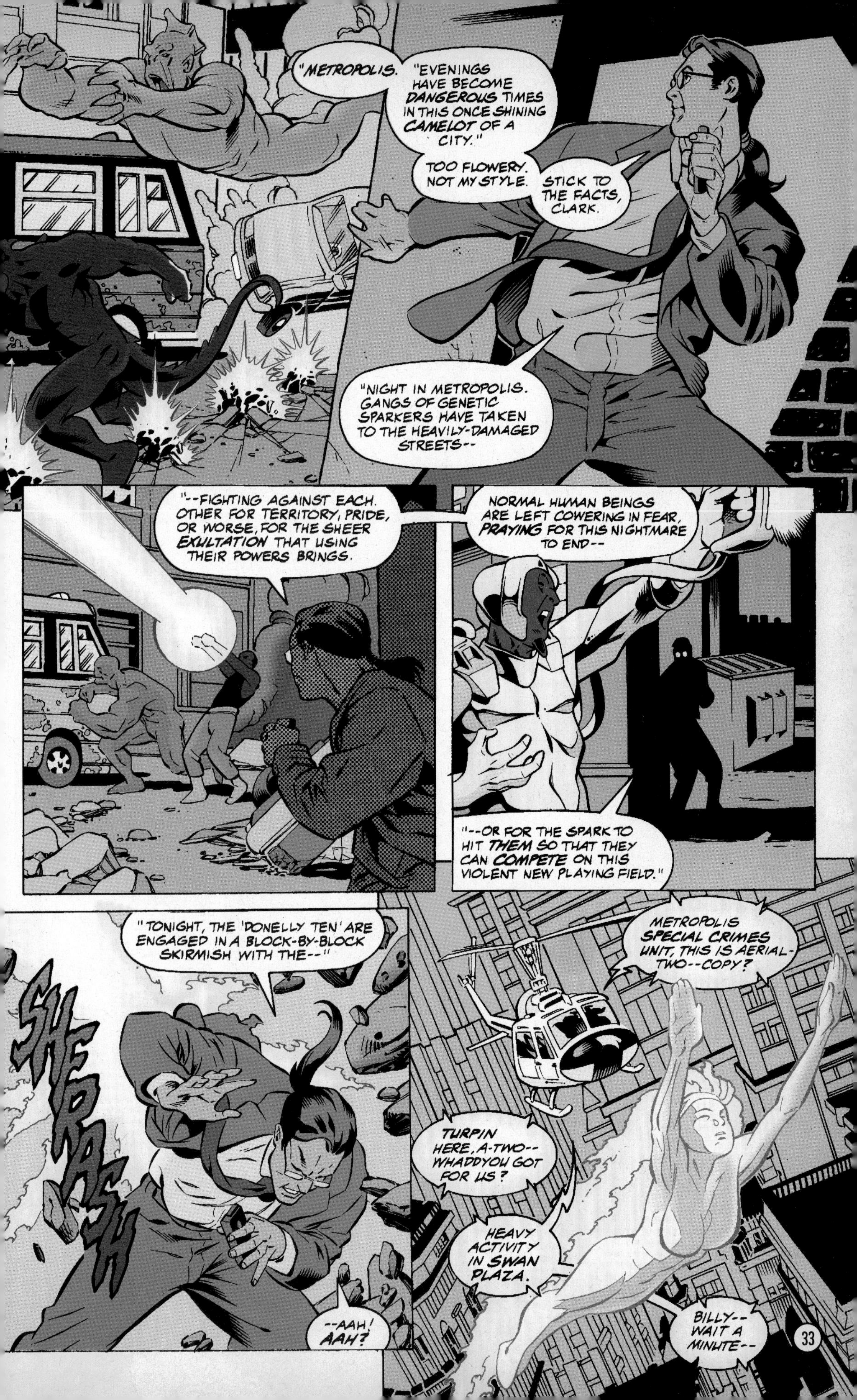
"METROPOLIS.
"EVENINGS HAVE BECOME DANGEROUS TIMES IN THIS ONCE SHINING CAMELOT OF A CITY."
TOO FLOWERY. NOT MY STYLE.
STICK TO THE FACTS, CLARK.
"NIGHT IN METROPOLIS. GANGS OF GENETIC SPARKERS HAVE TAKEN TO THE HEAVILY-DAMAGED STREETS--
"--FIGHTING AGAINST EACH. OTHER FOR TERRITORY, PRIDE, OR WORSE, FOR THE SHEER EXULTATION THAT USING THEIR POWERS BRINGS.
NORMAL HUMAN BEINGS ARE LEFT COWERING IN FEAR, PRAYING FOR THIS NIGHTMARE TO END--
"--OR FOR THE SPARK TO HIT THEM SO THAT THEY CAN COMPETE ON THIS VIOLENT NEW PLAYING FIELD."
"TONIGHT, THE 'DONELLY TEN' ARE ENGAGED IN A BLOCK-BY-BLOCK SKIRMISH WITH THE--"
SHRAASH
--AAH! AAH?
METROPOLIS SPECIAL CRIMES UNIT, THIS IS AERIAL-TWO--COPY?
TURPIN HERE, A-TWO-- WHADDYOU GOT FOR US?
HEAVY ACTIVITY IN SWAN PLAZA.
BILLY-- WAIT A MINUTE--

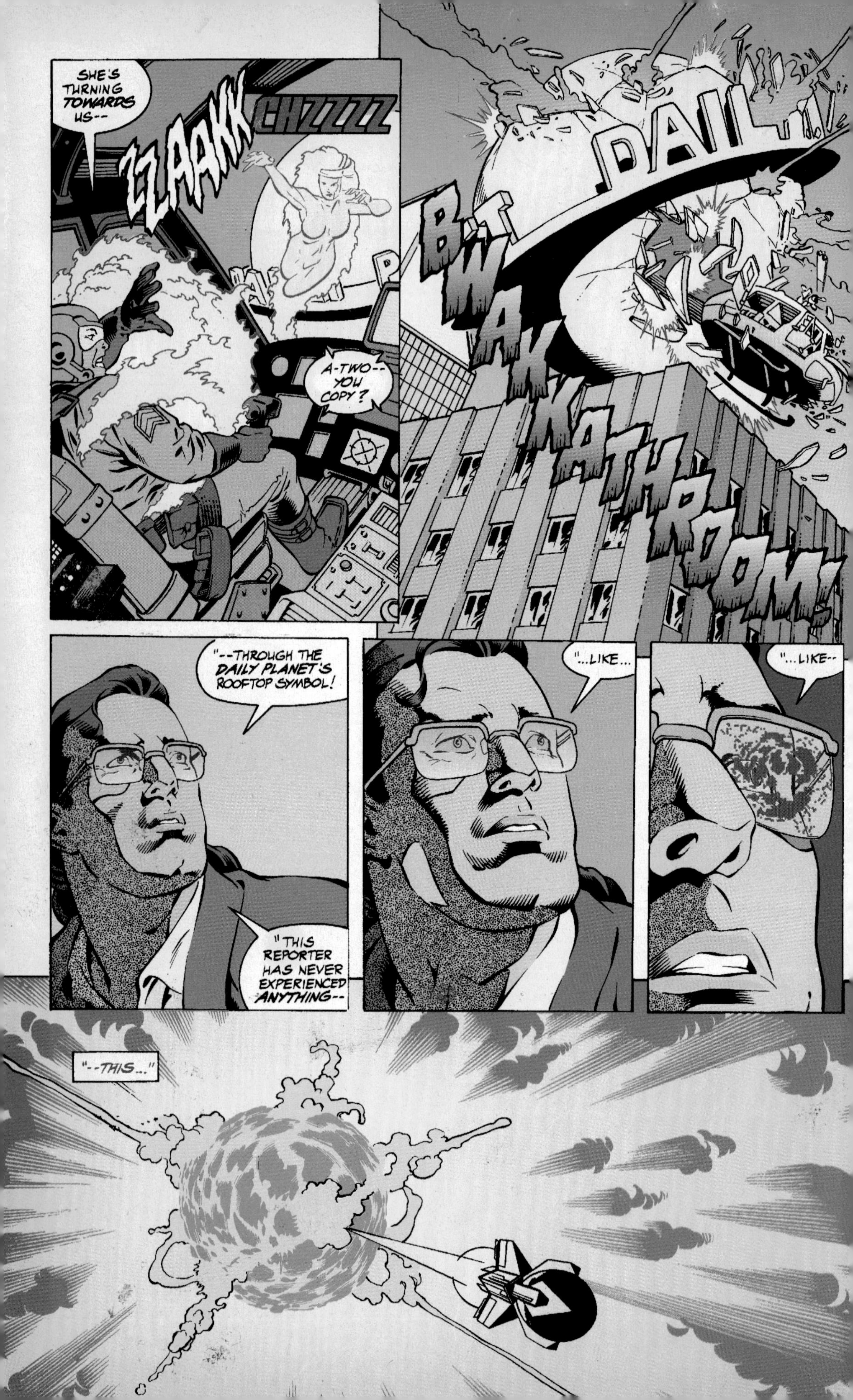
SHE'S TURNING TOWARDS US--
ZZAAKK
CHZZZZZ
A-TWO-- YOU COPY?
BWAKKATHROOM!
DAIL
"--THROUGH THE DAILY PLANET'S ROOFTOP SYMBOL!
"THIS REPORTER HAS NEVER EXPERIENCED ANYTHING--
"...LIKE...
"...LIKE--
"--THIS..."

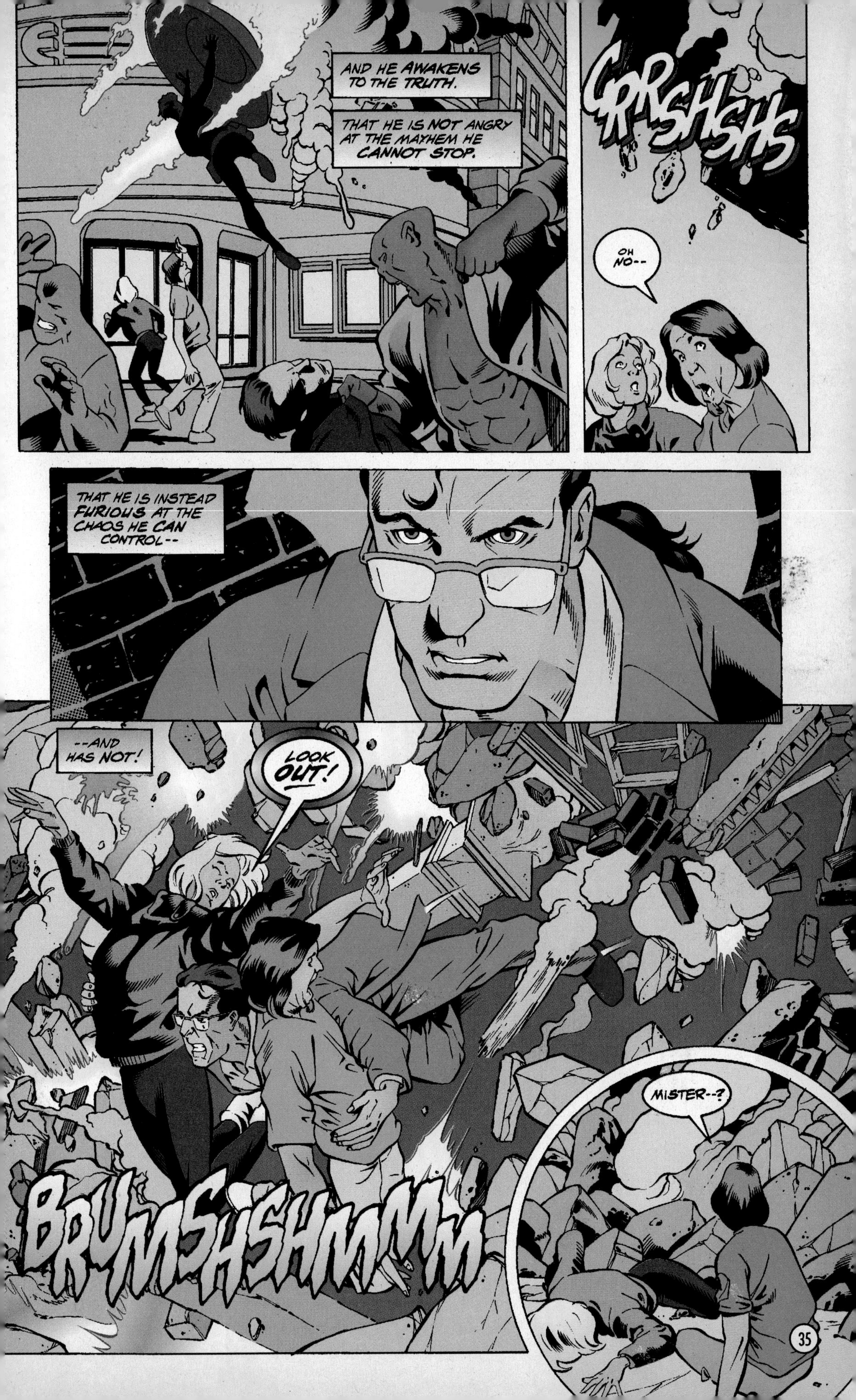
AND HE AWAKENS TO THE TRUTH.
THAT HE IS NOT ANGRY AT THE MAYHEM HE CANNOT STOP.
CRRSHSHS
OH NO--
THAT HE IS INSTEAD FURIOUS AT THE CHAOS HE CAN CONTROL--
--AND HAS NOT!
LOOK OUT!
MISTER--?
BRUMSHSHMMM

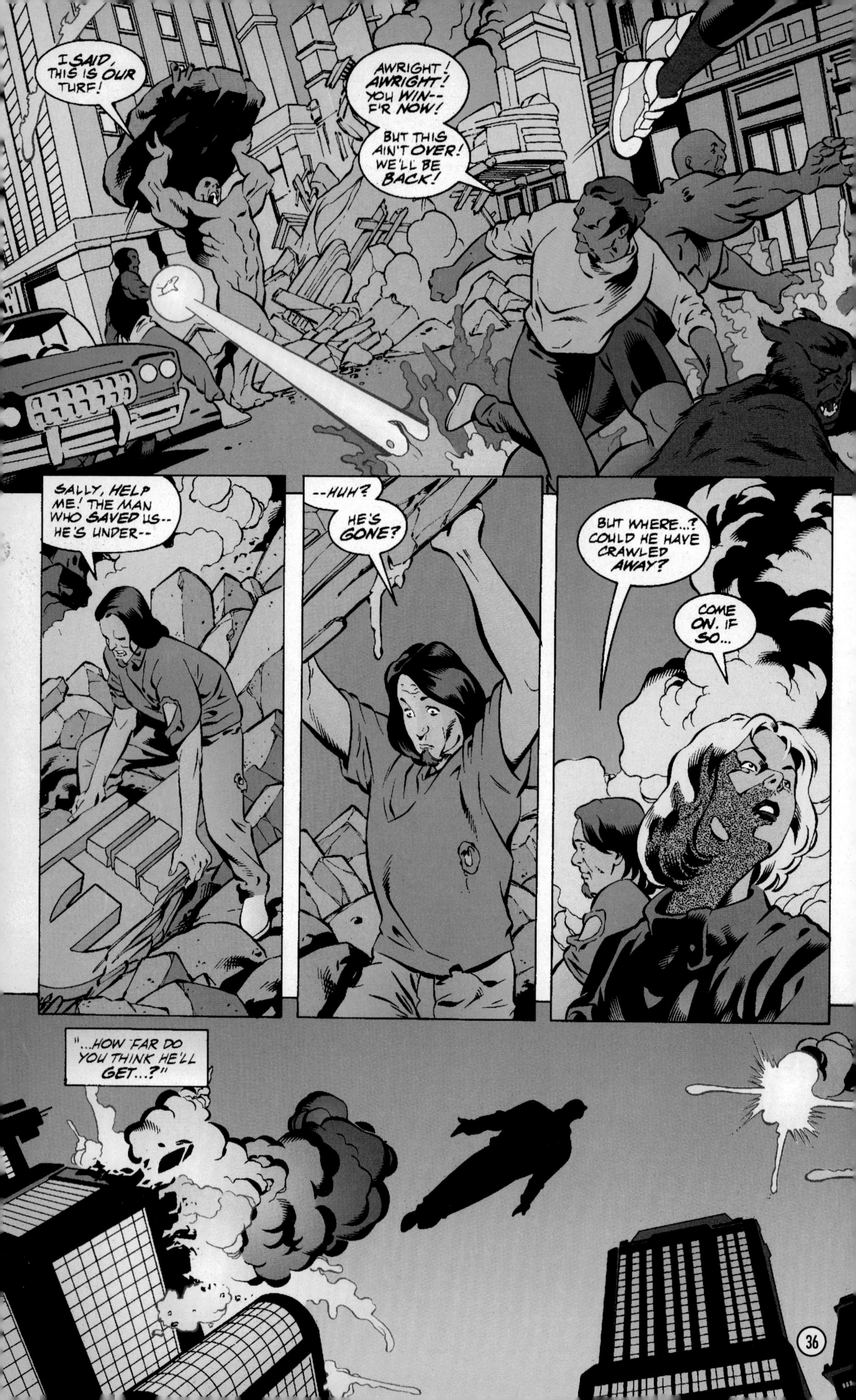
I SAID, THIS IS OUR TURF!
AWRIGHT! AWRIGHT! YOU WIN-- F'R NOW!
BUT THIS AIN'T OVER! WE'LL BE BACK!
SALLY, HELP ME! THE MAN WHO SAVED US-- HE'S UNDER--
--HUH?
HE'S GONE?
BUT WHERE...? COULD HE HAVE CRAWLED AWAY?
COME ON. IF SO...
"...HOW FAR DO YOU THINK HE'LL GET...?"
36

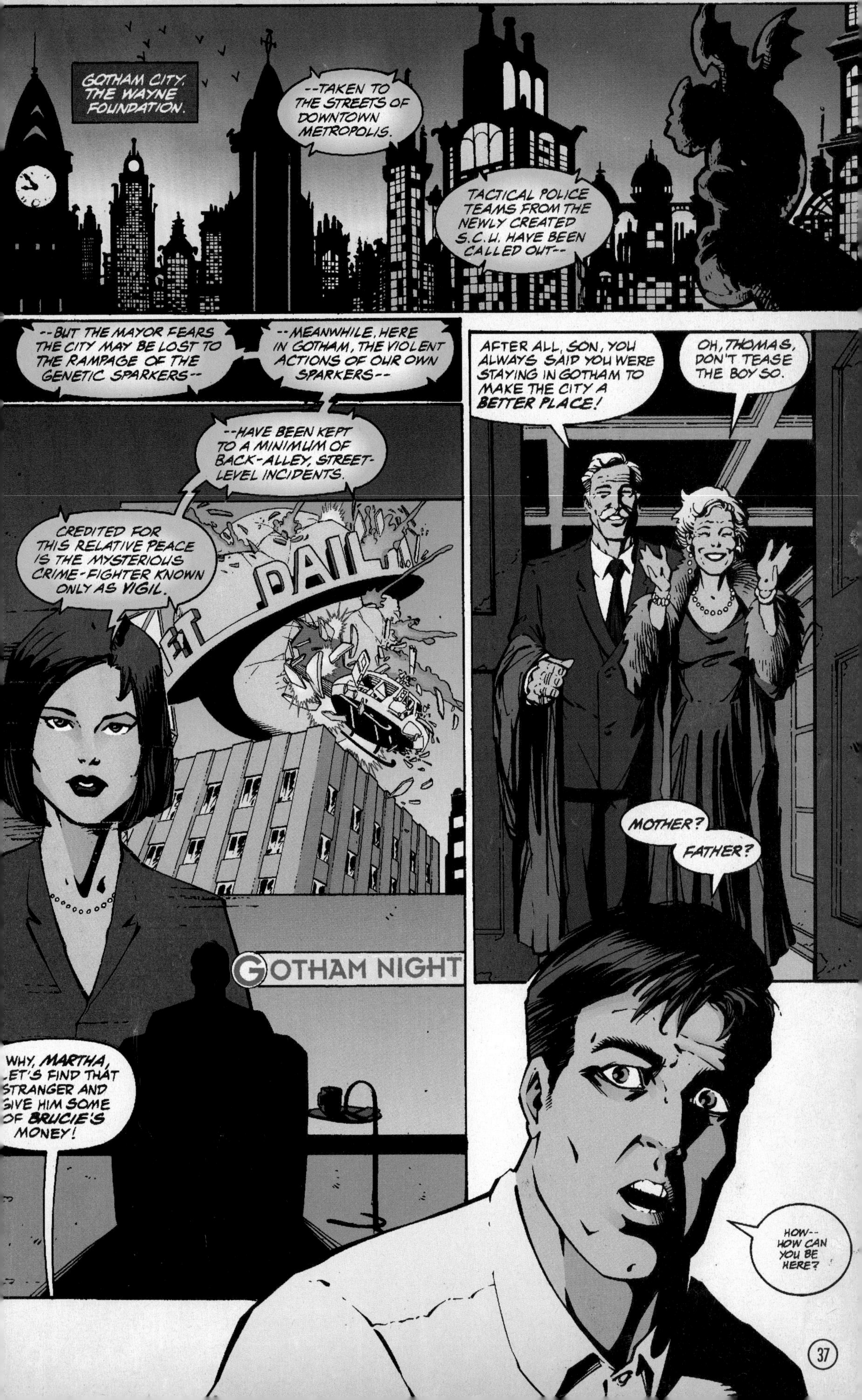
GOTHAM CITY. THE WAYNE FOUNDATION.
--TAKEN TO THE STREETS OF DOWNTOWN METROPOLIS.
TACTICAL POLICE TEAMS FROM THE NEWLY CREATED S.C.U. HAVE BEEN CALLED OUT--
--BUT THE MAYOR FEARS THE CITY MAY BE LOST TO THE RAMPAGE OF THE GENETIC SPARKERS--
--MEANWHILE, HERE IN GOTHAM, THE VIOLENT ACTIONS OF OUR OWN SPARKERS--
--HAVE BEEN KEPT TO A MINIMUM OF BACK-ALLEY, STREET-LEVEL INCIDENTS.
CREDITED FOR THIS RELATIVE PEACE IS THE MYSTERIOUS CRIME-FIGHTER KNOWN ONLY AS VIGIL.
GOTHAM NIGHT
AFTER ALL, SON, YOU ALWAYS SAID YOU WERE STAYING IN GOTHAM TO MAKE THE CITY A BETTER PLACE!
OH, THOMAS, DON'T TEASE THE BOY SO.
MOTHER?
FATHER?
WHY, MARTHA, LET'S FIND THAT STRANGER AND GIVE HIM SOME OF BRUCIE'S MONEY!
HOW-- HOW CAN YOU BE HERE?

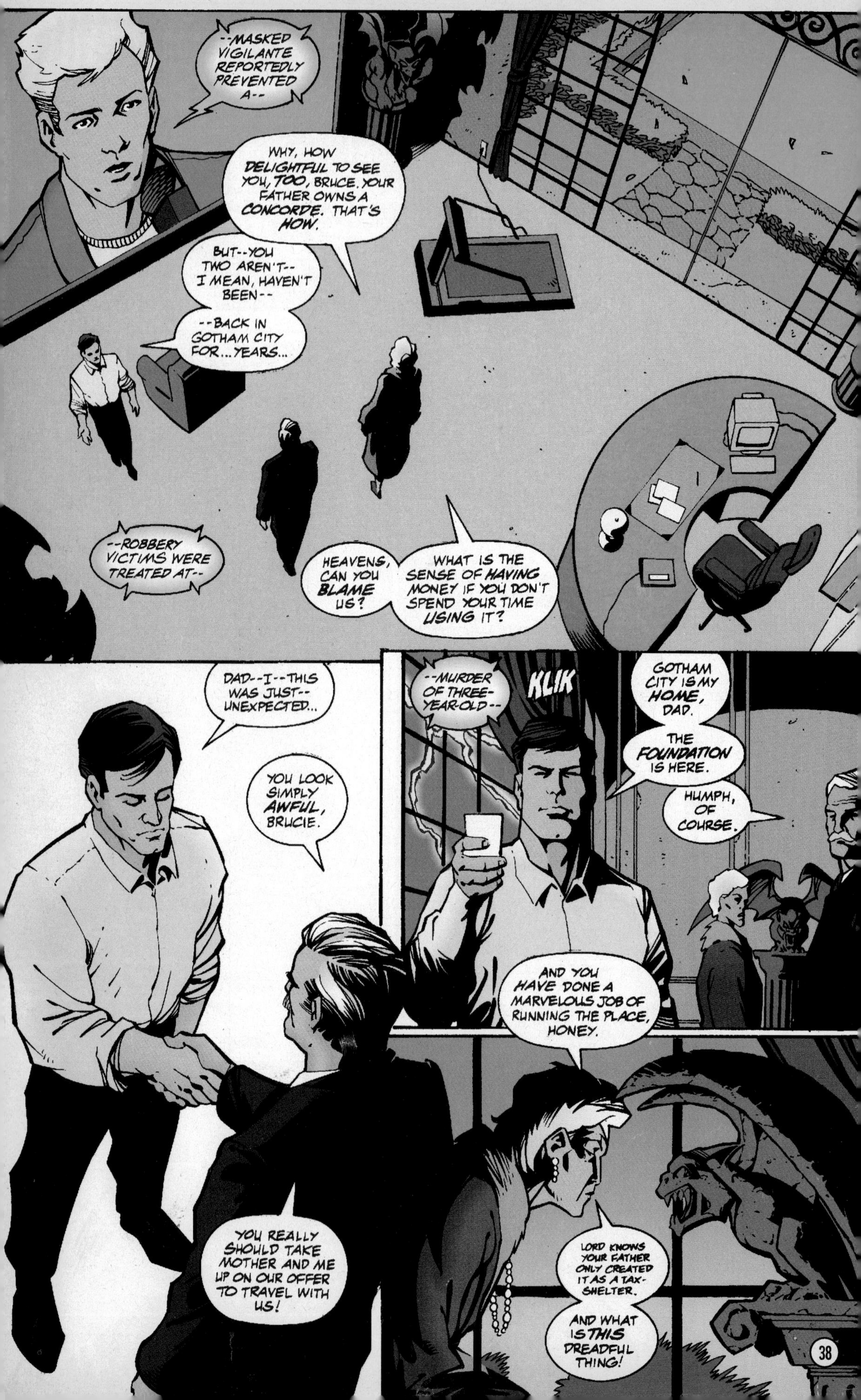
--MASKED VIGILANTE REPORTEDLY PREVENTED A--
WHY, HOW DELIGHTFUL TO SEE YOU, TOO, BRUCE. YOUR FATHER OWNS A CONCORDE. THAT'S HOW.
BUT--YOU TWO AREN'T-- I MEAN, HAVEN'T BEEN--
--BACK IN GOTHAM CITY FOR... YEARS...
--ROBBERY VICTIMS WERE TREATED AT--
HEAVENS, CAN YOU BLAME US?
WHAT IS THE SENSE OF HAVING MONEY IF YOU DON'T SPEND YOUR TIME USING IT?
DAD--I--THIS WAS JUST-- UNEXPECTED...
YOU LOOK SIMPLY AWFUL, BRUCIE.
--MURDER OF THREE-YEAR-OLD--
KLIK
GOTHAM CITY IS MY HOME, DAD.
THE FOUNDATION IS HERE.
HUMPH, OF COURSE.
AND YOU HAVE DONE A MARVELOUS JOB OF RUNNING THE PLACE, HONEY.
YOU REALLY SHOULD TAKE MOTHER AND ME UP ON OUR OFFER TO TRAVEL WITH US!
LORD KNOWS YOUR FATHER ONLY CREATED IT AS A TAX-SHELTER.
AND WHAT IS THIS DREADFUL THING!

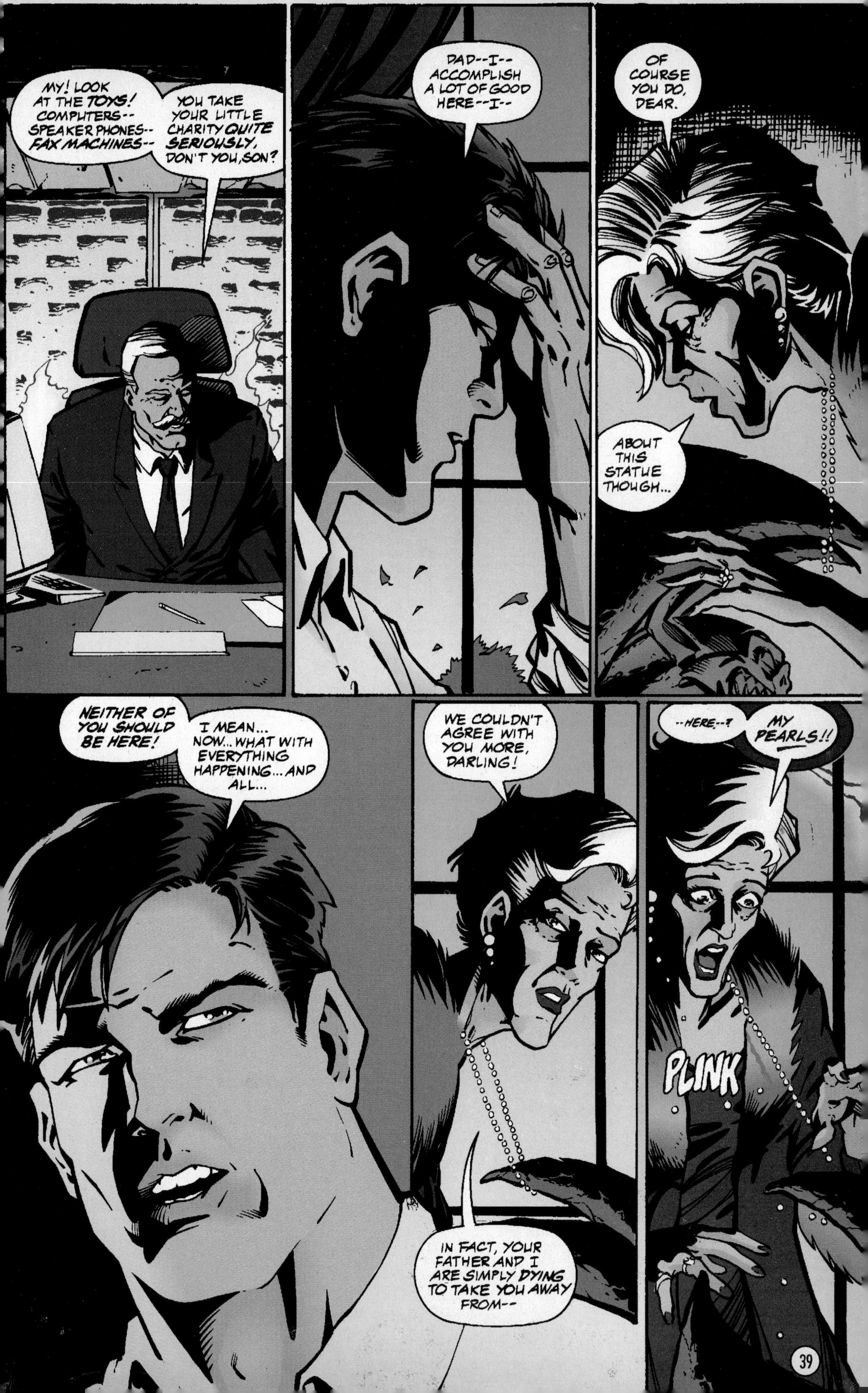
MY! LOOK AT THE TOYS! COMPUTERS-- SPEAKER PHONES-- FAX MACHINES--
YOU TAKE YOUR LITTLE CHARITY QUITE SERIOUSLY, DON'T YOU, SON?
DAD--I-- ACCOMPLISH A LOT OF GOOD HERE--I--
OF COURSE YOU DO, DEAR.
ABOUT THIS STATUE THOUGH...
NEITHER OF YOU SHOULD BE HERE!
I MEAN... NOW... WHAT WITH EVERYTHING HAPPENING... AND ALL...
WE COULDN'T AGREE WITH YOU MORE, DARLING!
IN FACT, YOUR FATHER AND I ARE SIMPLY DYING TO TAKE YOU AWAY FROM--
--HERE--?
MY PEARLS!!
PLINK

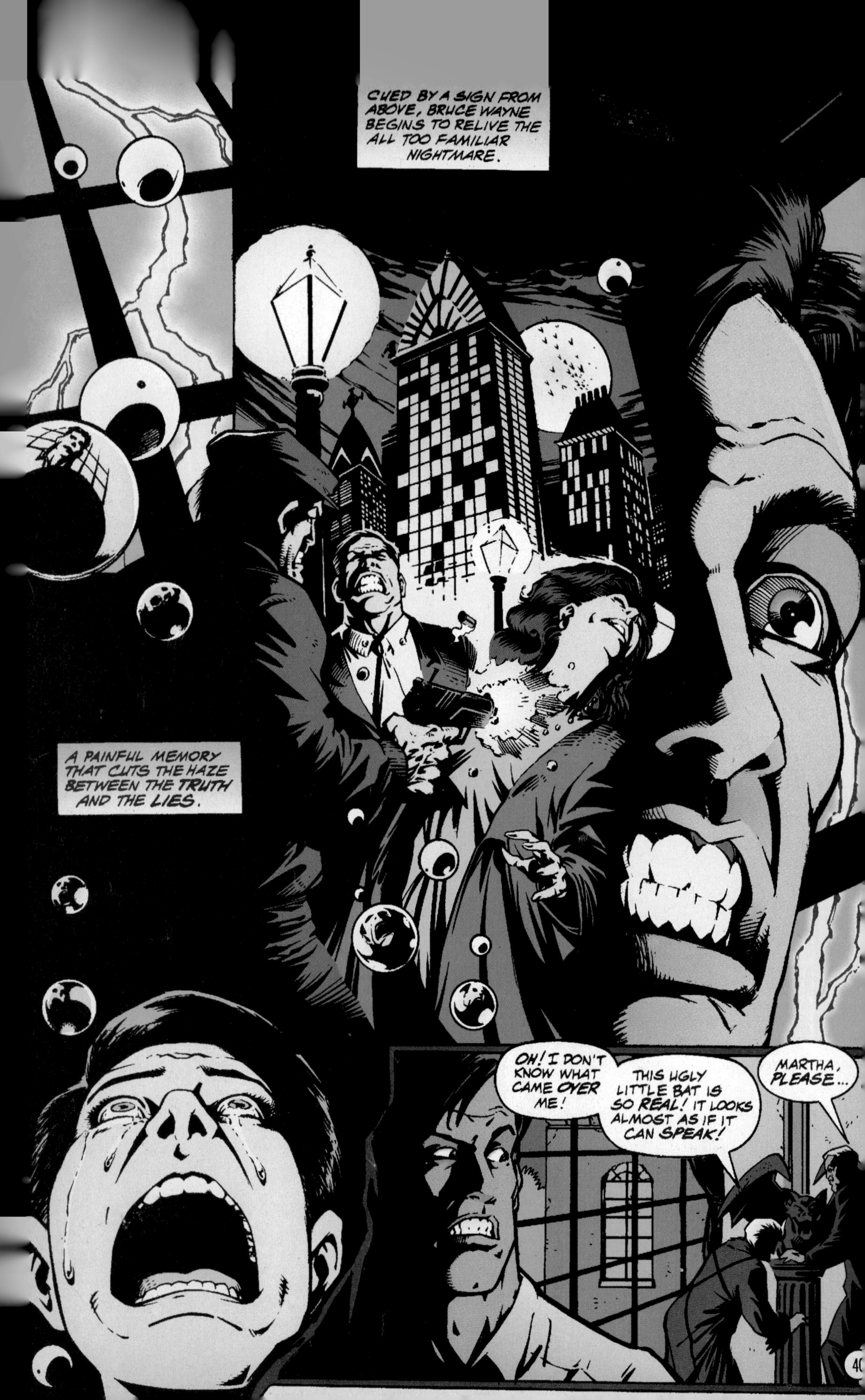
CUED BY A SIGN FROM ABOVE, BRUCE WAYNE BEGINS TO RELIVE THE ALL TOO FAMILIAR NIGHTMARE.
A PAINFUL MEMORY THAT CUTS THE HAZE BETWEEN THE TRUTH AND THE LIES.
OH! I DON'T KNOW WHAT CAME OVER ME!
THIS UGLY LITTLE BAT IS SO REAL! IT LOOKS ALMOST AS IF IT CAN SPEAK!
MARTHA, PLEASE...

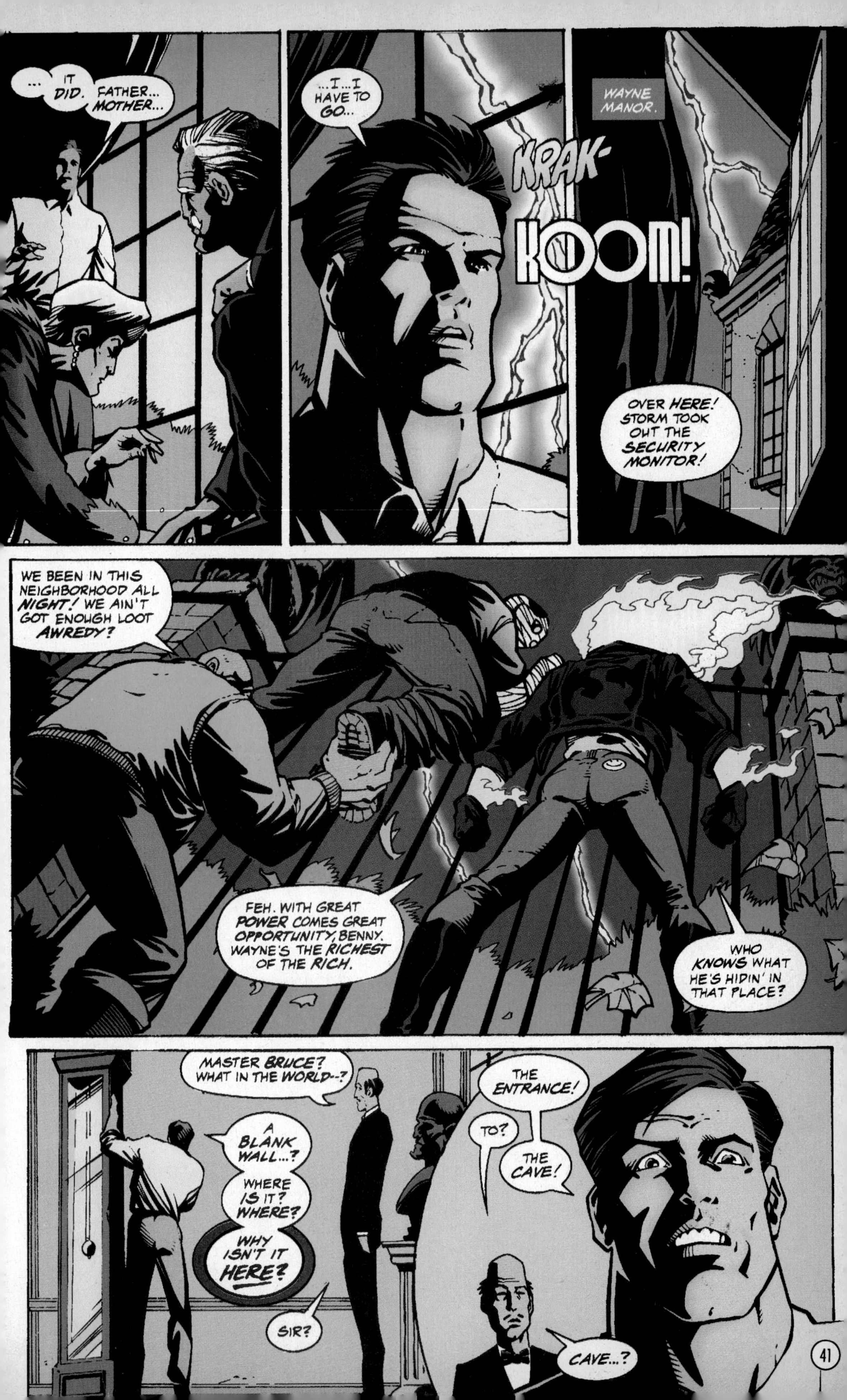

... IT DID.
FATHER... MOTHER...
...I...I HAVE TO GO...
WAYNE MANOR.
KRAK-KOOM!
OVER HERE! STORM TOOK OUT THE SECURITY MONITOR!
WE BEEN IN THIS NEIGHBORHOOD ALL NIGHT! WE AIN'T GOT ENOUGH LOOT AWREDY?
FEH. WITH GREAT POWER COMES GREAT OPPORTUNITY, BENNY. WAYNE'S THE RICHEST OF THE RICH.
WHO KNOWS WHAT HE'S HIDIN' IN THAT PLACE?
MASTER BRUCE? WHAT IN THE WORLD--?
A BLANK WALL...?
WHERE IS IT? WHERE?
WHY ISN'T IT HERE?
SIR?
THE ENTRANCE!
TO?
THE CAVE!
CAVE...?

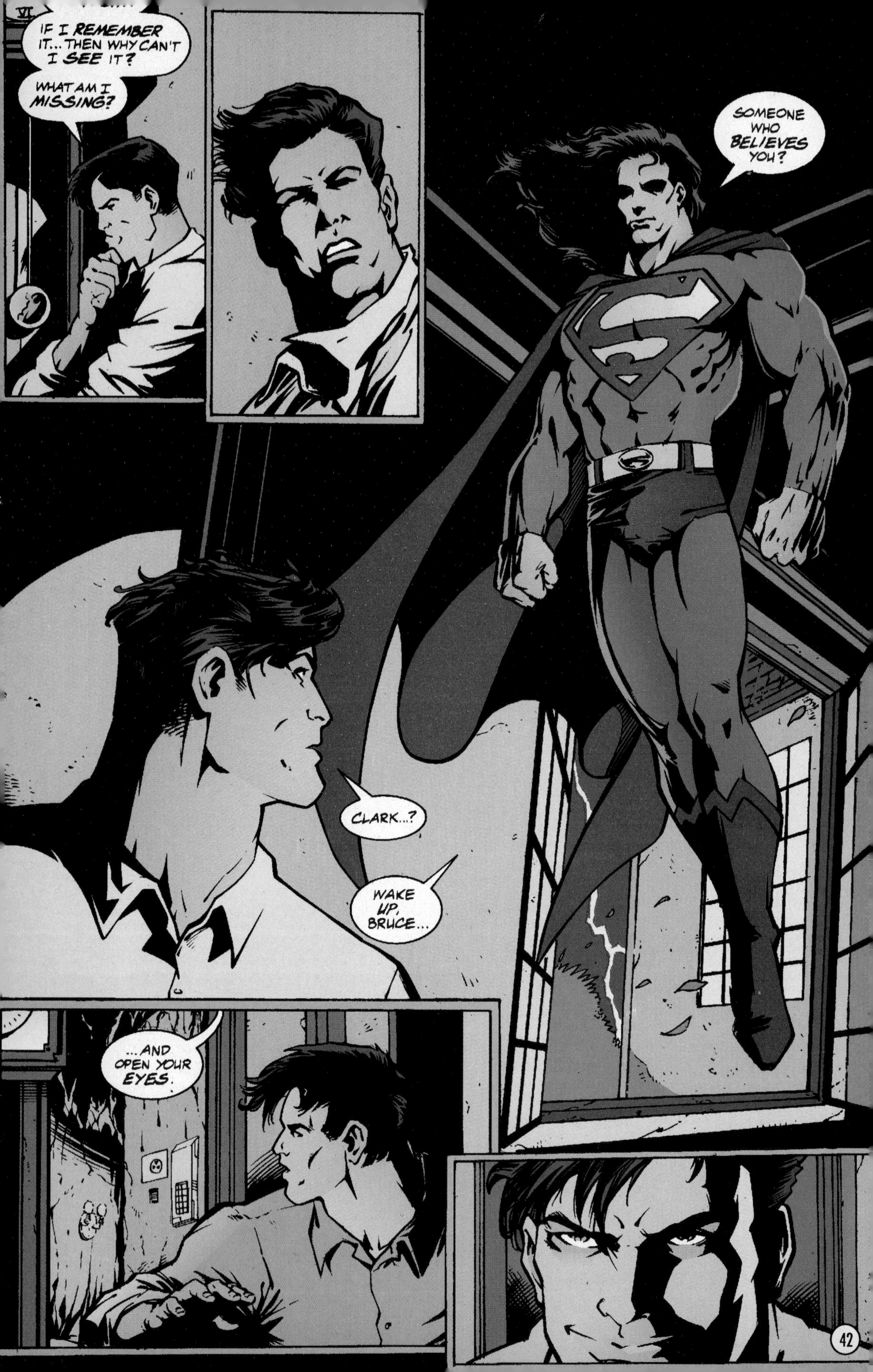
IF I REMEMBER IT... THEN WHY CAN'T I SEE IT?
WHAT AM I MISSING?
SOMEONE WHO BELIEVES YOU?
CLARK...?
WAKE UP, BRUCE...
...AND OPEN YOUR EYES.

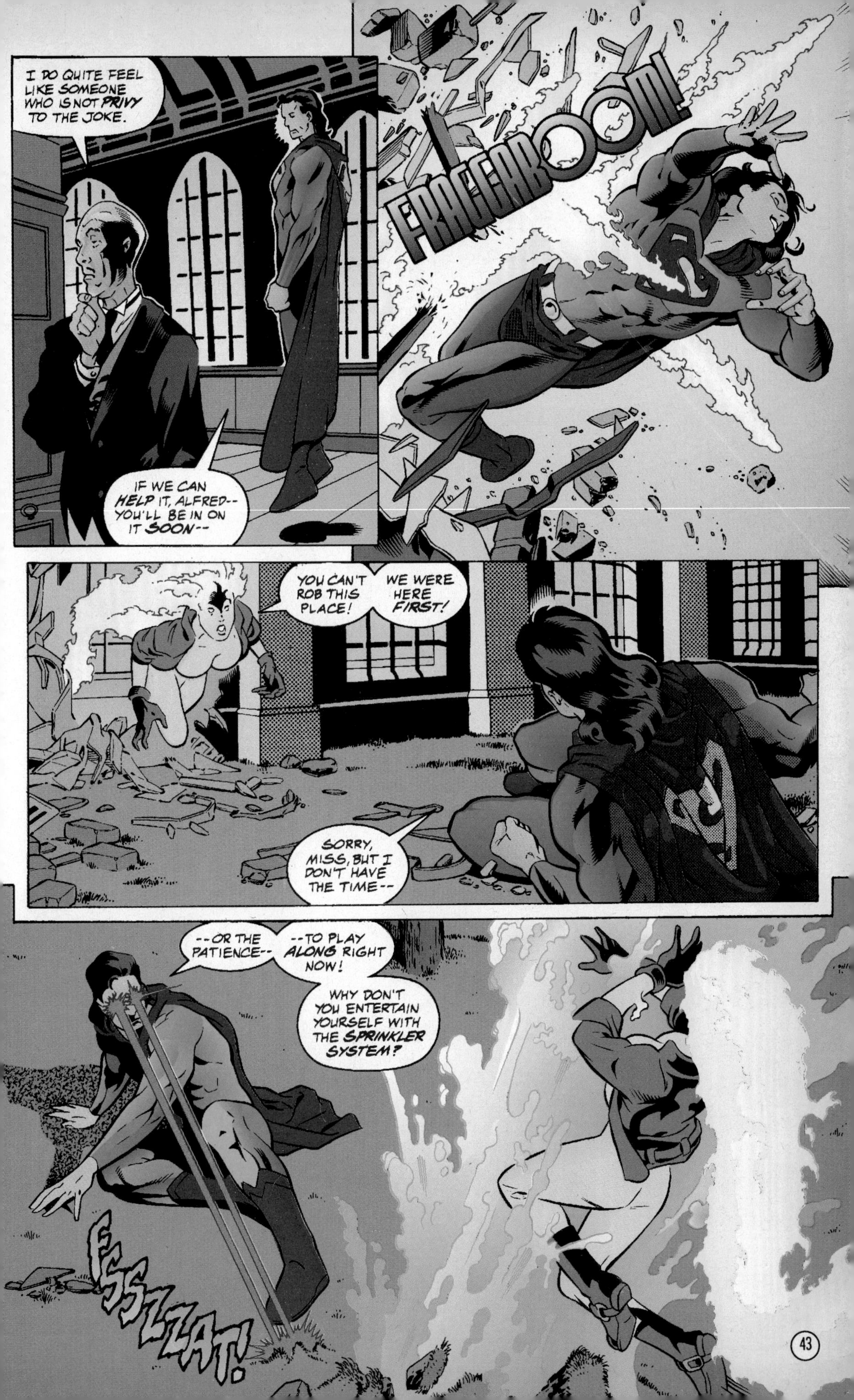

I DO QUITE FEEL LIKE SOMEONE WHO IS NOT PRIVY TO THE JOKE.
IF WE CAN HELP IT, ALFRED-- YOU'LL BE IN ON IT SOON--
FRAGGABOOM!
YOU CAN'T ROB THIS PLACE!
WE WERE HERE FIRST!
SORRY, MISS, BUT I DON'T HAVE THE TIME--
--OR THE PATIENCE--
--TO PLAY ALONG RIGHT NOW!
WHY DON'T YOU ENTERTAIN YOURSELF WITH THE SPRINKLER SYSTEM?
FSSZZAT!

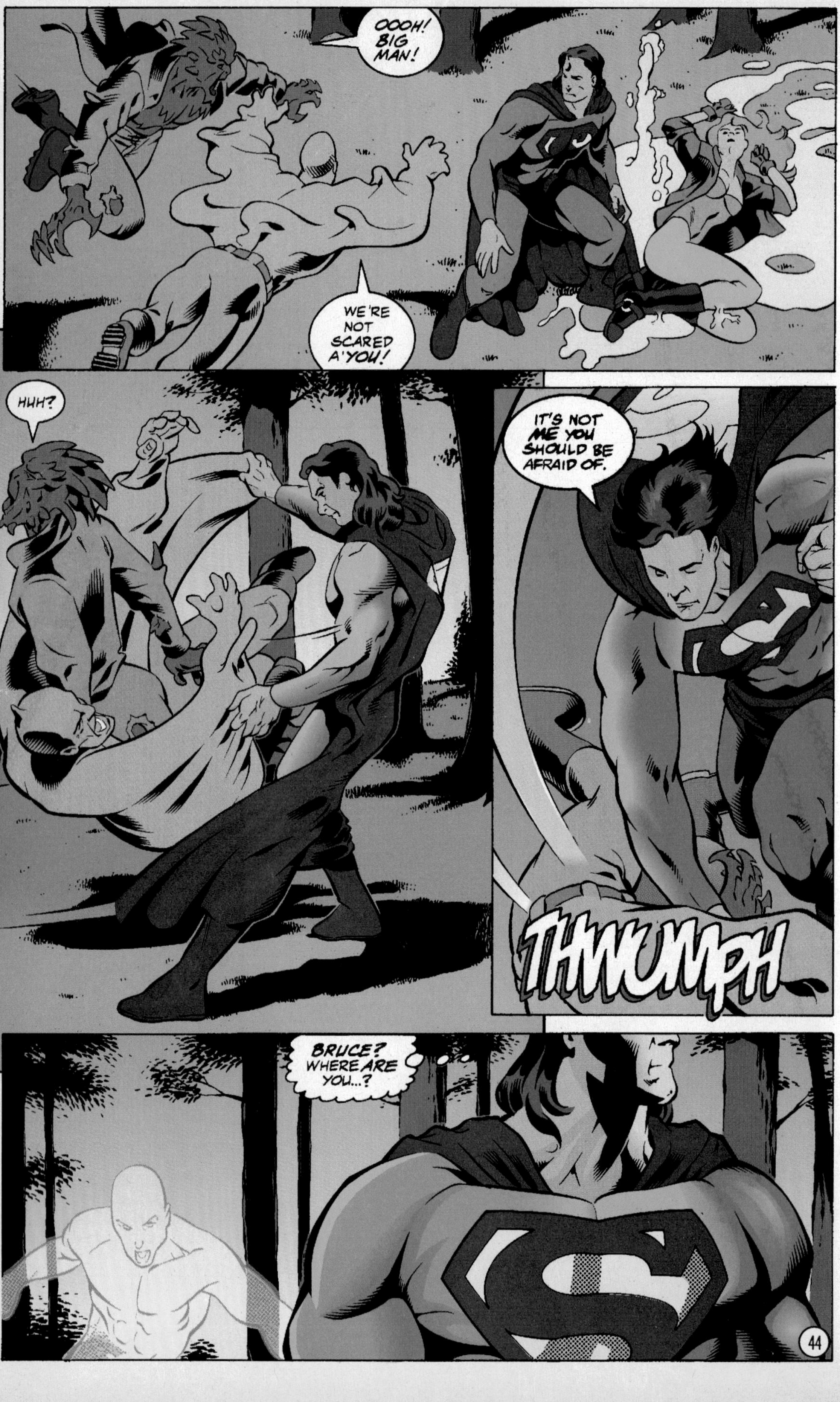

OOOH! BIG MAN!
WE'RE NOT SCARED A'YOU!
HUH?
IT'S NOT ME YOU SHOULD BE AFRAID OF.
THWUMPH
BRUCE? WHERE ARE YOU...?

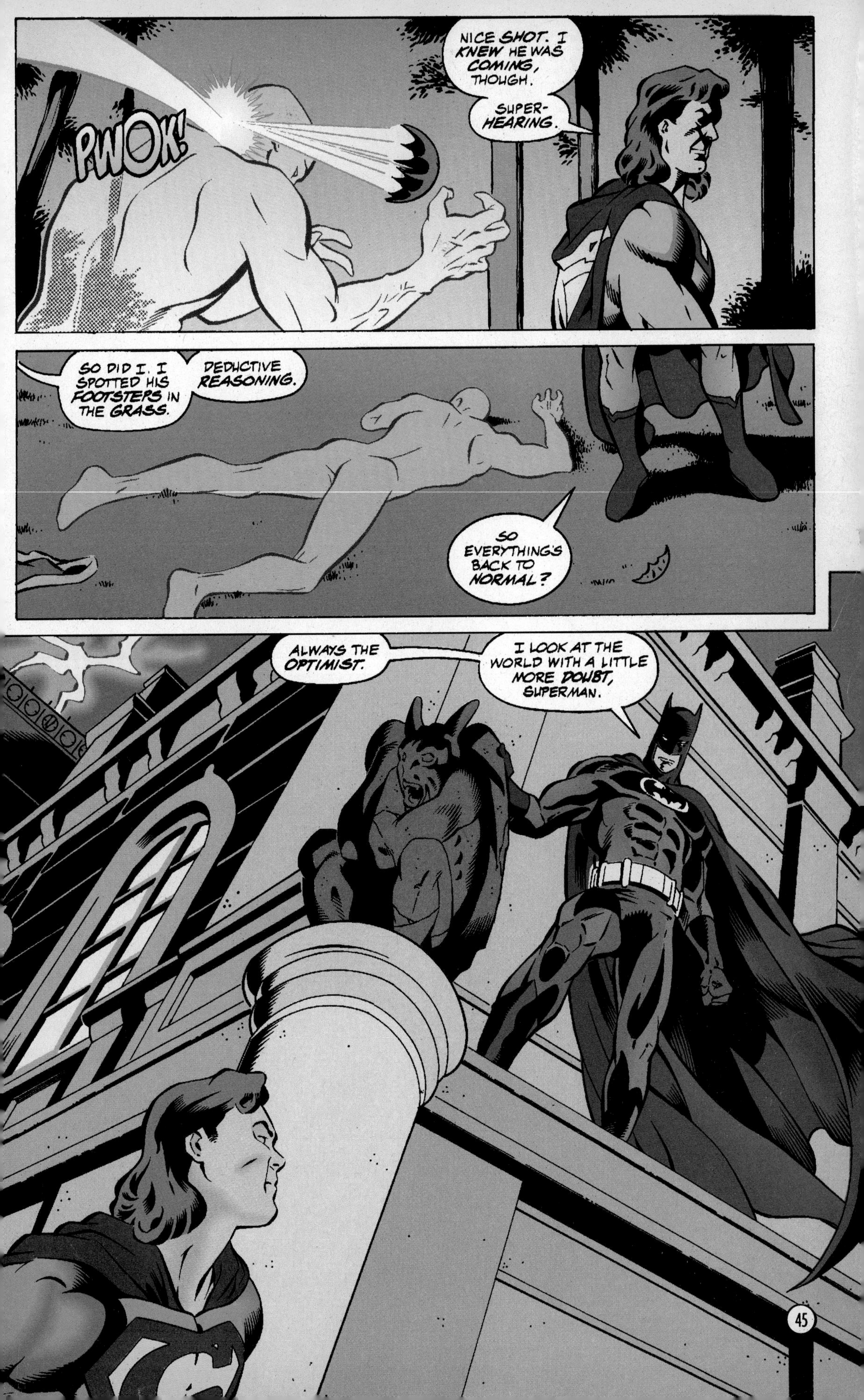
PWOK!
NICE SHOT. I KNEW HE WAS COMING, THOUGH.
SUPER-HEARING.
SO DID I. I SPOTTED HIS FOOTSTEPS IN THE GRASS.
DEDUCTIVE REASONING.
SO EVERYTHING'S BACK TO NORMAL?
ALWAYS THE OPTIMIST.
I LOOK AT THE WORLD WITH A LITTLE MORE DOUBT, SUPERMAN.

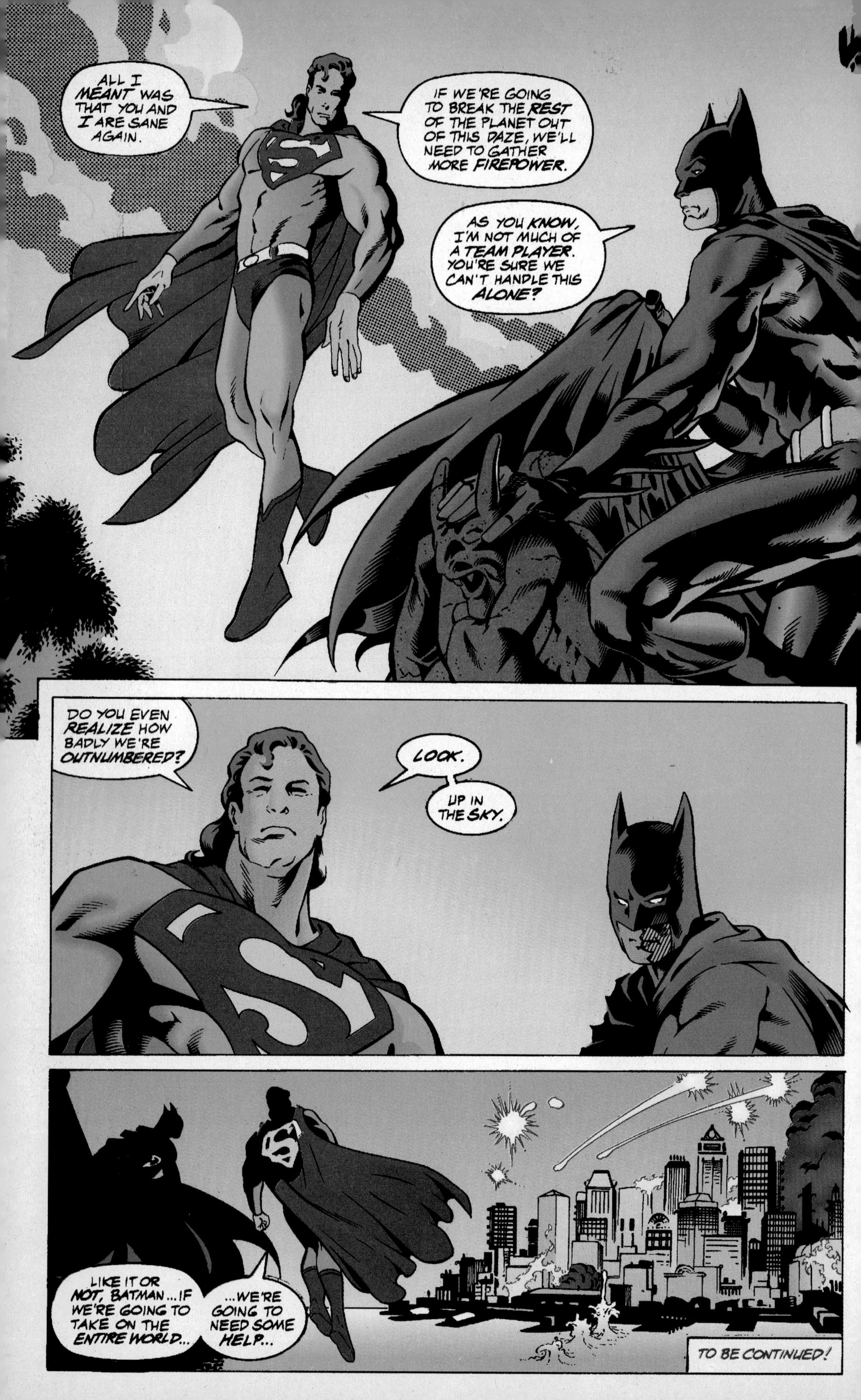
ALL I MEANT WAS THAT YOU AND I ARE SANE AGAIN.
IF WE'RE GOING TO BREAK THE REST OF THE PLANET OUT OF THIS DAZE, WE'LL NEED TO GATHER MORE FIREPOWER.
AS YOU KNOW, I'M NOT MUCH OF A TEAM PLAYER. YOU'RE SURE WE CAN'T HANDLE THIS ALONE?
DO YOU EVEN REALIZE HOW BADLY WE'RE OUTNUMBERED?
LOOK.
UP IN THE SKY.
LIKE IT OR NOT, BATMAN...IF WE'RE GOING TO TAKE ON THE ENTIRE WORLD...
...WE'RE GOING TO NEED SOME HELP...
TO BE CONTINUED!

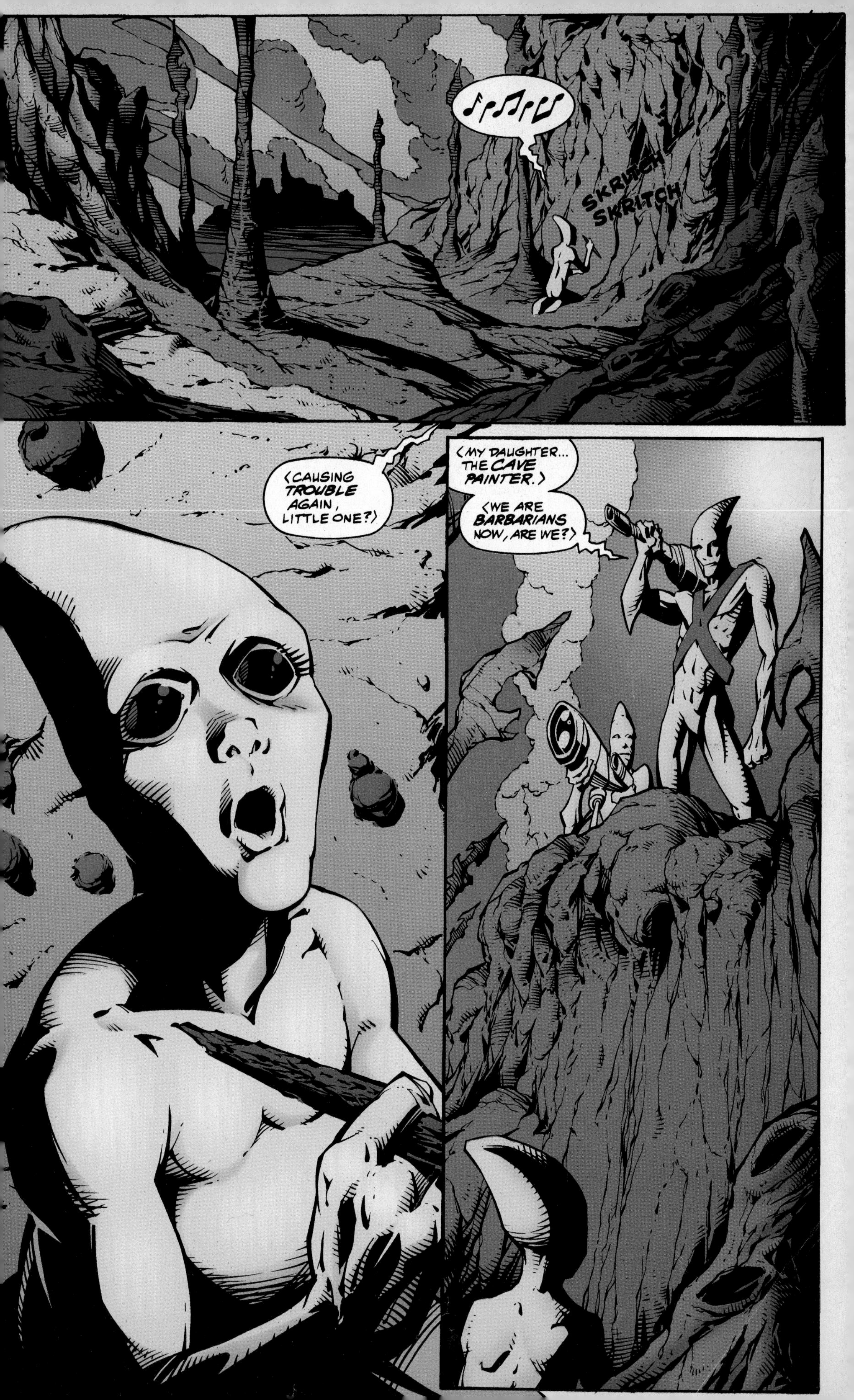
SKRITCH
SKRITCH
<CAUSING TROUBLE AGAIN, LITTLE ONE?>
<MY DAUGHTER... THE CAVE PAINTER.>
<WE ARE BARBARIANS NOW, ARE WE?>

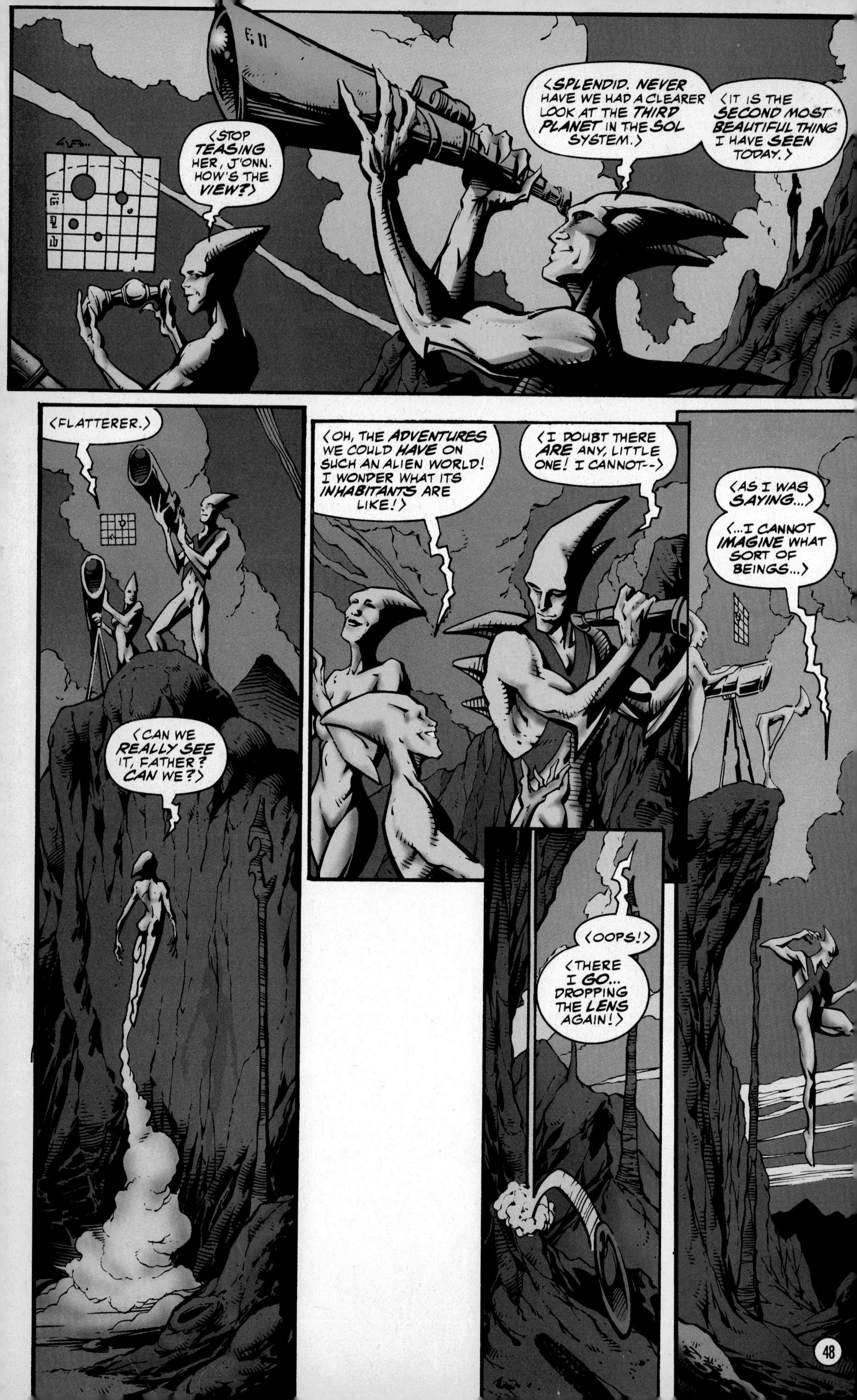

<STOP TEASING HER, J'ONN. HOW'S THE VIEW?>
<SPLENDID. NEVER HAVE WE HAD A CLEARER LOOK AT THE THIRD PLANET IN THE SOL SYSTEM.>
<IT IS THE SECOND MOST BEAUTIFUL THING I HAVE SEEN TODAY.>
<FLATTERER.>
<CAN WE REALLY SEE IT, FATHER? CAN WE?>
<OH, THE ADVENTURES WE COULD HAVE ON SUCH AN ALIEN WORLD! I WONDER WHAT ITS INHABITANTS ARE LIKE!>
<I DOUBT THERE ARE ANY, LITTLE ONE! I CANNOT-->
<OOPS!>
<THERE I GO... DROPPING THE LENS AGAIN!>
<AS I WAS SAYING...>
<...I CANNOT IMAGINE WHAT SORT OF BEINGS...>

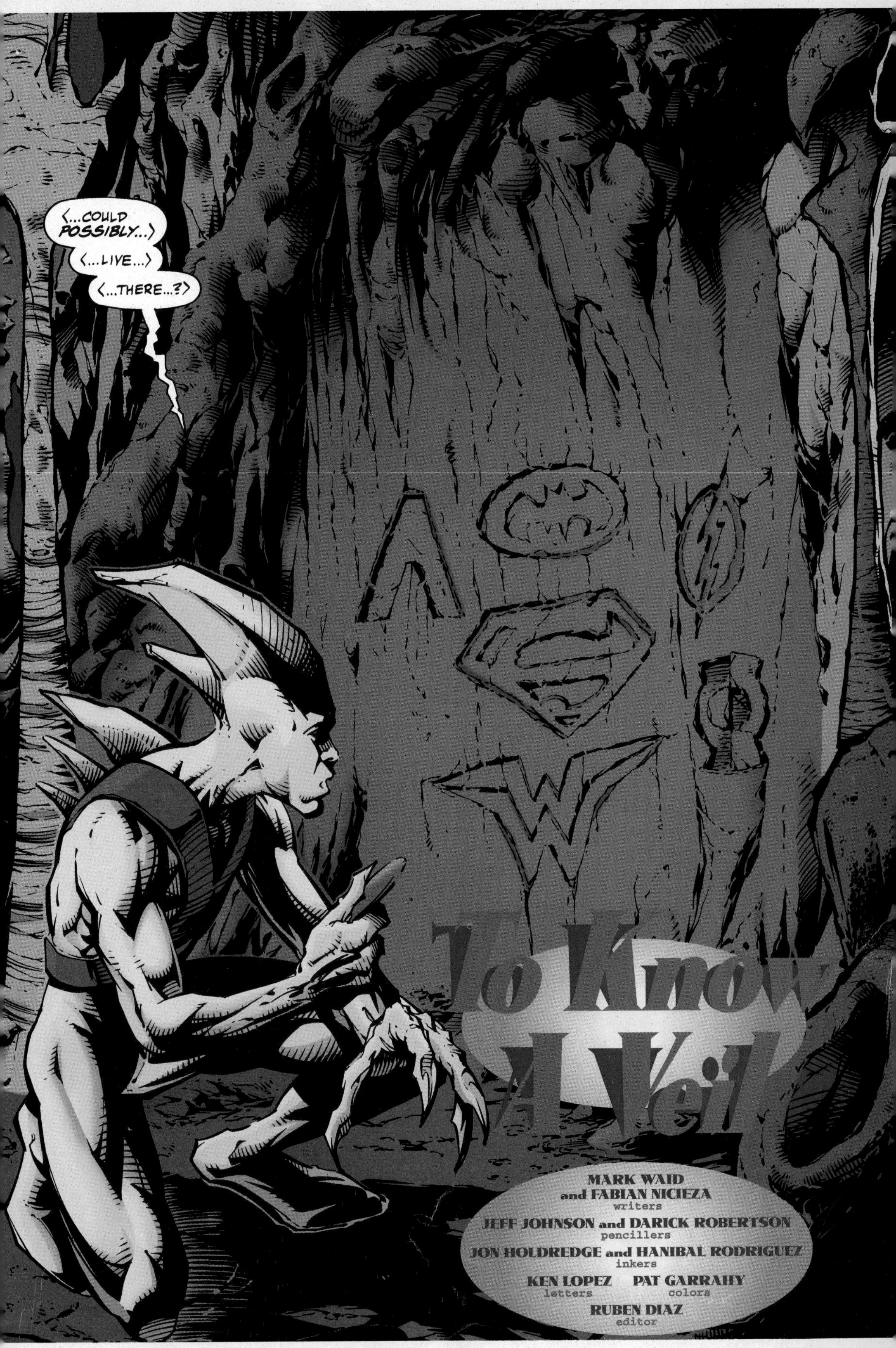

<...COULD POSSIBLY...>
<...LIVE...>
<...THERE...?>
To Know A Veil
MARK WAID and FABIAN NICIEZA writers
JEFF JOHNSON and DARICK ROBERTSON pencillers
JON HOLDREDGE and HANIBAL RODRIGUEZ inkers
KEN LOPEZ letters
PAT GARRAHY colors
RUBEN DIAZ editor

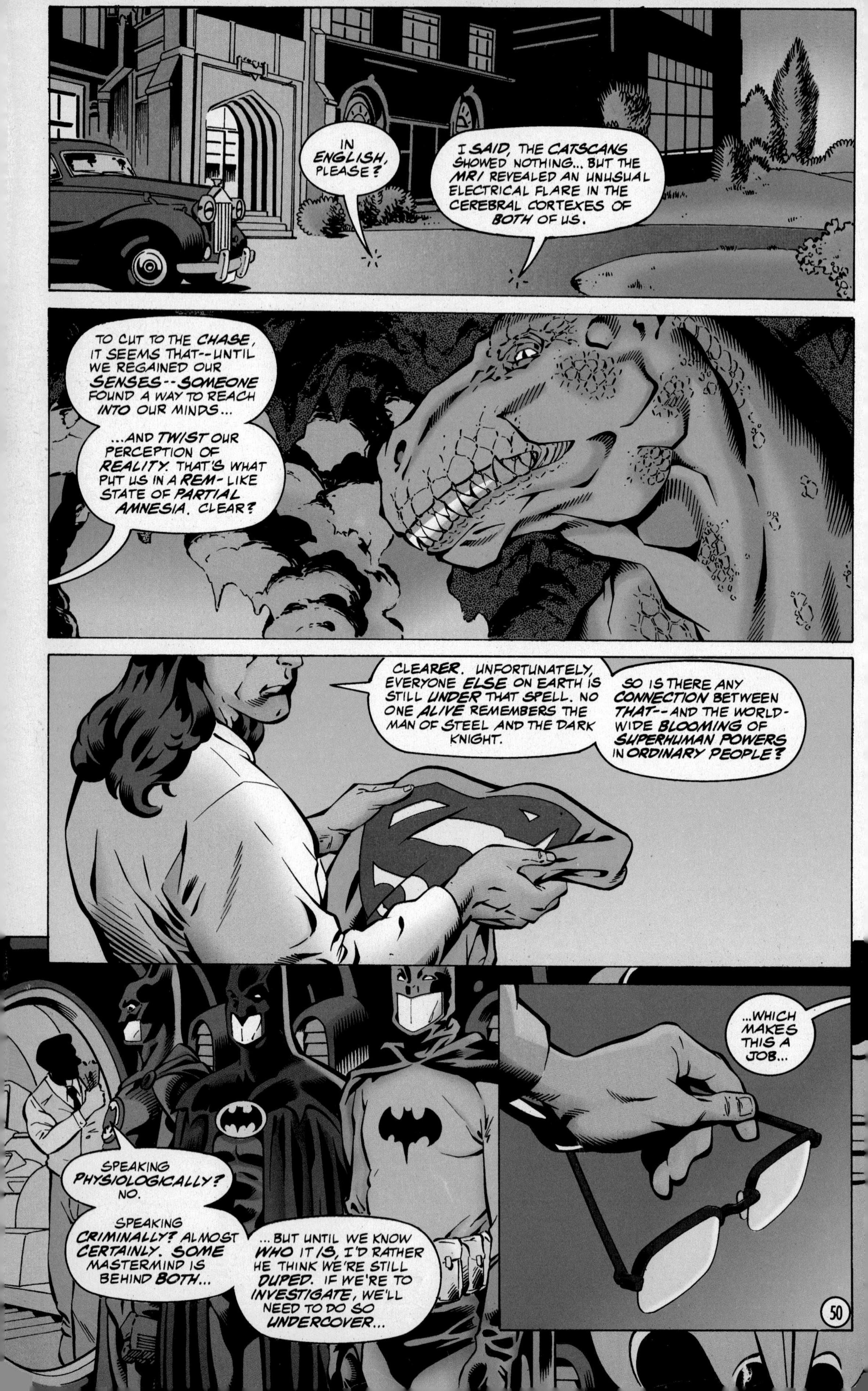

IN ENGLISH, PLEASE?
I SAID, THE CATSCANS SHOWED NOTHING... BUT THE MRI REVEALED AN UNUSUAL ELECTRICAL FLARE IN THE CEREBRAL CORTEXES OF BOTH OF US.
TO CUT TO THE CHASE, IT SEEMS THAT--UNTIL WE REGAINED OUR SENSES--SOMEONE FOUND A WAY TO REACH INTO OUR MINDS...
...AND TWIST OUR PERCEPTION OF REALITY. THAT'S WHAT PUT US IN A REM-LIKE STATE OF PARTIAL AMNESIA. CLEAR?
CLEARER. UNFORTUNATELY, EVERYONE ELSE ON EARTH IS STILL UNDER THAT SPELL. NO ONE ALIVE REMEMBERS THE MAN OF STEEL AND THE DARK KNIGHT.
SO IS THERE ANY CONNECTION BETWEEN THAT--AND THE WORLD-WIDE BLOOMING OF SUPERHUMAN POWERS IN ORDINARY PEOPLE?
SPEAKING PHYSIOLOGICALLY? NO.
SPEAKING CRIMINALLY? ALMOST CERTAINLY. SOME MASTERMIND IS BEHIND BOTH...
...BUT UNTIL WE KNOW WHO IT IS, I'D RATHER HE THINK WE'RE STILL DUPED. IF WE'RE TO INVESTIGATE, WE'LL NEED TO DO SO UNDERCOVER...
...WHICH MAKES THIS A JOB...

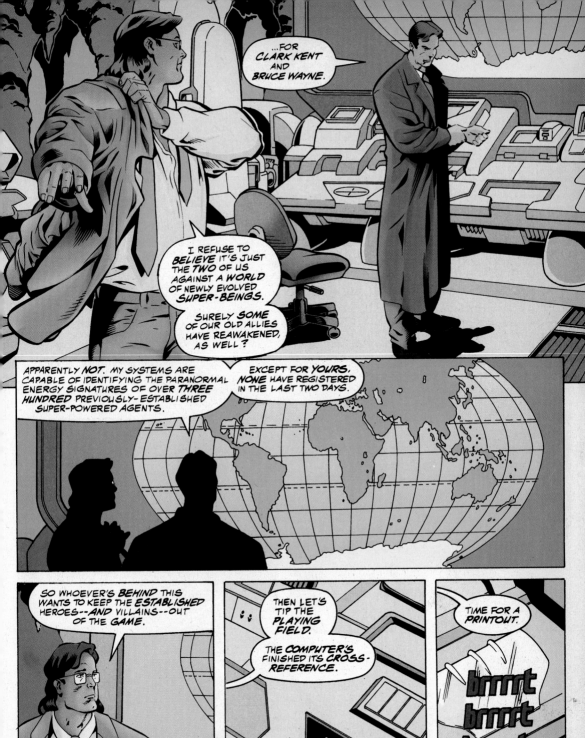

...FOR **CLARK KENT** AND **BRUCE WAYNE.**

I REFUSE TO **BELIEVE** IT'S JUST THE **TWO** OF US AGAINST A **WORLD** OF NEWLY EVOLVED **SUPER-BEINGS.**

SURELY **SOME** OF OUR OLD ALLIES HAVE REAWAKENED, AS WELL?

APPARENTLY **NOT.** MY SYSTEMS ARE CAPABLE OF IDENTIFYING THE PARANORMAL ENERGY SIGNATURES OF OVER **THREE HUNDRED** PREVIOUSLY-ESTABLISHED SUPER-POWERED AGENTS.

EXCEPT FOR **YOURS,** **NONE** HAVE REGISTERED IN THE LAST TWO DAYS.

SO WHOEVER'S **BEHIND** THIS WANTS TO KEEP THE **ESTABLISHED** HEROES--AND VILLAINS--OUT OF THE **GAME.**

THEN LET'S **TIP** THE **PLAYING FIELD.**

THE **COMPUTER'S** FINISHED ITS **CROSS-REFERENCE.**

TIME FOR A **PRINTOUT.**

brrrrt

brrrrt

brrrrt

- Blue Valley
- **Diana Prince**
- Themyscira School for Gir
- 4012 Peters Manor
- Gateway City
- **Arthur Curry**
- 73 Norris Estates
- New Carthage

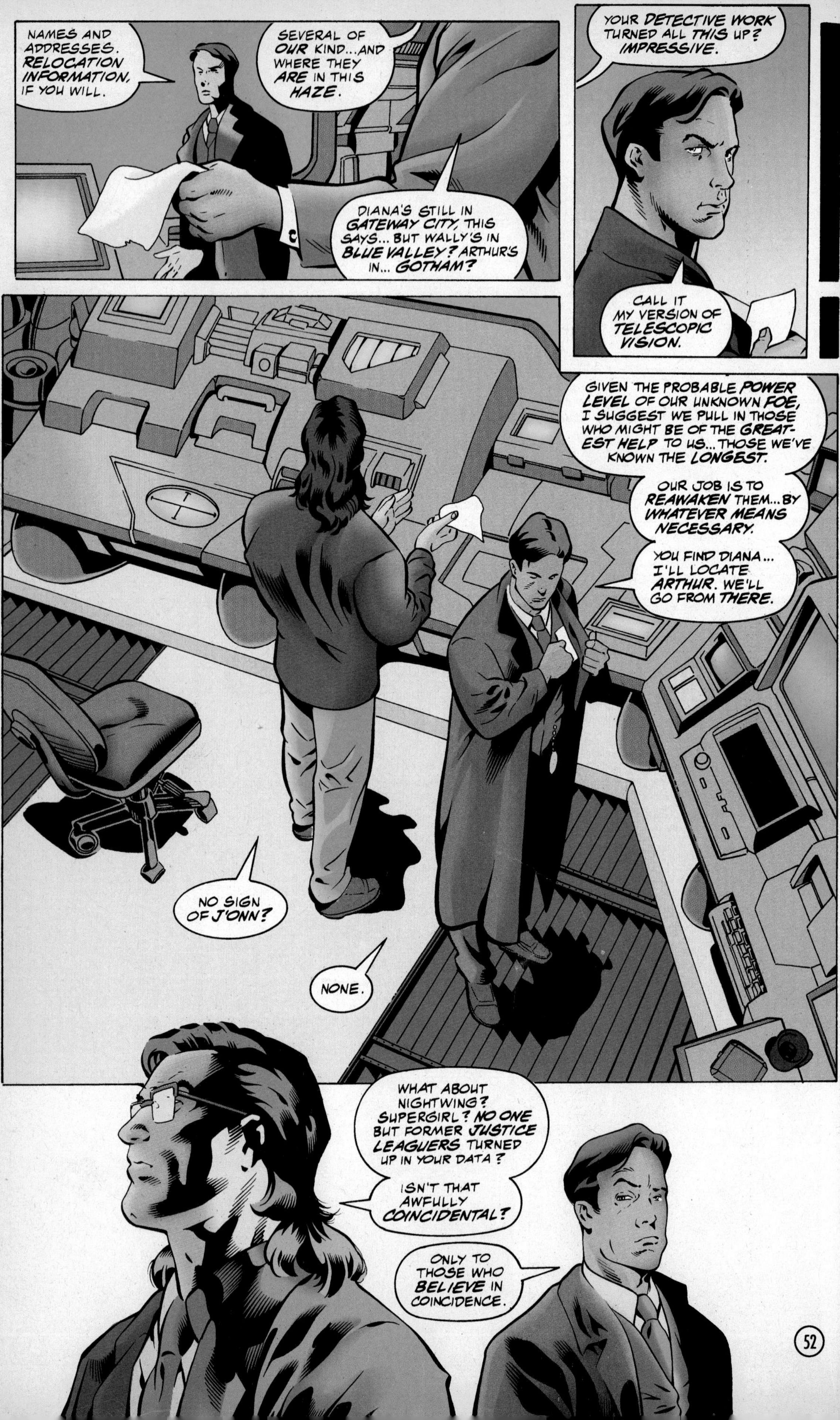
NAMES AND ADDRESSES. RELOCATION INFORMATION, IF YOU WILL.
SEVERAL OF OUR KIND...AND WHERE THEY ARE IN THIS HAZE.
DIANA'S STILL IN GATEWAY CITY, THIS SAYS... BUT WALLY'S IN BLUE VALLEY? ARTHUR'S IN... GOTHAM?
YOUR DETECTIVE WORK TURNED ALL THIS UP? IMPRESSIVE.
CALL IT MY VERSION OF TELESCOPIC VISION.
GIVEN THE PROBABLE POWER LEVEL OF OUR UNKNOWN FOE, I SUGGEST WE PULL IN THOSE WHO MIGHT BE OF THE GREATEST HELP TO US... THOSE WE'VE KNOWN THE LONGEST.
OUR JOB IS TO REAWAKEN THEM... BY WHATEVER MEANS NECESSARY.
YOU FIND DIANA... I'LL LOCATE ARTHUR. WE'LL GO FROM THERE.
NO SIGN OF J'ONN?
NONE.
WHAT ABOUT NIGHTWING? SUPERGIRL? NO ONE BUT FORMER JUSTICE LEAGUERS TURNED UP IN YOUR DATA?
ISN'T THAT AWFULLY COINCIDENTAL?
ONLY TO THOSE WHO BELIEVE IN COINCIDENCE.

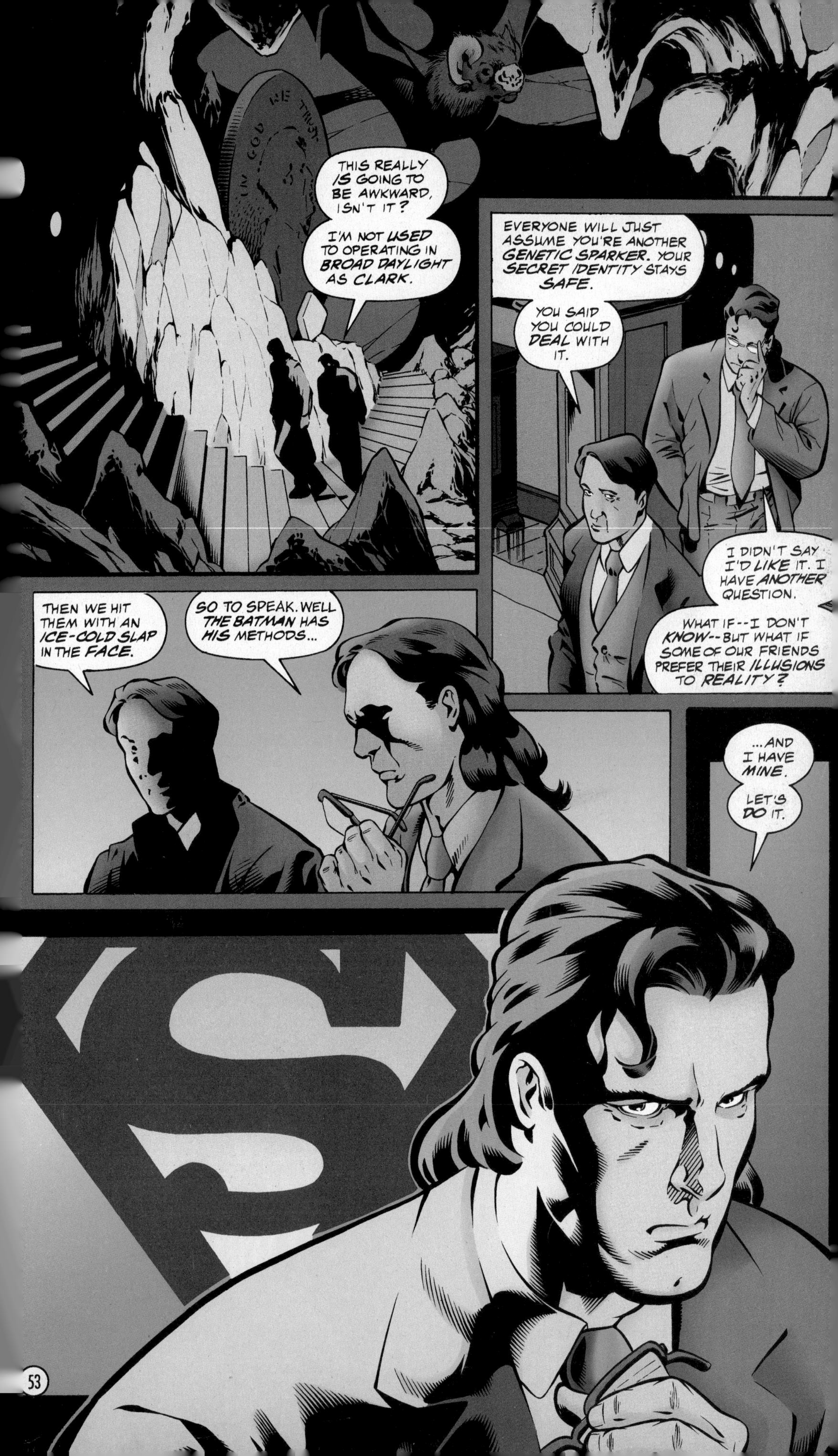

THIS REALLY IS GOING TO BE AWKWARD, ISN'T IT?
I'M NOT USED TO OPERATING IN BROAD DAYLIGHT AS CLARK.
EVERYONE WILL JUST ASSUME YOU'RE ANOTHER GENETIC SPARKER. YOUR SECRET IDENTITY STAYS SAFE.
YOU SAID YOU COULD DEAL WITH IT.
I DIDN'T SAY I'D LIKE IT. I HAVE ANOTHER QUESTION.
WHAT IF--I DON'T KNOW--BUT WHAT IF SOME OF OUR FRIENDS PREFER THEIR ILLUSIONS TO REALITY?
THEN WE HIT THEM WITH AN ICE-COLD SLAP IN THE FACE.
SO TO SPEAK. WELL THE BATMAN HAS HIS METHODS...
...AND I HAVE MINE.
LET'S DO IT.

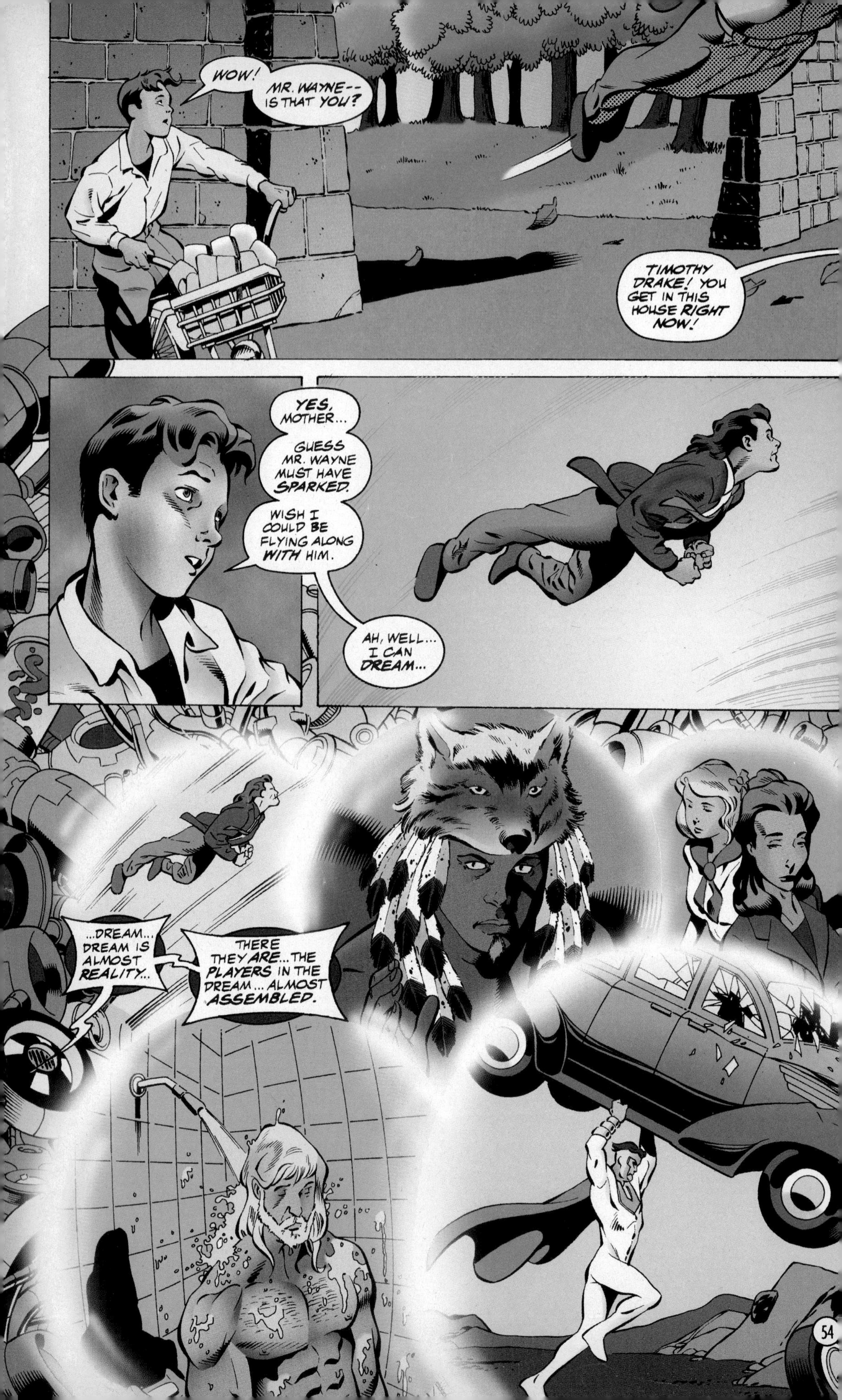
WOW!
MR. WAYNE-- IS THAT YOU?
TIMOTHY DRAKE! YOU GET IN THIS HOUSE RIGHT NOW!
YES, MOTHER...
GUESS MR. WAYNE MUST HAVE SPARKED.
WISH I COULD BE FLYING ALONG WITH HIM.
AH, WELL... I CAN DREAM...
...DREAM... DREAM IS ALMOST REALITY...
THERE THEY ARE... THE PLAYERS IN THE DREAM... ALMOST ASSEMBLED.

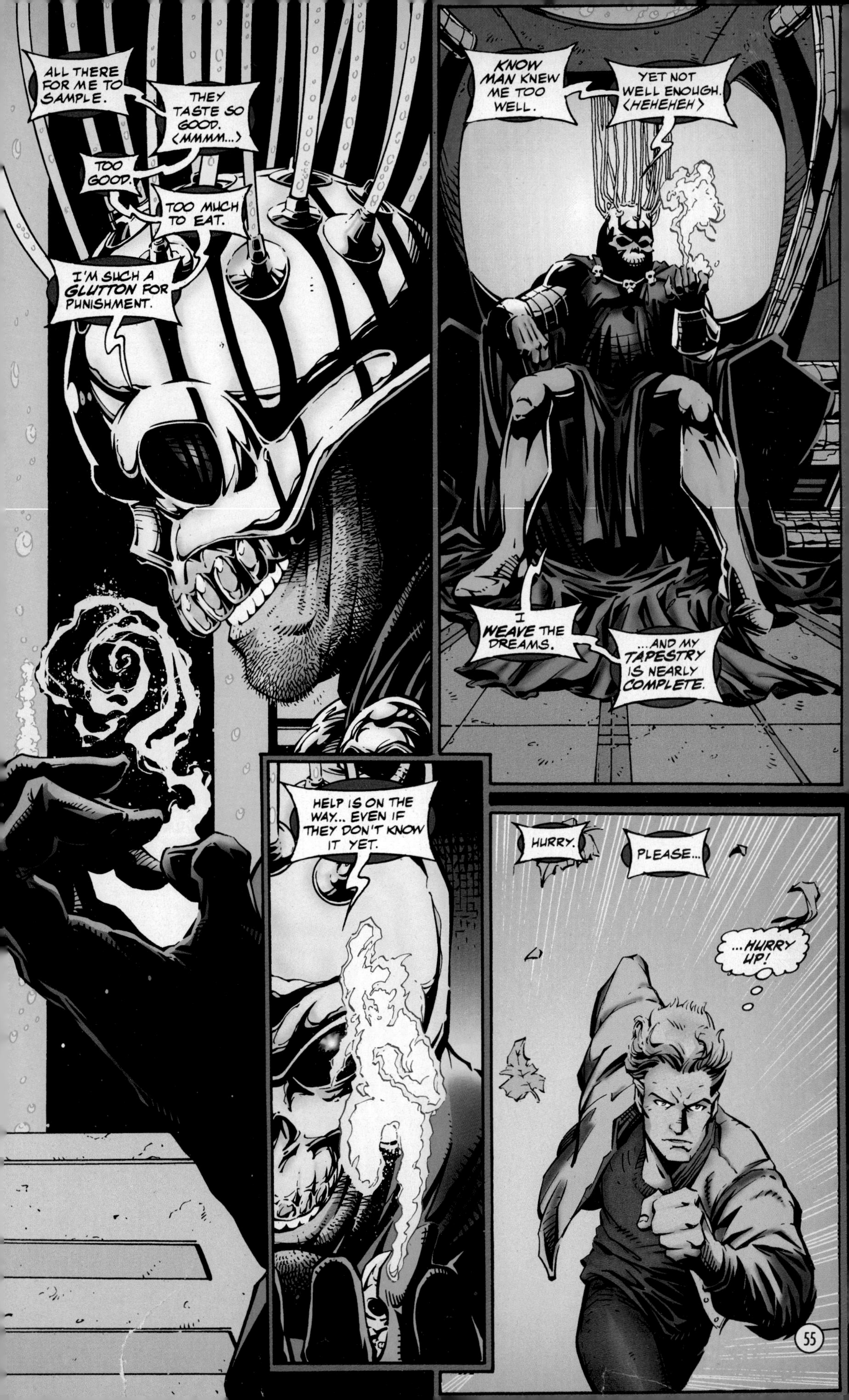
ALL THERE FOR ME TO SAMPLE.
THEY TASTE SO GOOD. ⟨MMMM...⟩
TOO GOOD.
TOO MUCH TO EAT.
I'M SUCH A GLUTTON FOR PUNISHMENT.
KNOW MAN KNEW ME TOO WELL.
YET NOT WELL ENOUGH. ⟨HEHEHEH⟩
I WEAVE THE DREAMS.
...AND MY TAPESTRY IS NEARLY COMPLETE.
HELP IS ON THE WAY... EVEN IF THEY DON'T KNOW IT YET.
HURRY.
PLEASE...
...HURRY UP!

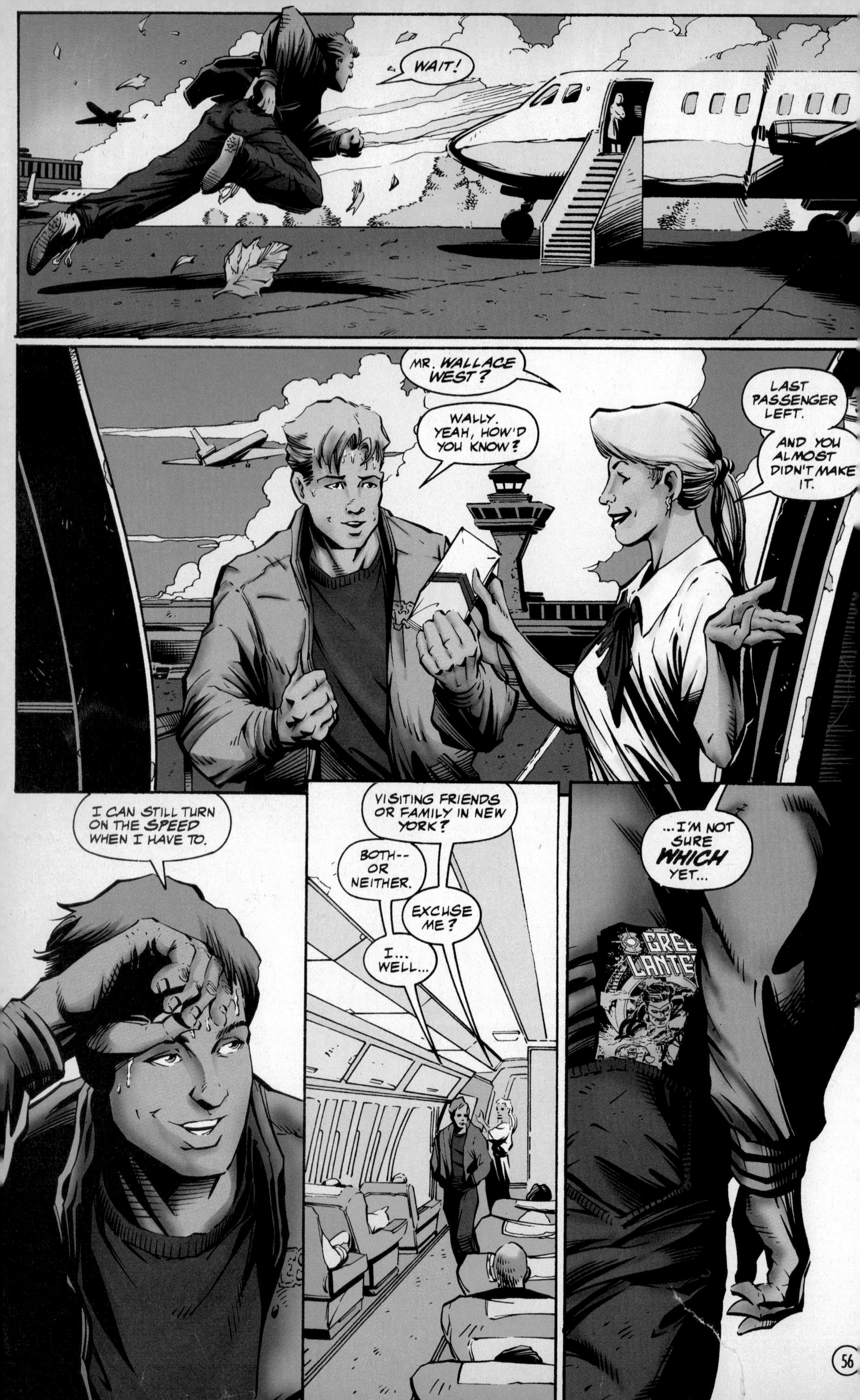

WAIT!
MR. WALLACE WEST?
WALLY. YEAH, HOW'D YOU KNOW?
LAST PASSENGER LEFT.
AND YOU ALMOST DIDN'T MAKE IT.
I CAN STILL TURN ON THE SPEED WHEN I HAVE TO.
VISITING FRIENDS OR FAMILY IN NEW YORK?
BOTH-- OR NEITHER.
EXCUSE ME?
I... WELL...
...I'M NOT SURE WHICH YET...

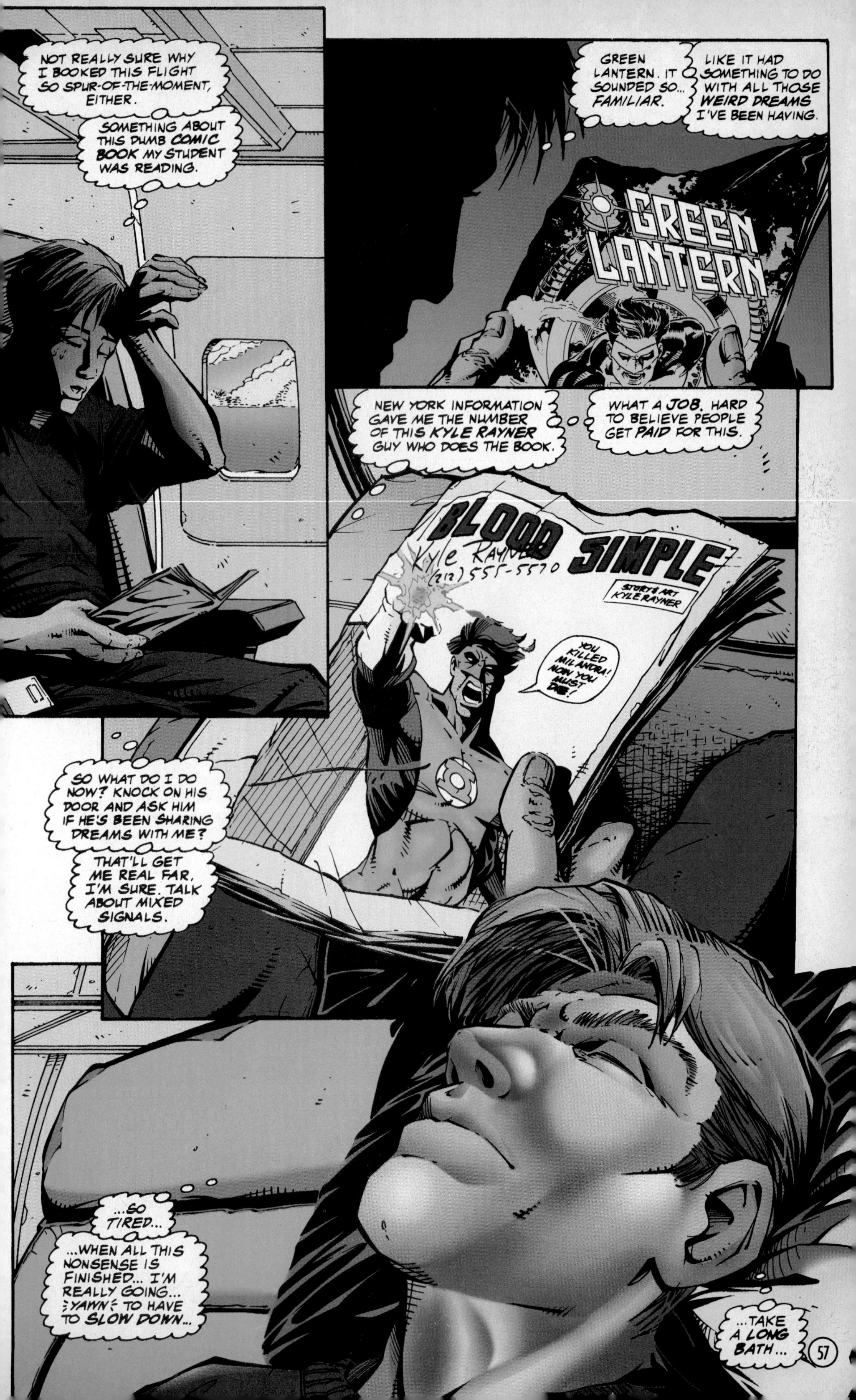
NOT REALLY SURE WHY I BOOKED THIS FLIGHT SO SPUR-OF-THE-MOMENT, EITHER.
SOMETHING ABOUT THIS DUMB COMIC BOOK MY STUDENT WAS READING.
GREEN LANTERN. IT SOUNDED SO... FAMILIAR.
LIKE IT HAD SOMETHING TO DO WITH ALL THOSE WEIRD DREAMS I'VE BEEN HAVING.
GREEN LANTERN
NEW YORK INFORMATION GAVE ME THE NUMBER OF THIS KYLE RAYNER GUY WHO DOES THE BOOK.
WHAT A JOB. HARD TO BELIEVE PEOPLE GET PAID FOR THIS.
BLOOD SIMPLE
Kyle Rayner (212) 555-5570
STORY & ART KYLE RAYNER
YOU KILLED MILANDRA! NOW YOU MUST DIE!
SO WHAT DO I DO NOW? KNOCK ON HIS DOOR AND ASK HIM IF HE'S BEEN SHARING DREAMS WITH ME?
THAT'LL GET ME REAL FAR, I'M SURE. TALK ABOUT MIXED SIGNALS.
...SO TIRED...
...WHEN ALL THIS NONSENSE IS FINISHED... I'M REALLY GOING... YAWN TO HAVE TO SLOW DOWN...
...TAKE A LONG BATH...

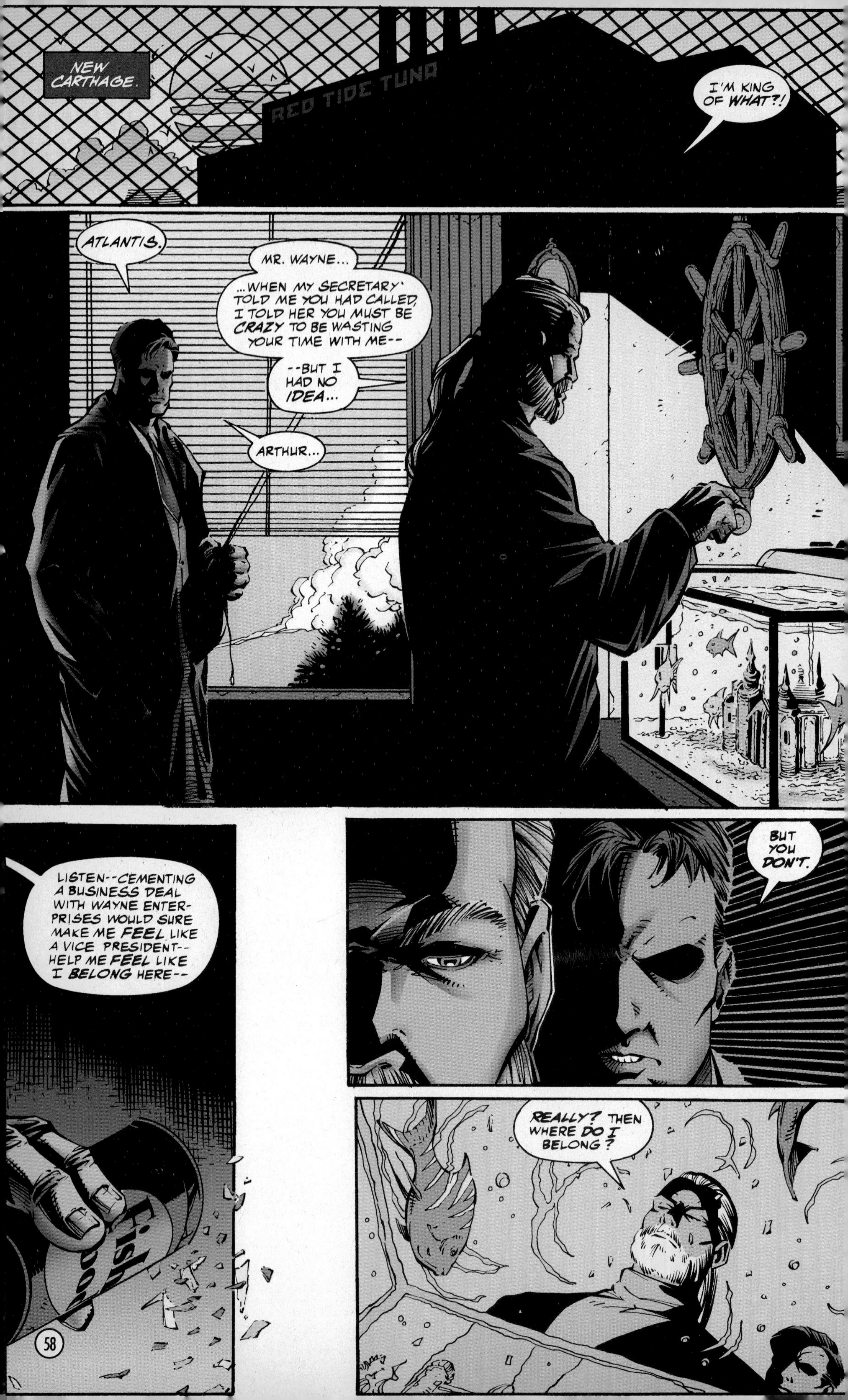
NEW CARTHAGE.
RED TIDE TUNA
I'M KING OF WHAT?!
ATLANTIS.
MR. WAYNE...
...WHEN MY SECRETARY TOLD ME YOU HAD CALLED, I TOLD HER YOU MUST BE CRAZY TO BE WASTING YOUR TIME WITH ME--
--BUT I HAD NO IDEA...
ARTHUR...
LISTEN--CEMENTING A BUSINESS DEAL WITH WAYNE ENTERPRISES WOULD SURE MAKE ME FEEL LIKE A VICE PRESIDENT--HELP ME FEEL LIKE I BELONG HERE--
BUT YOU DON'T.
REALLY? THEN WHERE DO I BELONG?

SPLWISHSH!!

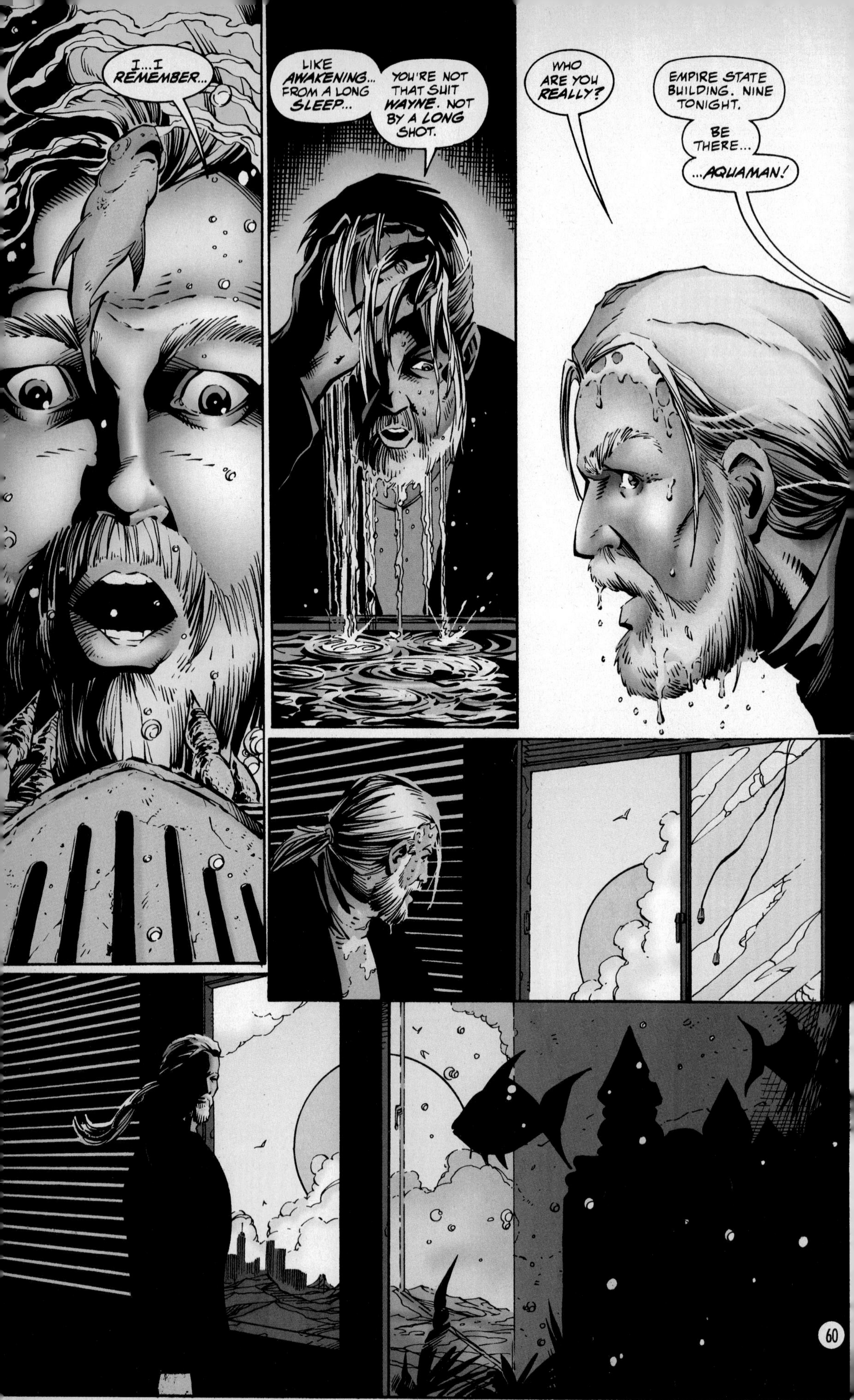
I...I REMEMBER...
LIKE AWAKENING... FROM A LONG SLEEP...
YOU'RE NOT THAT SUIT WAYNE. NOT BY A LONG SHOT.
WHO ARE YOU REALLY?
EMPIRE STATE BUILDING. NINE TONIGHT.
BE THERE...
...AQUAMAN!

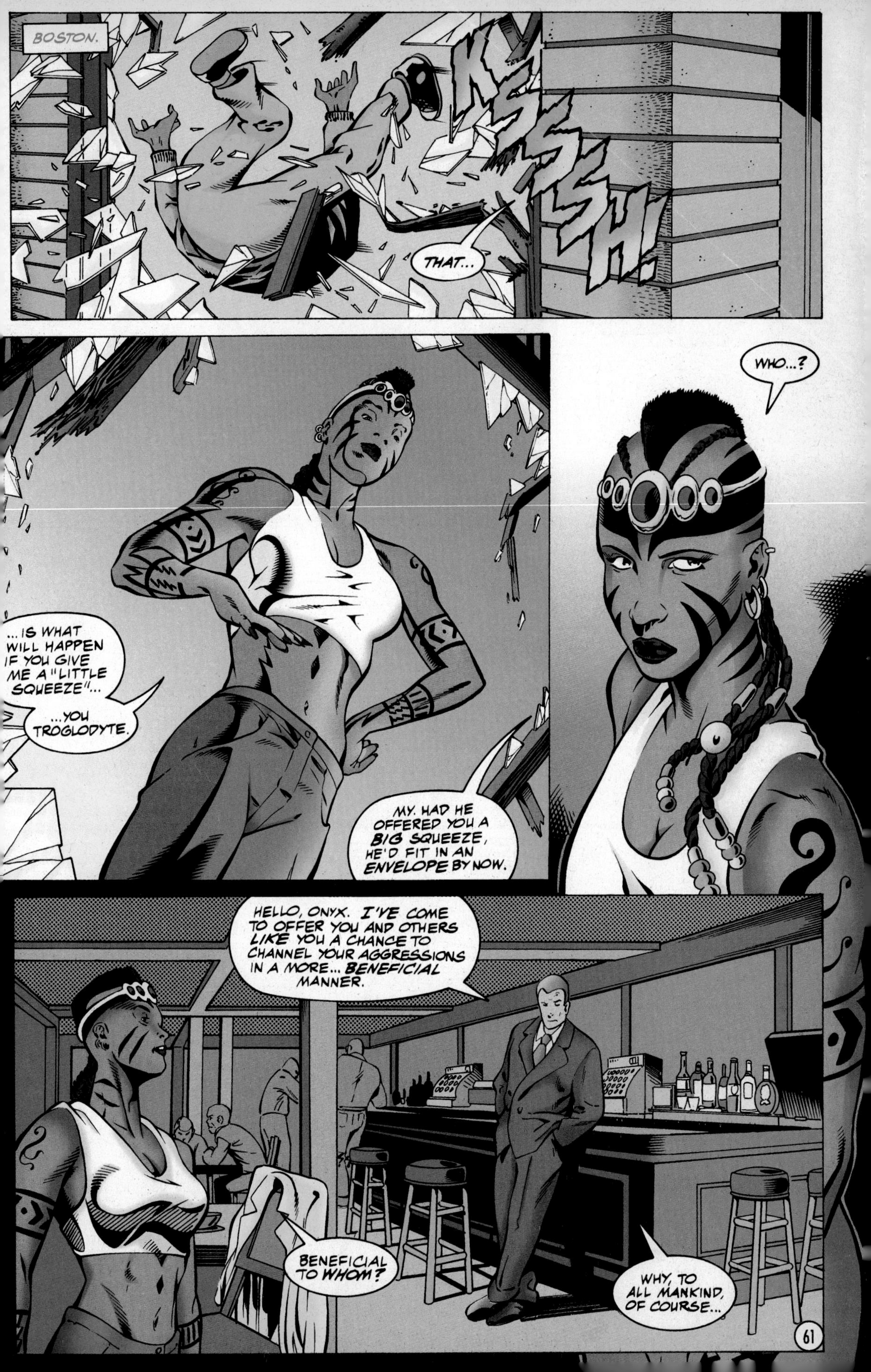

BOSTON.
KSSSH!
THAT...
...IS WHAT WILL HAPPEN IF YOU GIVE ME A "LITTLE SQUEEZE"...
...YOU TROGLODYTE.
MY. HAD HE OFFERED YOU A BIG SQUEEZE, HE'D FIT IN AN ENVELOPE BY NOW.
WHO...?
HELLO, ONYX. I'VE COME TO OFFER YOU AND OTHERS LIKE YOU A CHANCE TO CHANNEL YOUR AGGRESSIONS IN A MORE... BENEFICIAL MANNER.
BENEFICIAL TO WHOM?
WHY, TO ALL MANKIND, OF COURSE...

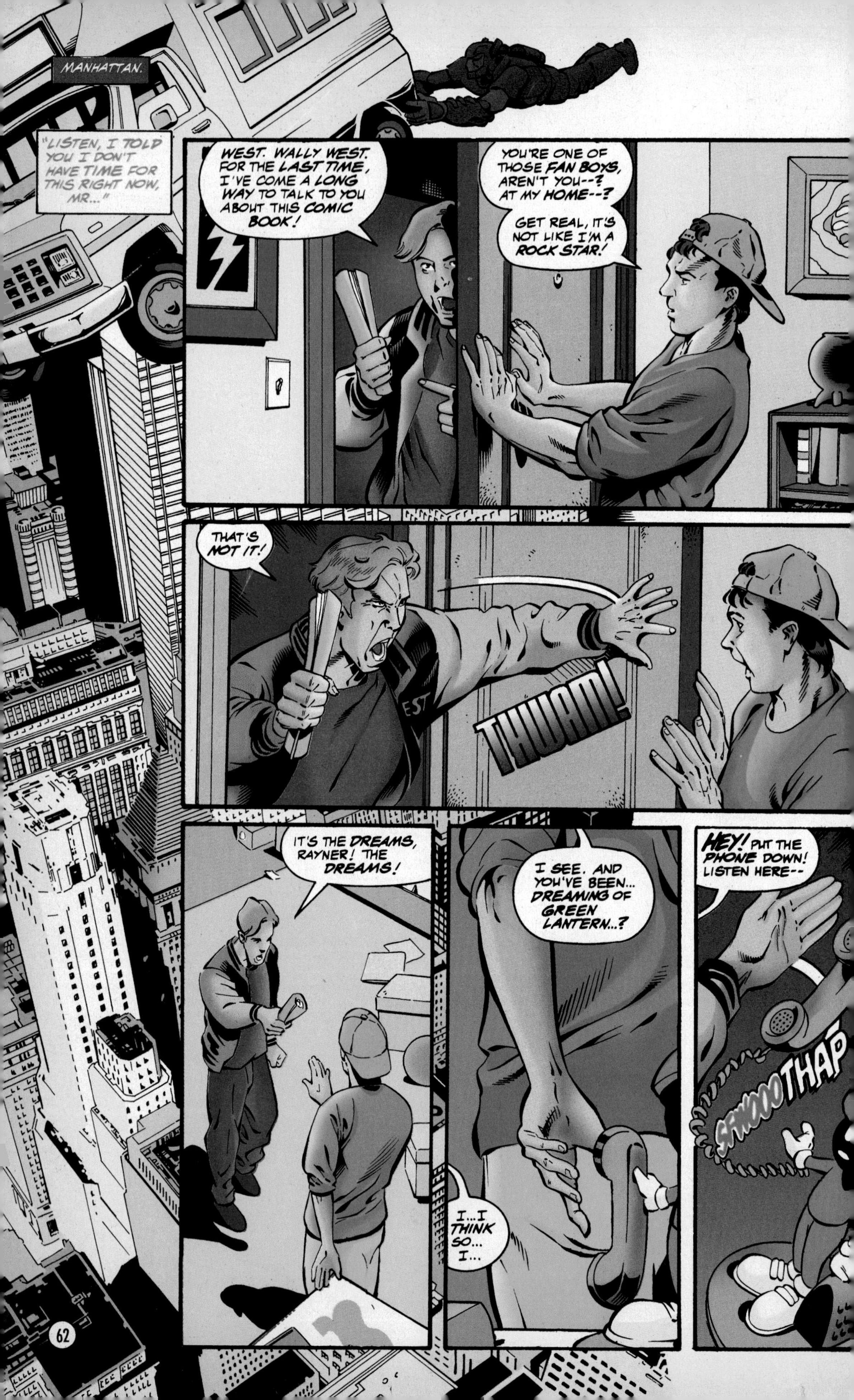

MANHATTAN.
"LISTEN, I TOLD YOU I DON'T HAVE TIME FOR THIS RIGHT NOW, MR..."
WEST. WALLY WEST. FOR THE LAST TIME, I'VE COME A LONG WAY TO TALK TO YOU ABOUT THIS COMIC BOOK!
YOU'RE ONE OF THOSE FAN BOYS, AREN'T YOU--? AT MY HOME--?
GET REAL, IT'S NOT LIKE I'M A ROCK STAR!
THAT'S NOT IT!
THWAM!
IT'S THE DREAMS, RAYNER! THE DREAMS!
I SEE. AND YOU'VE BEEN... DREAMING OF GREEN LANTERN...?
I...I THINK SO... I...
HEY! PUT THE PHONE DOWN! LISTEN HERE--
SFWOOOTHAP

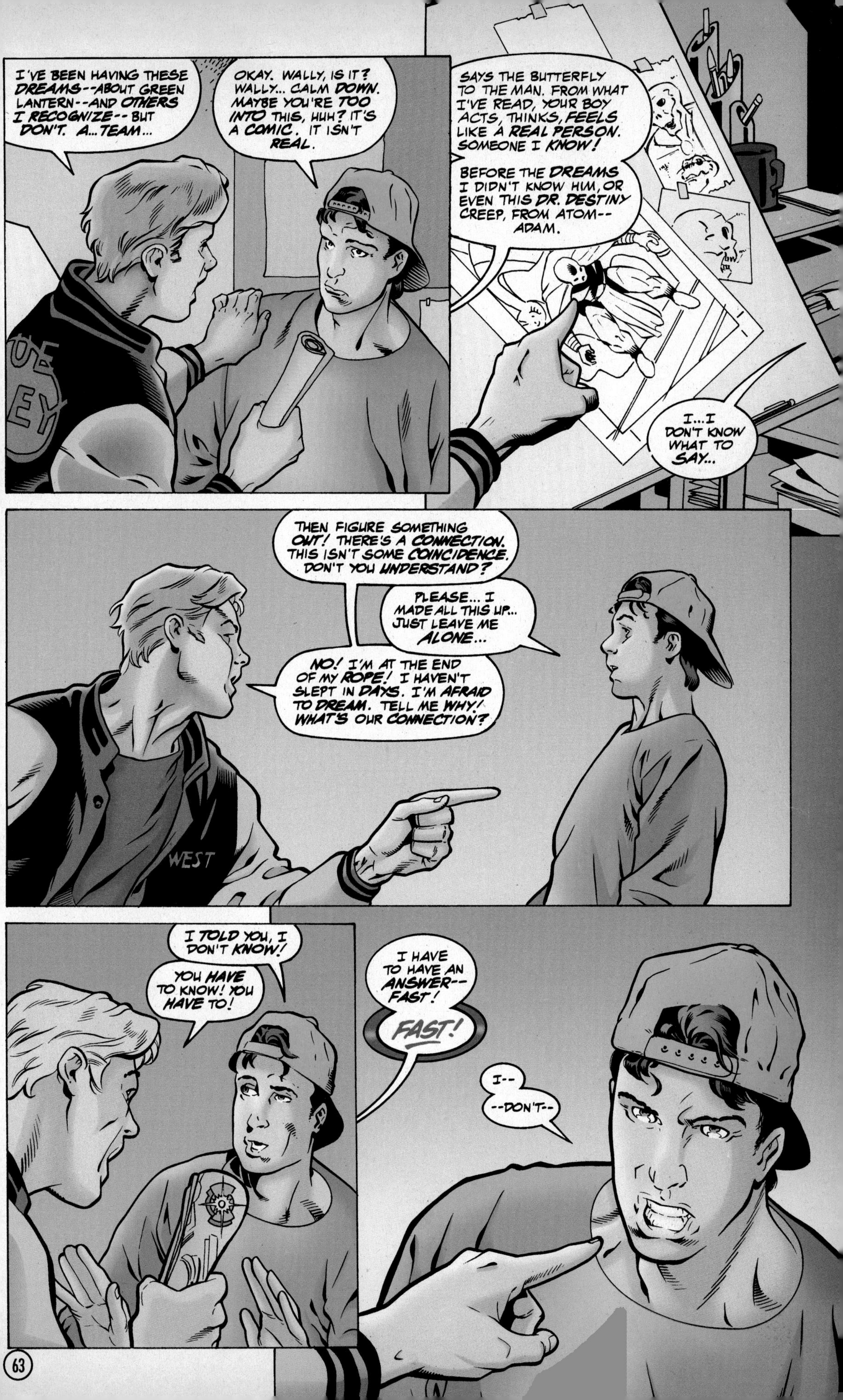
I'VE BEEN HAVING THESE DREAMS--ABOUT GREEN LANTERN--AND OTHERS I RECOGNIZE--BUT DON'T. A...TEAM...
OKAY. WALLY, IS IT? WALLY... CALM DOWN. MAYBE YOU'RE TOO INTO THIS, HUH? IT'S A COMIC. IT ISN'T REAL.
SAYS THE BUTTERFLY TO THE MAN. FROM WHAT I'VE READ, YOUR BOY ACTS, THINKS, FEELS LIKE A REAL PERSON. SOMEONE I KNOW!
BEFORE THE DREAMS I DIDN'T KNOW HIM, OR EVEN THIS DR. DESTINY CREEP, FROM ATOM--ADAM.
I...I DON'T KNOW WHAT TO SAY...
THEN FIGURE SOMETHING OUT! THERE'S A CONNECTION. THIS ISN'T SOME COINCIDENCE. DON'T YOU UNDERSTAND?
PLEASE... I MADE ALL THIS UP... JUST LEAVE ME ALONE...
NO! I'M AT THE END OF MY ROPE! I HAVEN'T SLEPT IN DAYS. I'M AFRAID TO DREAM. TELL ME WHY! WHAT'S OUR CONNECTION?
WEST
I TOLD YOU, I DON'T KNOW!
YOU HAVE TO KNOW! YOU HAVE TO!
I HAVE TO HAVE AN ANSWER--FAST!
FAST!
I--
--DON'T--

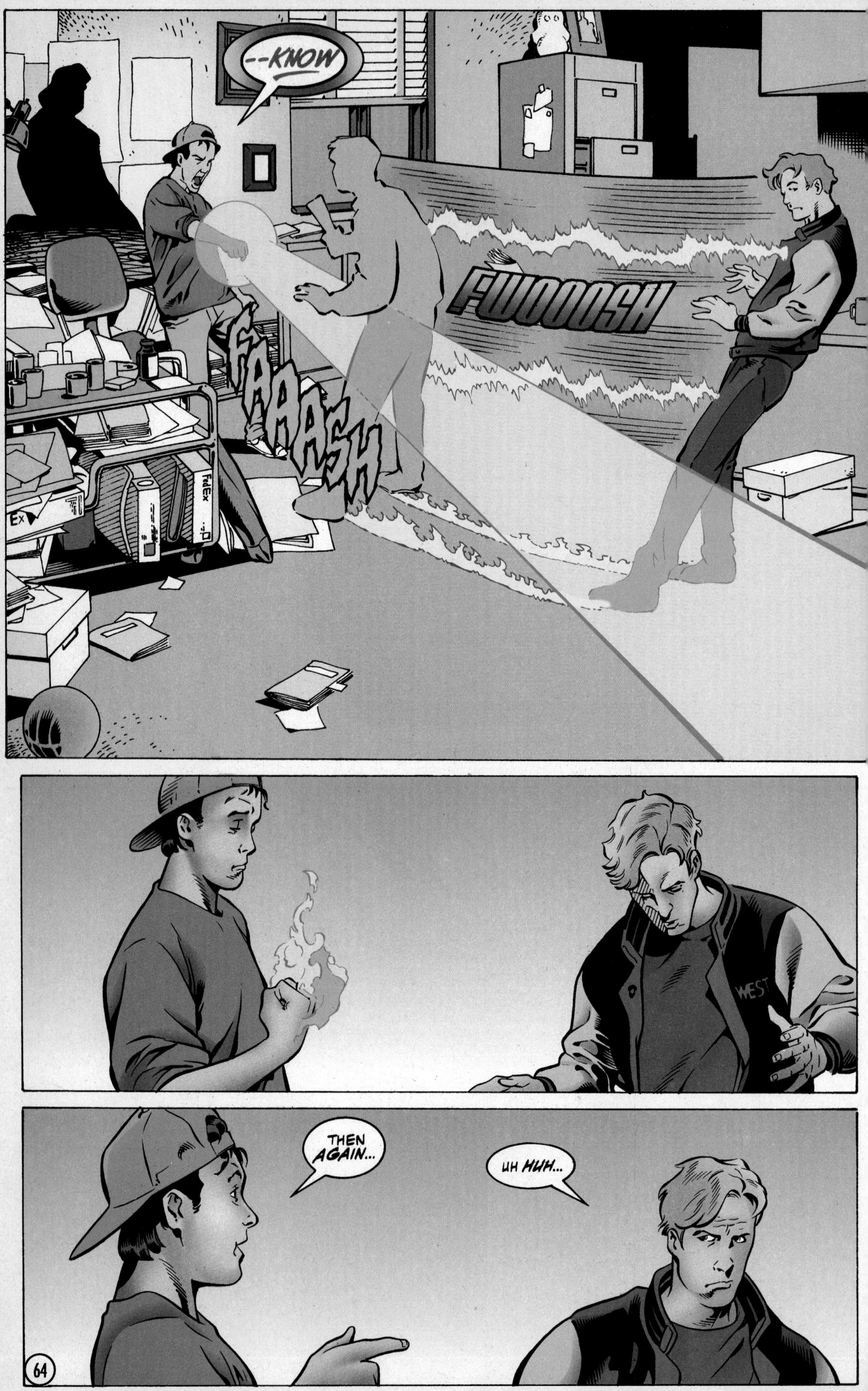
--KNOW
FAAASH
FWOOOOSH
WEST
THEN AGAIN...
UH HUH...

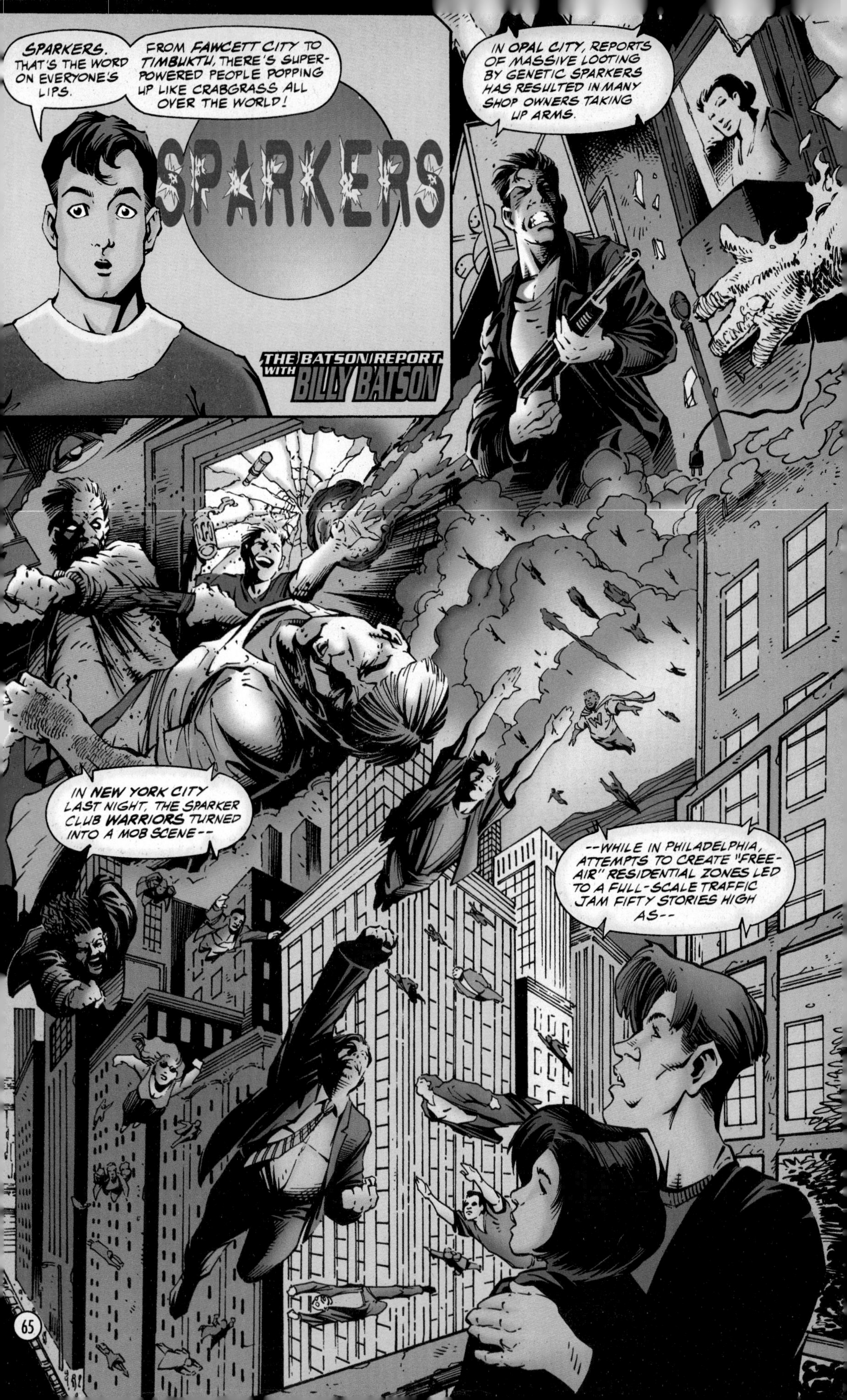
SPARKERS. THAT'S THE WORD ON EVERYONE'S LIPS.
FROM FAWCETT CITY TO TIMBUKTU, THERE'S SUPER-POWERED PEOPLE POPPING UP LIKE CRABGRASS ALL OVER THE WORLD!
SPARKERS
THE BATSON REPORT WITH BILLY BATSON
IN OPAL CITY, REPORTS OF MASSIVE LOOTING BY GENETIC SPARKERS HAS RESULTED IN MANY SHOP OWNERS TAKING UP ARMS.
IN NEW YORK CITY LAST NIGHT, THE SPARKER CLUB WARRIORS TURNED INTO A MOB SCENE--
--WHILE IN PHILADELPHIA, ATTEMPTS TO CREATE "FREE-AIR" RESIDENTIAL ZONES LED TO A FULL-SCALE TRAFFIC JAM FIFTY STORIES HIGH AS--

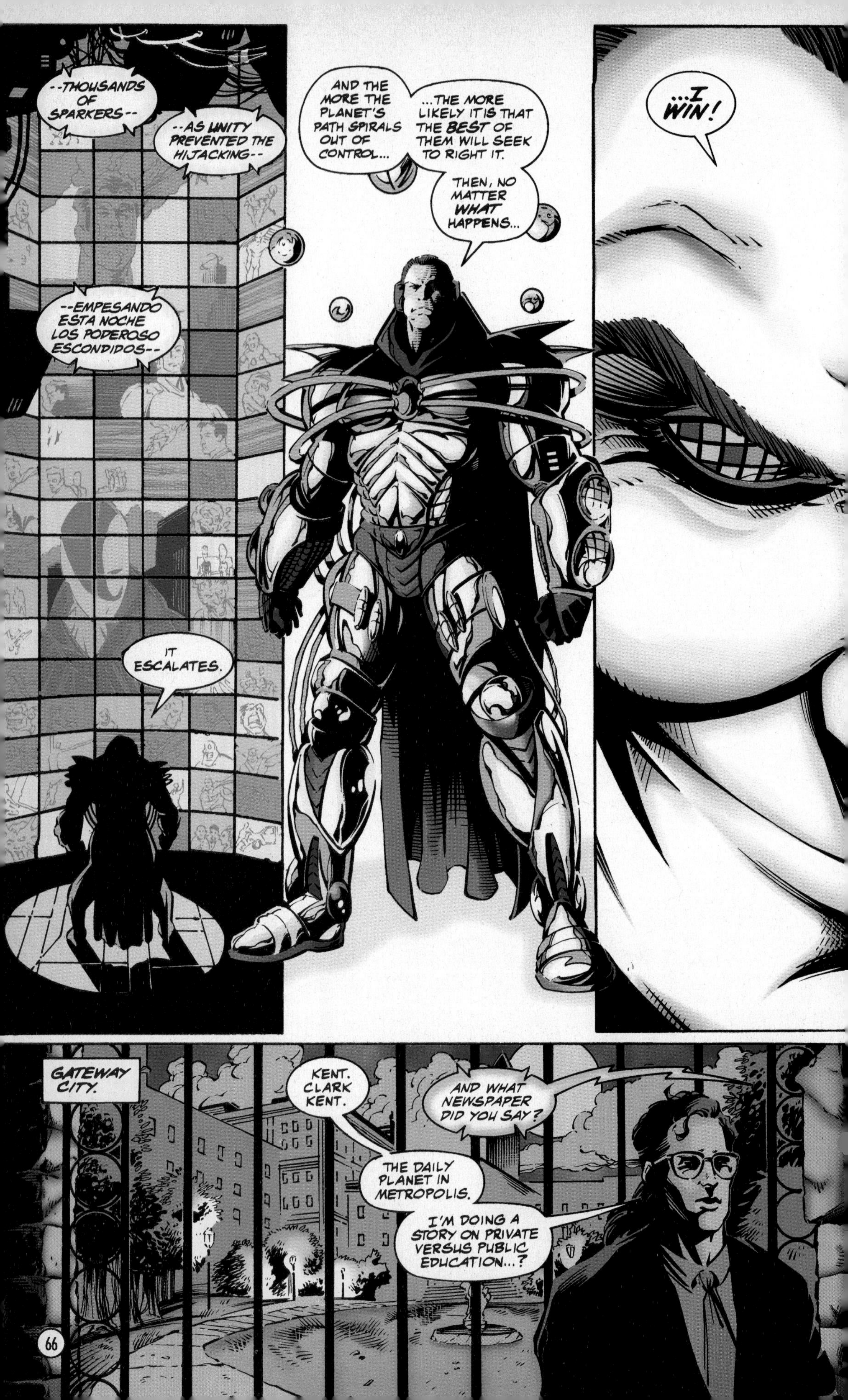
--THOUSANDS OF SPARKERS--
--AS UNITY PREVENTED THE HIJACKING--
--EMPESANDO ESTA NOCHE LOS PODEROSO ESCONDIDOS--
IT ESCALATES.
AND THE MORE THE PLANET'S PATH SPIRALS OUT OF CONTROL...
...THE MORE LIKELY IT IS THAT THE BEST OF THEM WILL SEEK TO RIGHT IT.
THEN, NO MATTER WHAT HAPPENS...
...I WIN!
GATEWAY CITY.
KENT. CLARK KENT.
AND WHAT NEWSPAPER DID YOU SAY?
THE DAILY PLANET IN METROPOLIS.
I'M DOING A STORY ON PRIVATE VERSUS PUBLIC EDUCATION...?

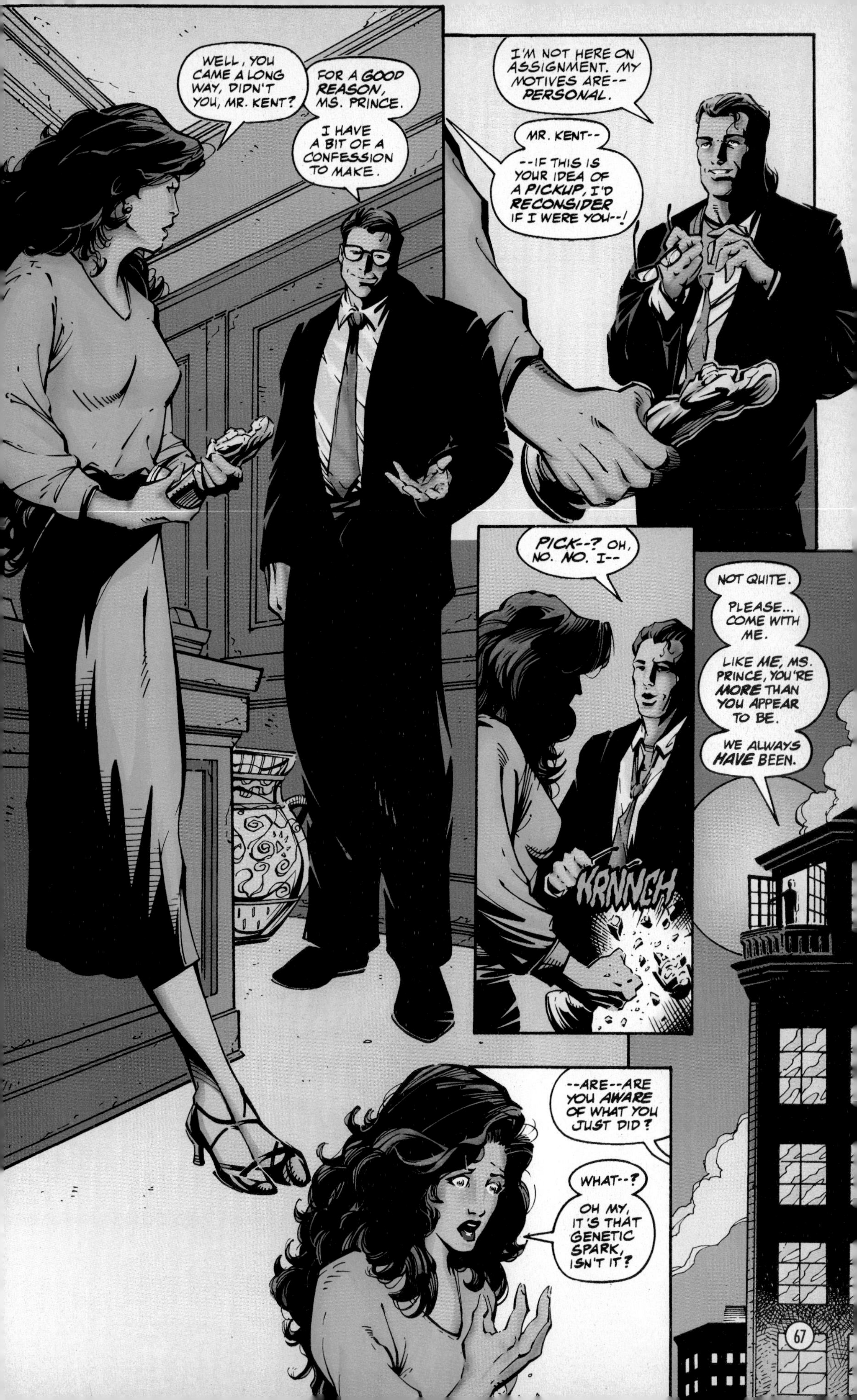
WELL, YOU CAME A LONG WAY, DIDN'T YOU, MR. KENT?
FOR A GOOD REASON, MS. PRINCE.
I HAVE A BIT OF A CONFESSION TO MAKE.
I'M NOT HERE ON ASSIGNMENT. MY MOTIVES ARE-- PERSONAL.
MR. KENT--
--IF THIS IS YOUR IDEA OF A PICKUP, I'D RECONSIDER IF I WERE YOU--!
PICK--? OH, NO. NO. I--
KRNNCH
--ARE--ARE YOU AWARE OF WHAT YOU JUST DID?
WHAT--?
OH MY, IT'S THAT GENETIC SPARK, ISN'T IT?
NOT QUITE.
PLEASE... COME WITH ME.
LIKE ME, MS. PRINCE, YOU'RE MORE THAN YOU APPEAR TO BE.
WE ALWAYS HAVE BEEN.

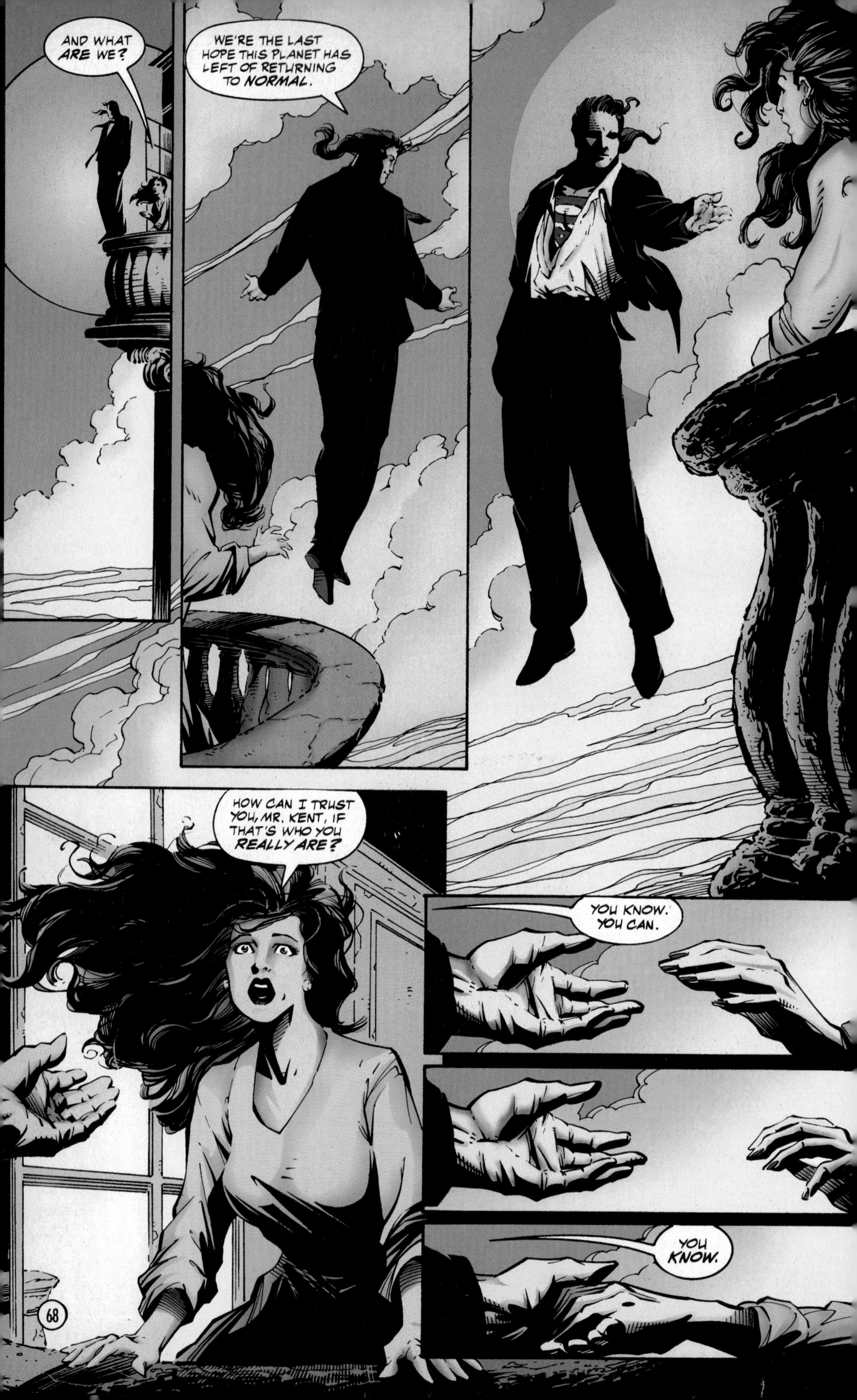

AND WHAT ARE WE?
WE'RE THE LAST HOPE THIS PLANET HAS LEFT OF RETURNING TO NORMAL.
HOW CAN I TRUST YOU, MR. KENT, IF THAT'S WHO YOU REALLY ARE?
YOU KNOW. YOU CAN.
YOU KNOW.

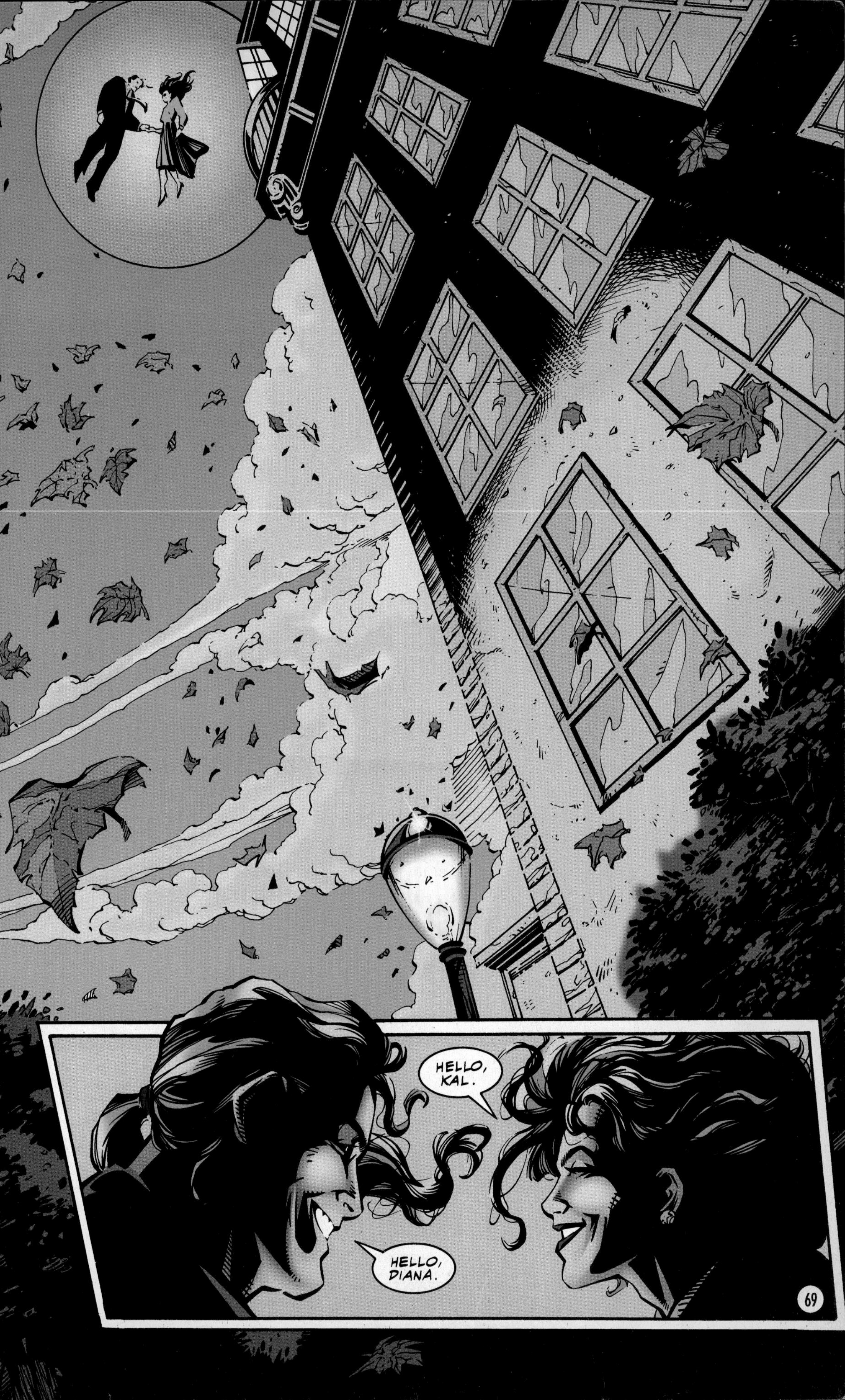
HELLO, KAL.
HELLO, DIANA.

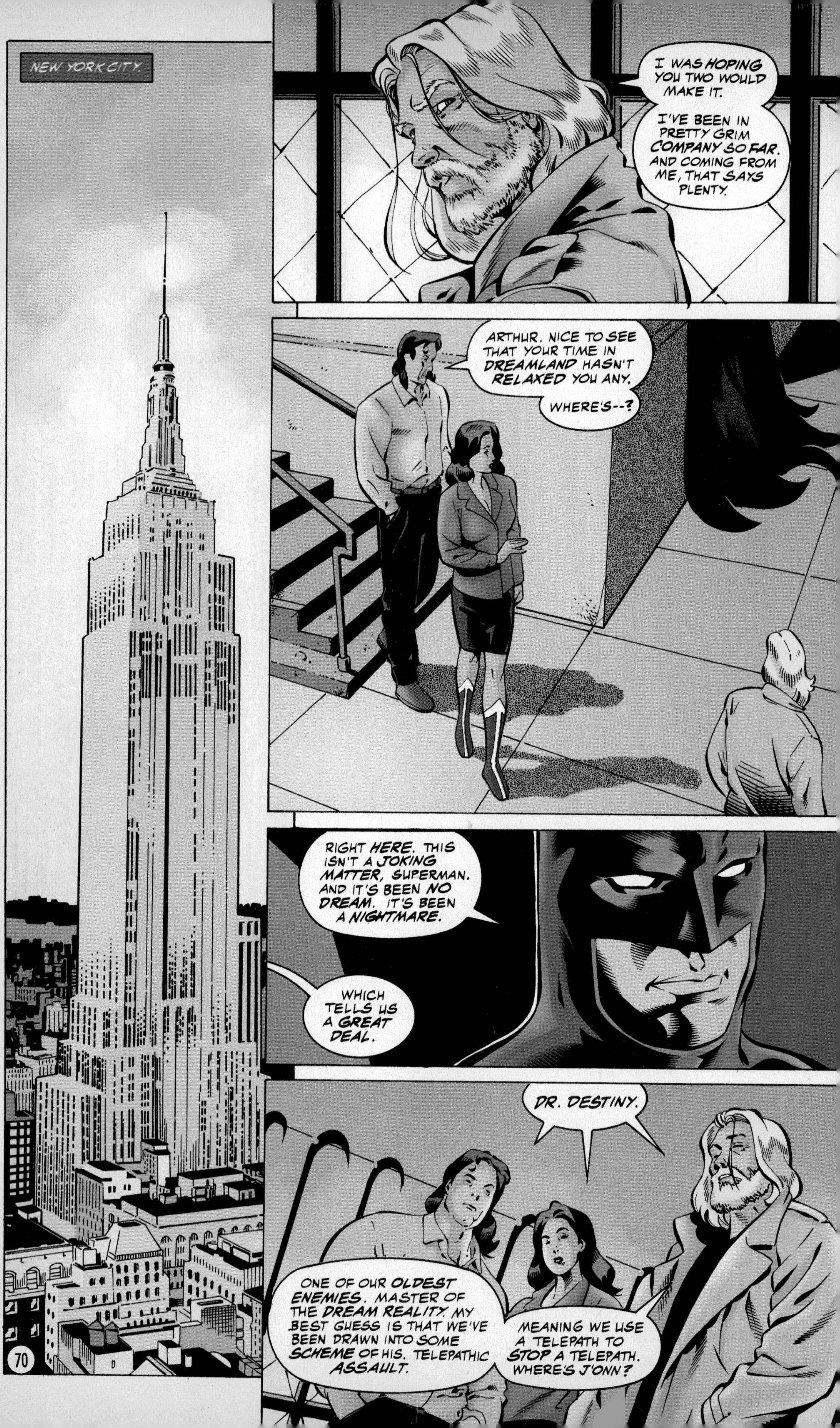
NEW YORK CITY.
I WAS HOPING YOU TWO WOULD MAKE IT.
I'VE BEEN IN PRETTY GRIM COMPANY SO FAR. AND COMING FROM ME, THAT SAYS PLENTY.
ARTHUR. NICE TO SEE THAT YOUR TIME IN DREAMLAND HASN'T RELAXED YOU ANY.
WHERE'S--?
RIGHT HERE. THIS ISN'T A JOKING MATTER, SUPERMAN. AND IT'S BEEN NO DREAM. IT'S BEEN A NIGHTMARE.
WHICH TELLS US A GREAT DEAL.
DR. DESTINY.
ONE OF OUR OLDEST ENEMIES. MASTER OF THE DREAM REALITY. MY BEST GUESS IS THAT WE'VE BEEN DRAWN INTO SOME SCHEME OF HIS. TELEPATHIC ASSAULT.
MEANING WE USE A TELEPATH TO STOP A TELEPATH. WHERE'S J'ONN?

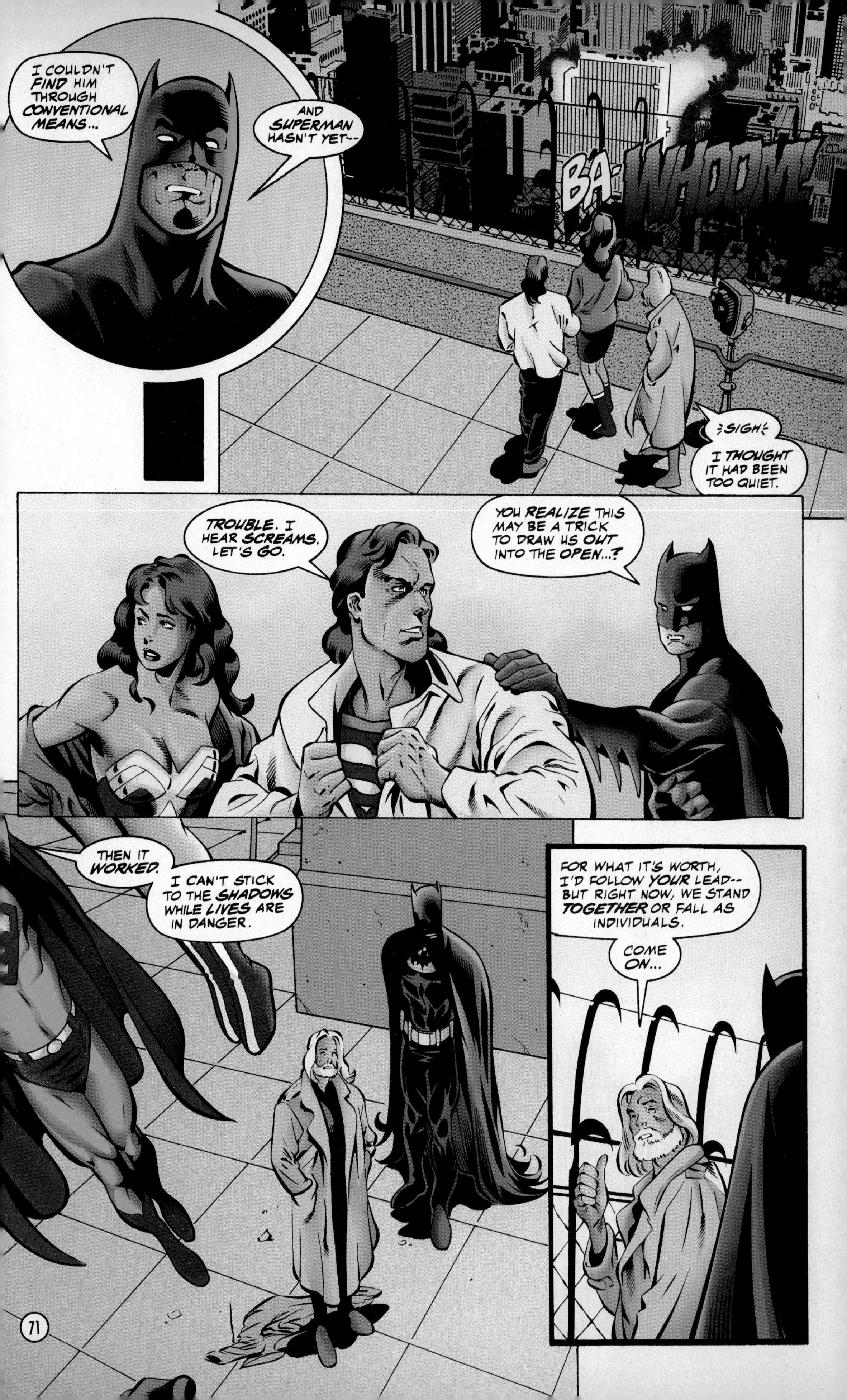

I COULDN'T FIND HIM THROUGH CONVENTIONAL MEANS...
AND SUPERMAN HASN'T YET--
BA-WHOOM!
≷SIGH≶ I THOUGHT IT HAD BEEN TOO QUIET.
TROUBLE. I HEAR SCREAMS. LET'S GO.
YOU REALIZE THIS MAY BE A TRICK TO DRAW US OUT INTO THE OPEN...?
THEN IT WORKED.
I CAN'T STICK TO THE SHADOWS WHILE LIVES ARE IN DANGER.
FOR WHAT IT'S WORTH, I'D FOLLOW YOUR LEAD--BUT RIGHT NOW, WE STAND TOGETHER OR FALL AS INDIVIDUALS.
COME ON...

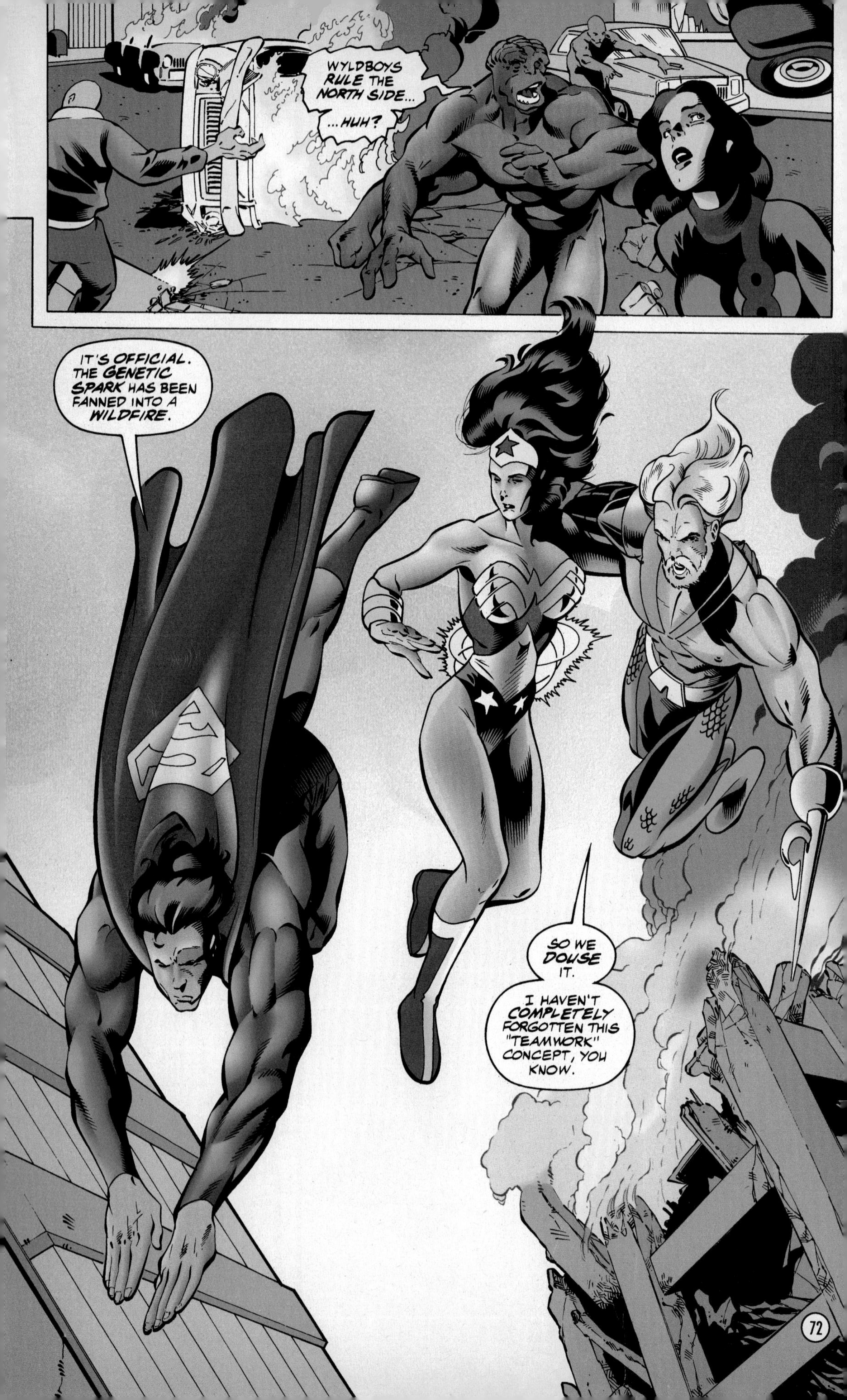
WYLDBOYS RULE THE NORTH SIDE...
...HUH?
IT'S OFFICIAL. THE GENETIC SPARK HAS BEEN FANNED INTO A WILDFIRE.
SO WE DOUSE IT.
I HAVEN'T COMPLETELY FORGOTTEN THIS "TEAMWORK" CONCEPT, YOU KNOW.
72

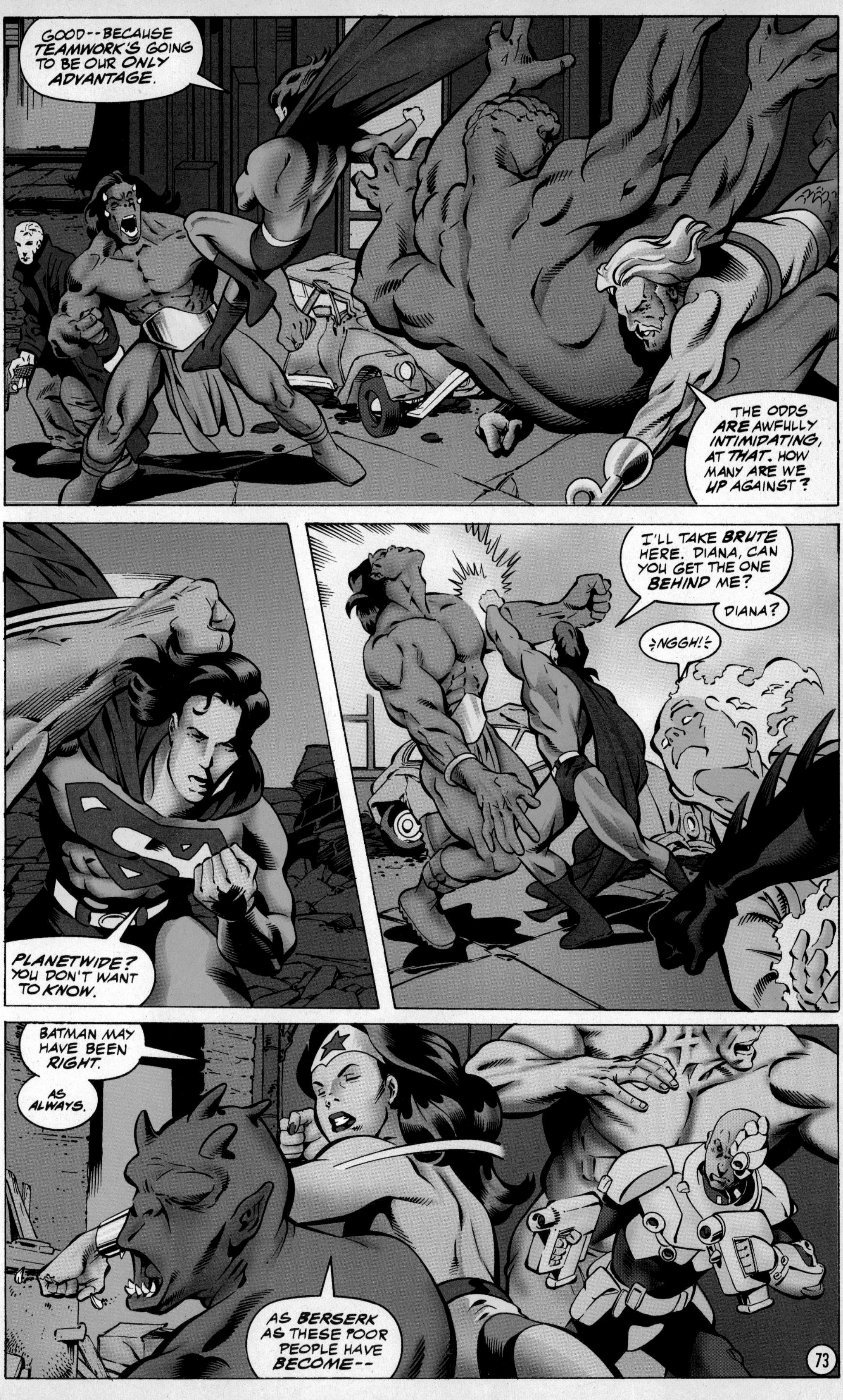
GOOD--BECAUSE TEAMWORK'S GOING TO BE OUR ONLY ADVANTAGE.
THE ODDS ARE AWFULLY INTIMIDATING, AT THAT. HOW MANY ARE WE UP AGAINST?
PLANETWIDE? YOU DON'T WANT TO KNOW.
I'LL TAKE BRUTE HERE. DIANA, CAN YOU GET THE ONE BEHIND ME?
DIANA?
NGGH!
BATMAN MAY HAVE BEEN RIGHT.
AS ALWAYS.
AS BERSERK AS THESE POOR PEOPLE HAVE BECOME--

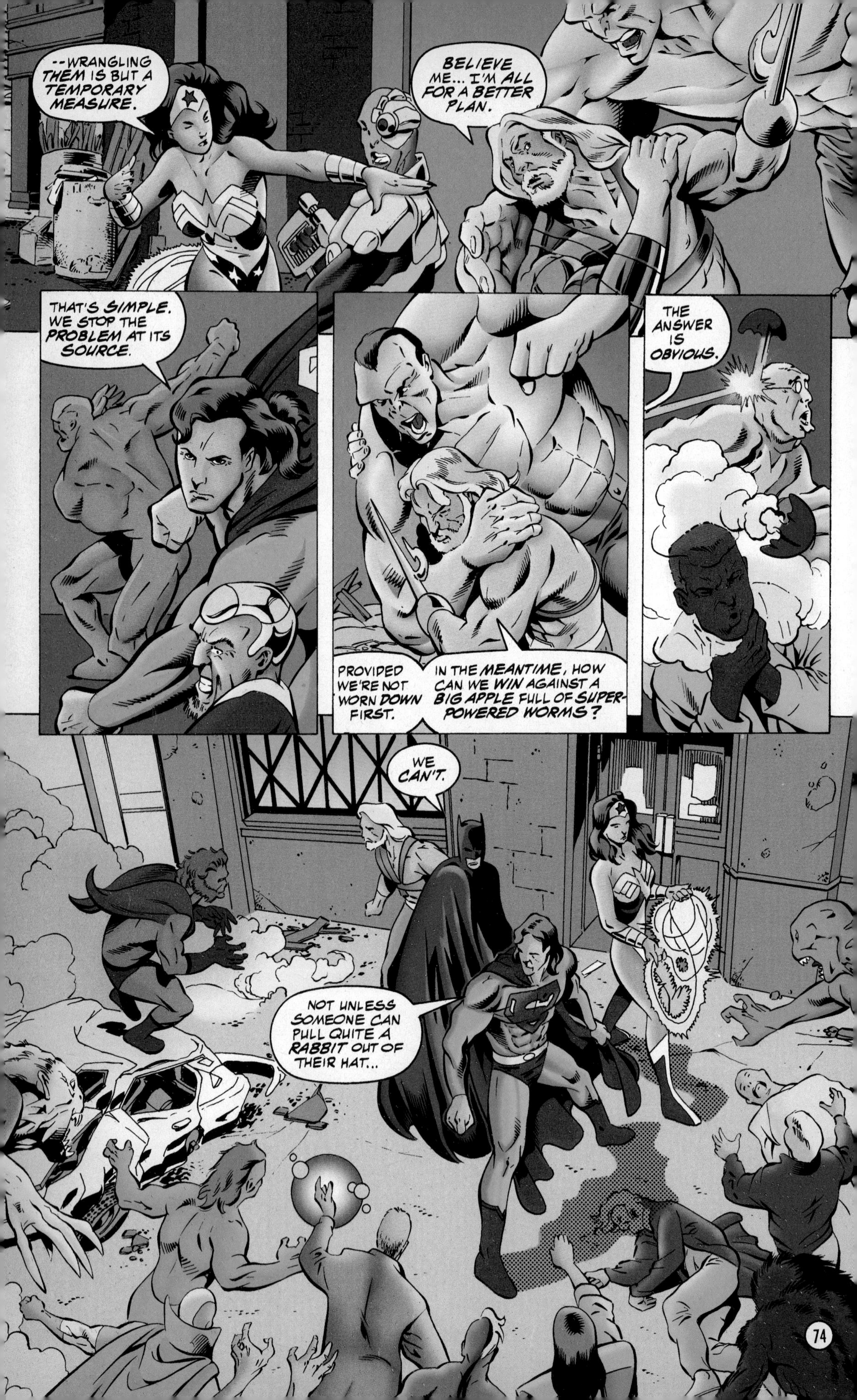
--WRANGLING THEM IS BUT A TEMPORARY MEASURE.
BELIEVE ME... I'M ALL FOR A BETTER PLAN.
THAT'S SIMPLE. WE STOP THE PROBLEM AT ITS SOURCE.
PROVIDED WE'RE NOT WORN DOWN FIRST.
IN THE MEANTIME, HOW CAN WE WIN AGAINST A BIG APPLE FULL OF SUPER-POWERED WORMS?
THE ANSWER IS OBVIOUS.
WE CAN'T.
NOT UNLESS SOMEONE CAN PULL QUITE A RABBIT OUT OF THEIR HAT...

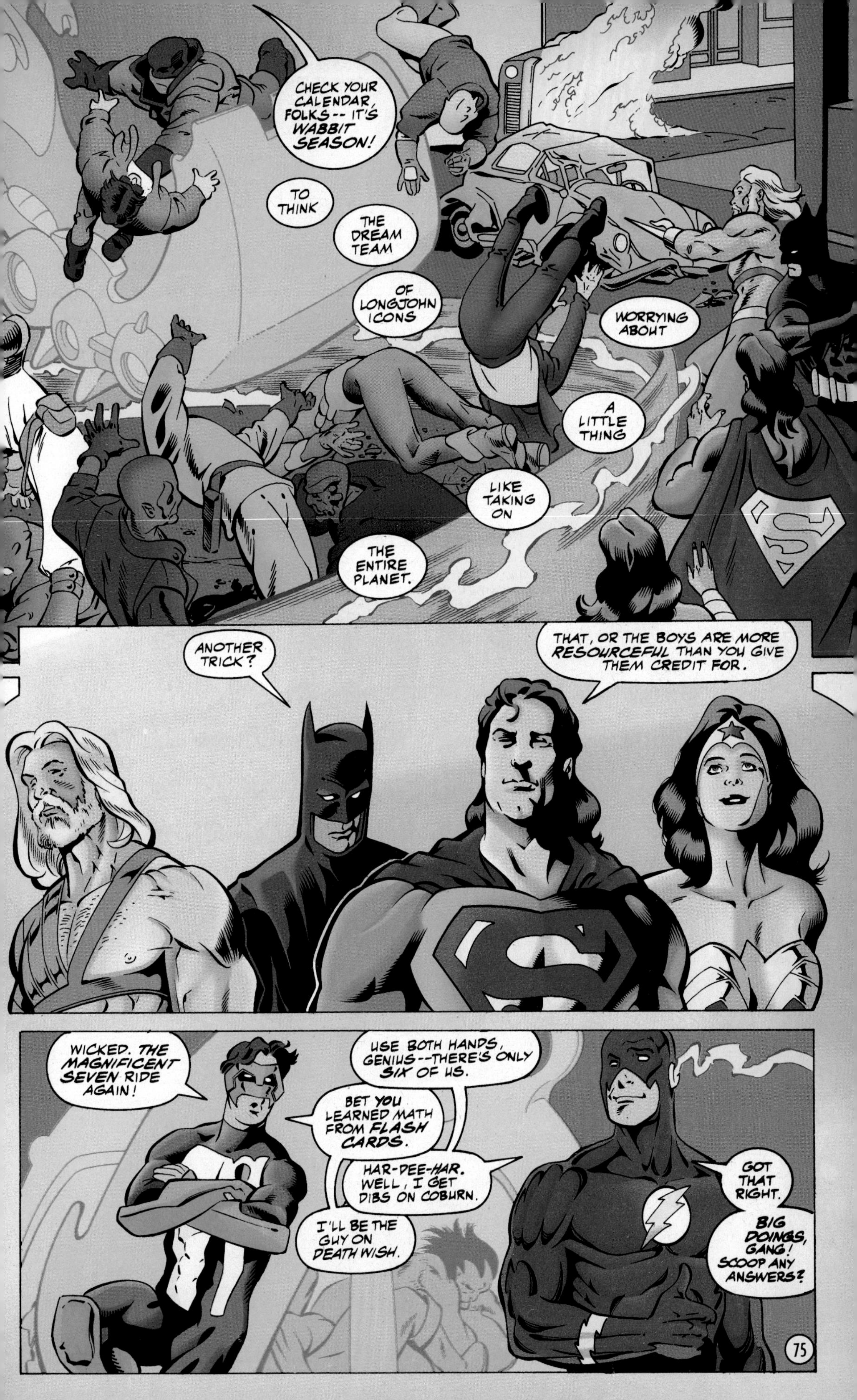

CHECK YOUR CALENDAR, FOLKS -- IT'S WABBIT SEASON!
TO THINK
THE DREAM TEAM
OF LONGJOHN ICONS
WORRYING ABOUT
A LITTLE THING
LIKE TAKING ON
THE ENTIRE PLANET.
ANOTHER TRICK?
THAT, OR THE BOYS ARE MORE RESOURCEFUL THAN YOU GIVE THEM CREDIT FOR.
WICKED. THE MAGNIFICENT SEVEN RIDE AGAIN!
USE BOTH HANDS, GENIUS--THERE'S ONLY SIX OF US.
BET YOU LEARNED MATH FROM FLASH CARDS.
HAR-DEE-HAR. WELL, I GET DIBS ON COBURN.
I'LL BE THE GUY ON DEATH WISH.
GOT THAT RIGHT.
BIG DOINGS, GANG! SCOOP ANY ANSWERS?

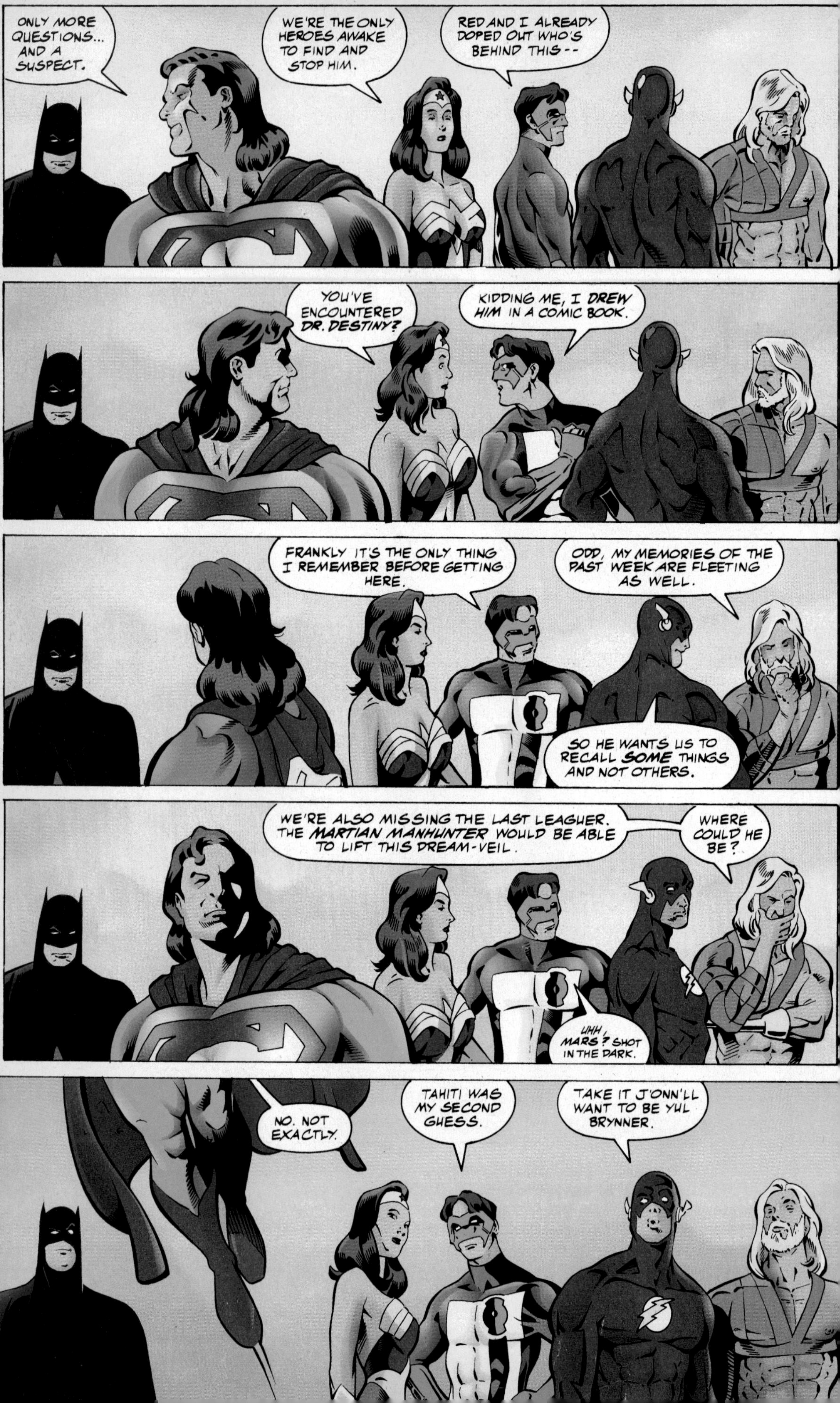
ONLY MORE QUESTIONS... AND A SUSPECT.
WE'RE THE ONLY HEROES AWAKE TO FIND AND STOP HIM.
RED AND I ALREADY DOPED OUT WHO'S BEHIND THIS--
YOU'VE ENCOUNTERED DR. DESTINY?
KIDDING ME, I DREW HIM IN A COMIC BOOK.
FRANKLY IT'S THE ONLY THING I REMEMBER BEFORE GETTING HERE.
ODD, MY MEMORIES OF THE PAST WEEK ARE FLEETING AS WELL.
SO HE WANTS US TO RECALL SOME THINGS AND NOT OTHERS.
WE'RE ALSO MISSING THE LAST LEAGUER. THE MARTIAN MANHUNTER WOULD BE ABLE TO LIFT THIS DREAM-VEIL.
WHERE COULD HE BE?
UHH, MARS? SHOT IN THE DARK.
NO. NOT EXACTLY.
TAHITI WAS MY SECOND GUESS.
TAKE IT J'ONN'LL WANT TO BE YUL BRYNNER.

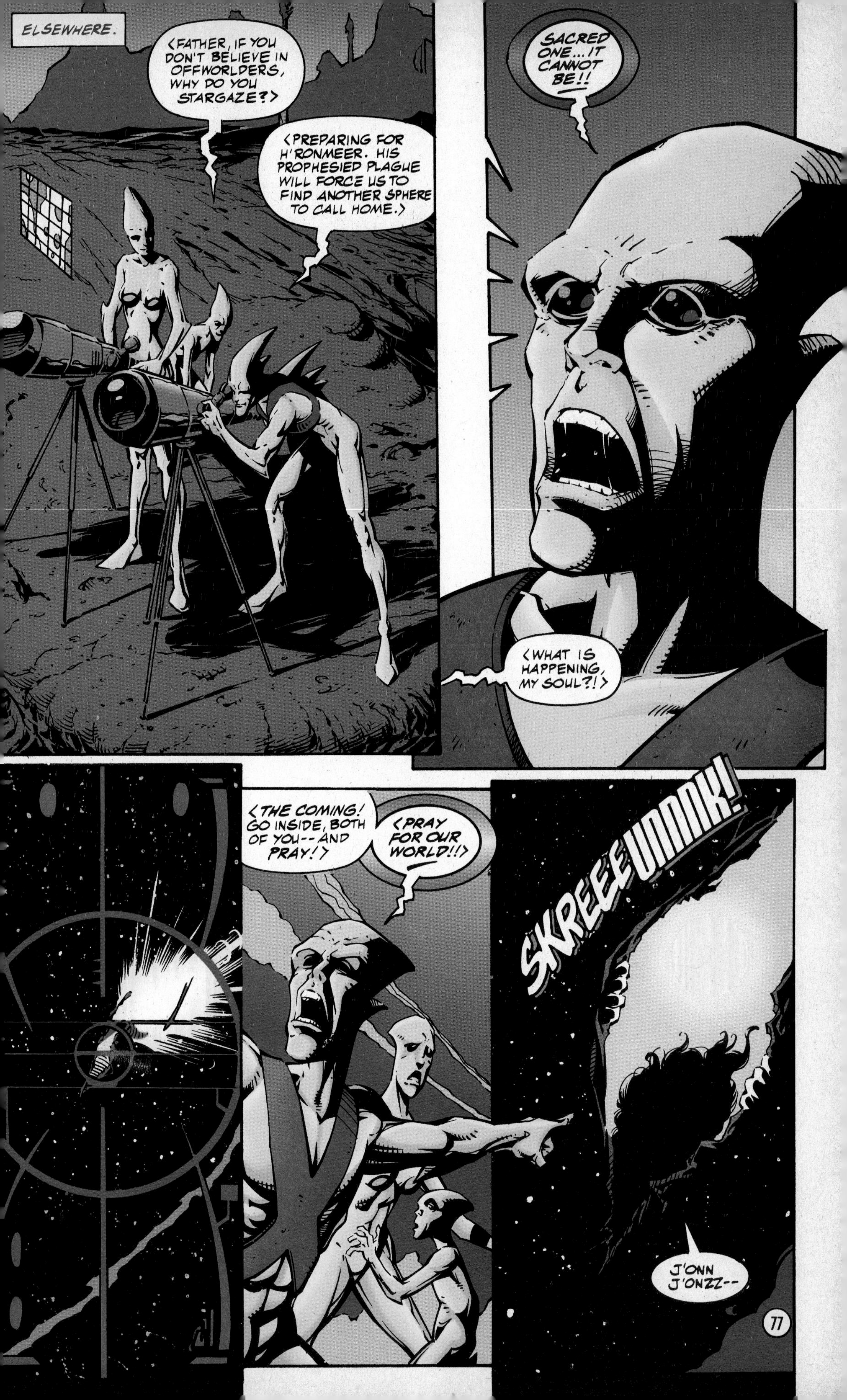
ELSEWHERE.
<FATHER, IF YOU DON'T BELIEVE IN OFFWORLDERS, WHY DO YOU STARGAZE?>
<PREPARING FOR H'RONMEER. HIS PROPHESIED PLAGUE WILL FORCE US TO FIND ANOTHER SPHERE TO CALL HOME.>
SACRED ONE... IT CANNOT BE!!
<WHAT IS HAPPENING, MY SOUL?!>
<THE COMING! GO INSIDE, BOTH OF YOU--AND PRAY!>
<PRAY FOR OUR WORLD!!>
SKREEEUNNNK!
J'ONN J'ONZZ--

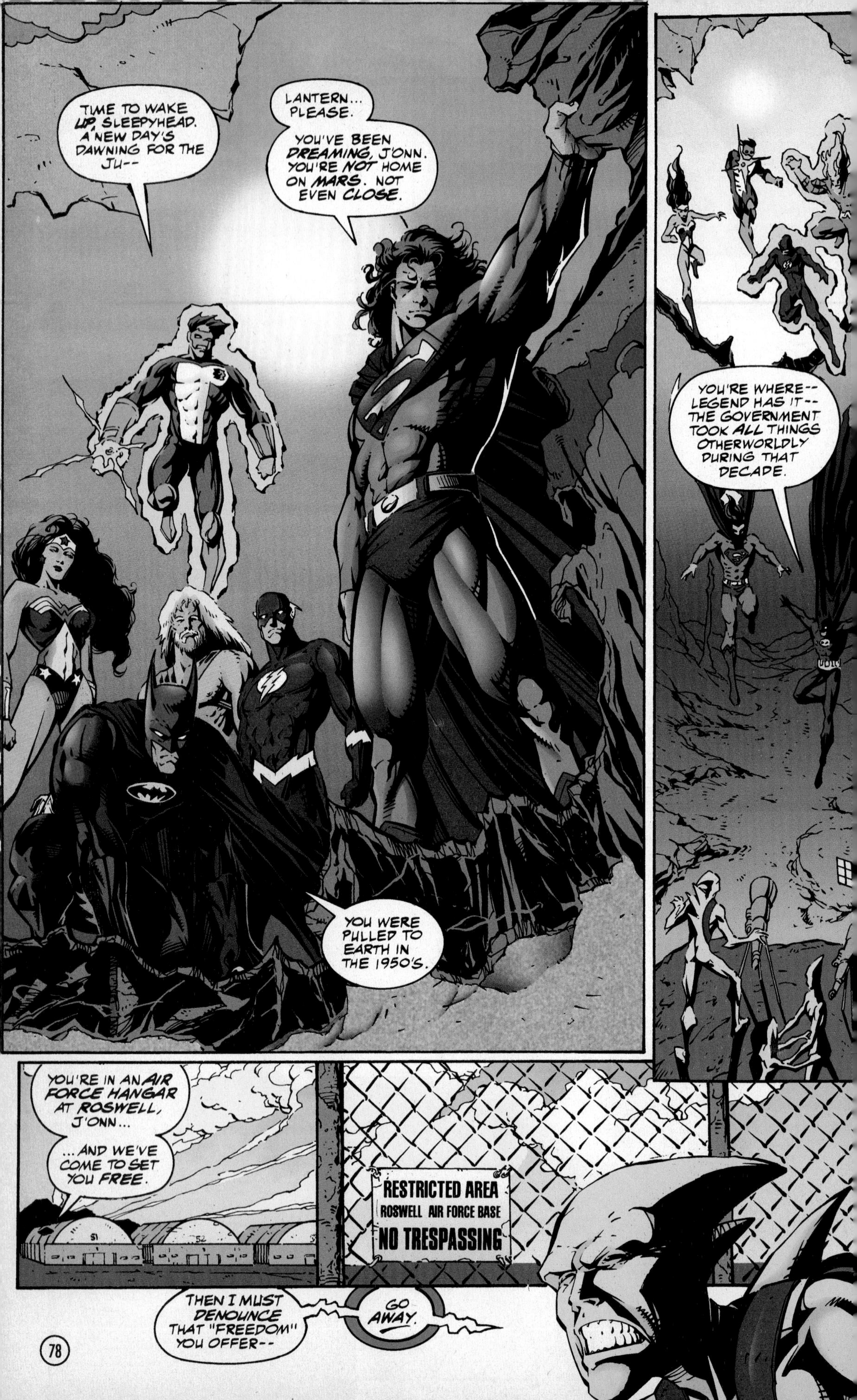

TIME TO WAKE UP, SLEEPYHEAD. A NEW DAY'S DAWNING FOR THE JU--
LANTERN... PLEASE.
YOU'VE BEEN DREAMING, J'ONN. YOU'RE NOT HOME ON MARS. NOT EVEN CLOSE.
YOU WERE PULLED TO EARTH IN THE 1950'S.
YOU'RE WHERE-- LEGEND HAS IT-- THE GOVERNMENT TOOK ALL THINGS OTHERWORLDLY DURING THAT DECADE.
YOU'RE IN AN AIR FORCE HANGAR AT ROSWELL, J'ONN...
...AND WE'VE COME TO SET YOU FREE.
RESTRICTED AREA
ROSWELL AIR FORCE BASE
NO TRESPASSING
THEN I MUST DENOUNCE THAT "FREEDOM" YOU OFFER--
GO AWAY.

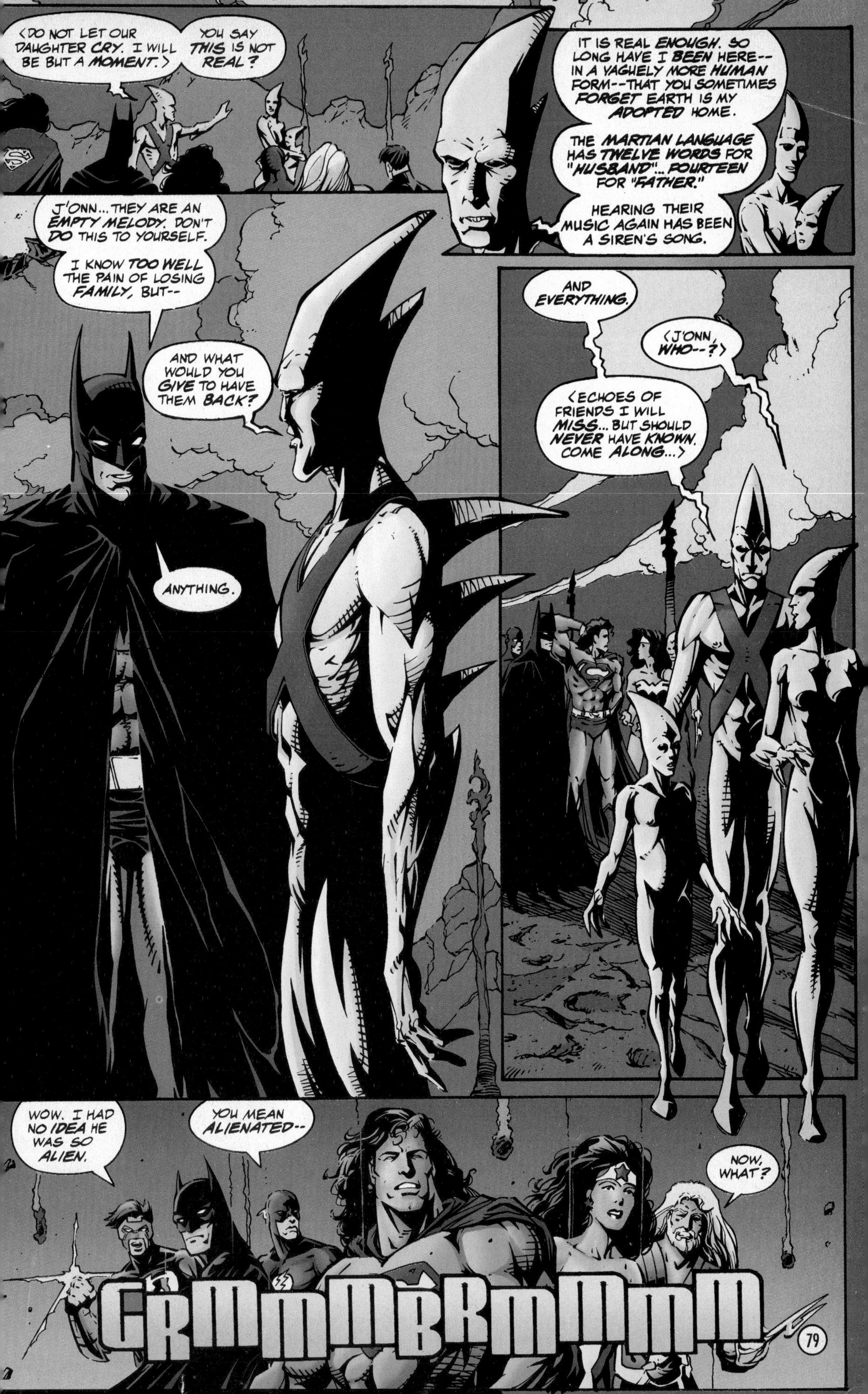

‹DO NOT LET OUR DAUGHTER CRY. I WILL BE BUT A MOMENT.›
YOU SAY THIS IS NOT REAL?
IT IS REAL ENOUGH. SO LONG HAVE I BEEN HERE-- IN A VAGUELY MORE HUMAN FORM--THAT YOU SOMETIMES FORGET EARTH IS MY ADOPTED HOME.
THE MARTIAN LANGUAGE HAS TWELVE WORDS FOR "HUSBAND"... FOURTEEN FOR "FATHER."
HEARING THEIR MUSIC AGAIN HAS BEEN A SIREN'S SONG.
J'ONN... THEY ARE AN EMPTY MELODY. DON'T DO THIS TO YOURSELF.
I KNOW TOO WELL THE PAIN OF LOSING FAMILY, BUT--
AND WHAT WOULD YOU GIVE TO HAVE THEM BACK?
ANYTHING.
AND EVERYTHING.
‹J'ONN, WHO--?›
‹ECHOES OF FRIENDS I WILL MISS... BUT SHOULD NEVER HAVE KNOWN. COME ALONG...›
WOW. I HAD NO IDEA HE WAS SO ALIEN.
YOU MEAN ALIENATED--
NOW, WHAT?
GRMMMBRMMMMM

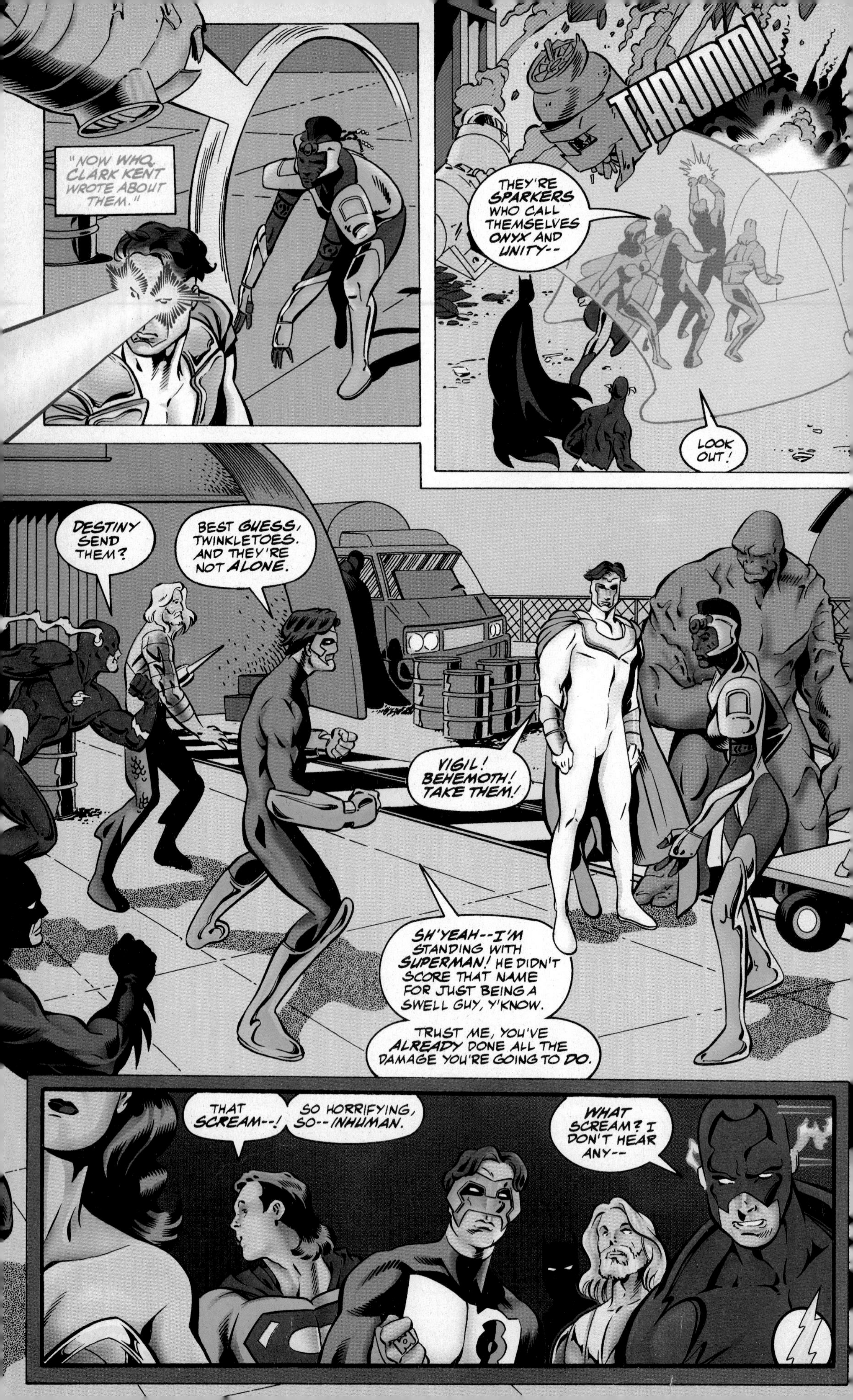
"NOW WHO. CLARK KENT WROTE ABOUT THEM."
THUMM!
THEY'RE SPARKERS WHO CALL THEMSELVES ONYX AND UNITY--
LOOK OUT!
DESTINY SEND THEM?
BEST GUESS, TWINKLETOES. AND THEY'RE NOT ALONE.
VIGIL! BEHEMOTH! TAKE THEM!
SH'YEAH--I'M STANDING WITH SUPERMAN! HE DIDN'T SCORE THAT NAME FOR JUST BEING A SWELL GUY, Y'KNOW.
TRUST ME, YOU'VE ALREADY DONE ALL THE DAMAGE YOU'RE GOING TO DO.
THAT SCREAM--!
SO HORRIFYING, SO--INHUMAN.
WHAT SCREAM? I DON'T HEAR ANY--

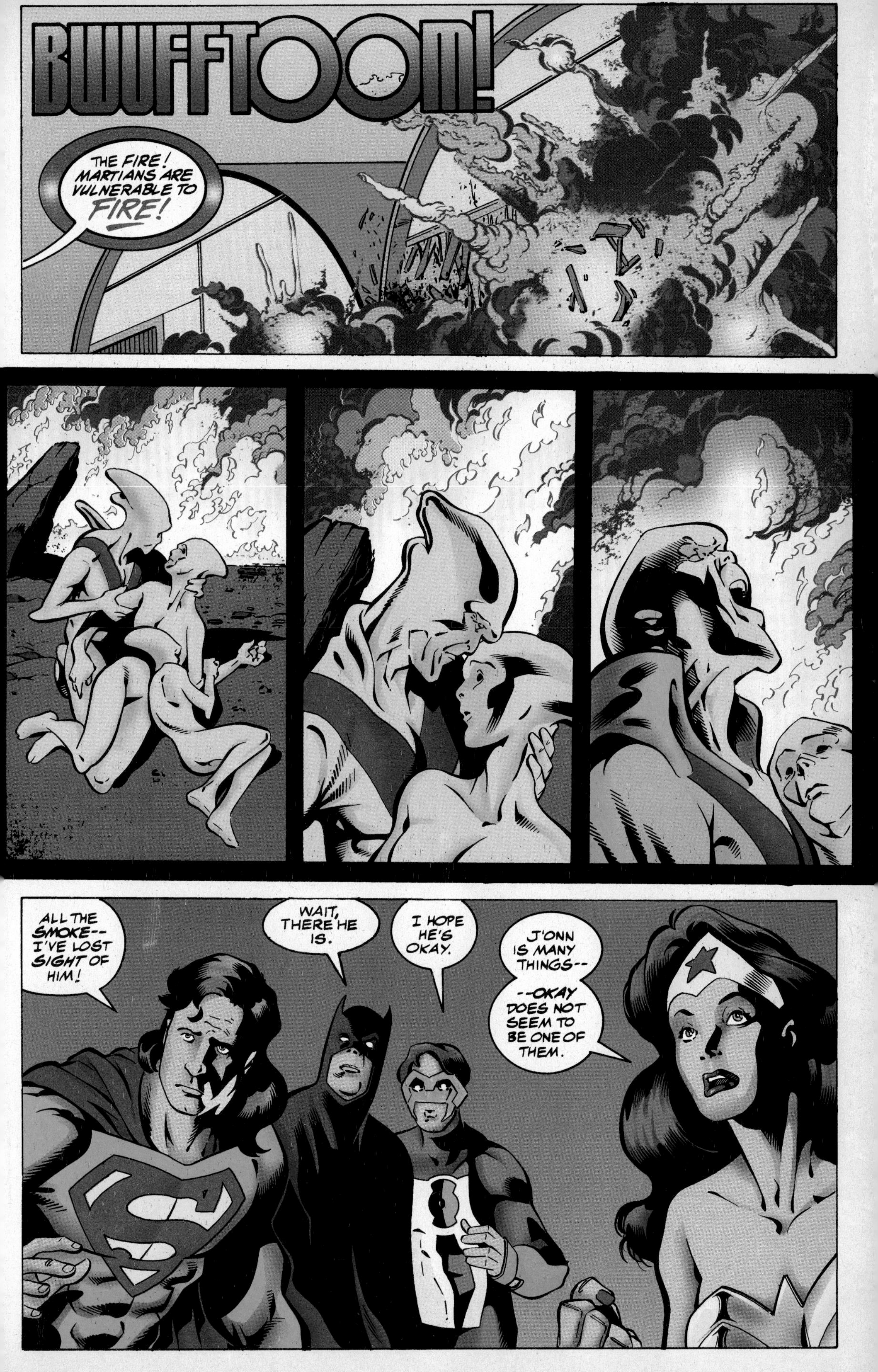
BWUFFTOOM!
THE FIRE! MARTIANS ARE VULNERABLE TO FIRE!
ALL THE SMOKE-- I'VE LOST SIGHT OF HIM!
WAIT, THERE HE IS.
I HOPE HE'S OKAY.
J'ONN IS MANY THINGS--
--OKAY DOES NOT SEEM TO BE ONE OF THEM.

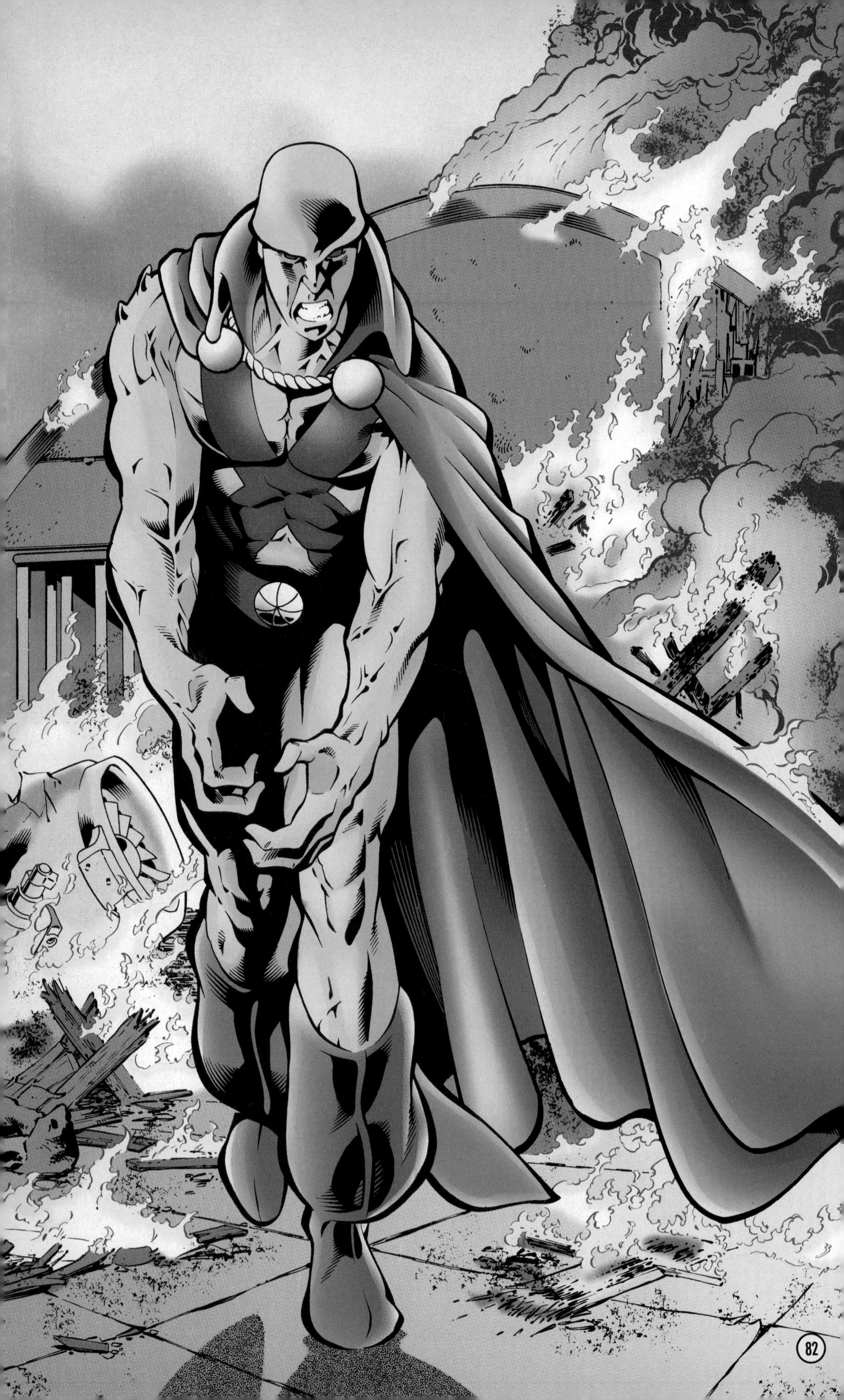

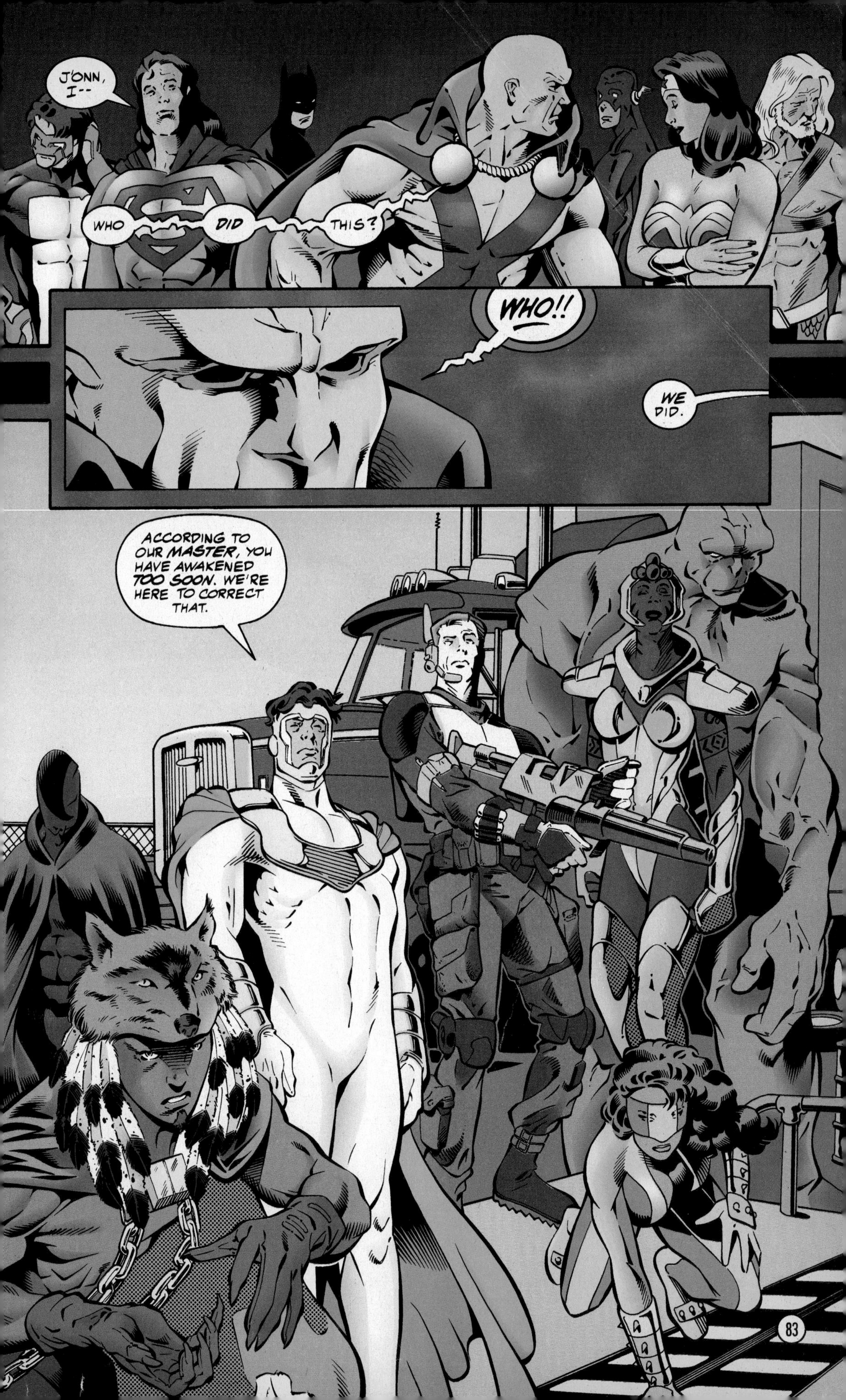
J'ONN, I--
WHO DID THIS?
WHO!!
WE DID.
ACCORDING TO OUR MASTER, YOU HAVE AWAKENED TOO SOON. WE'RE HERE TO CORRECT THAT.

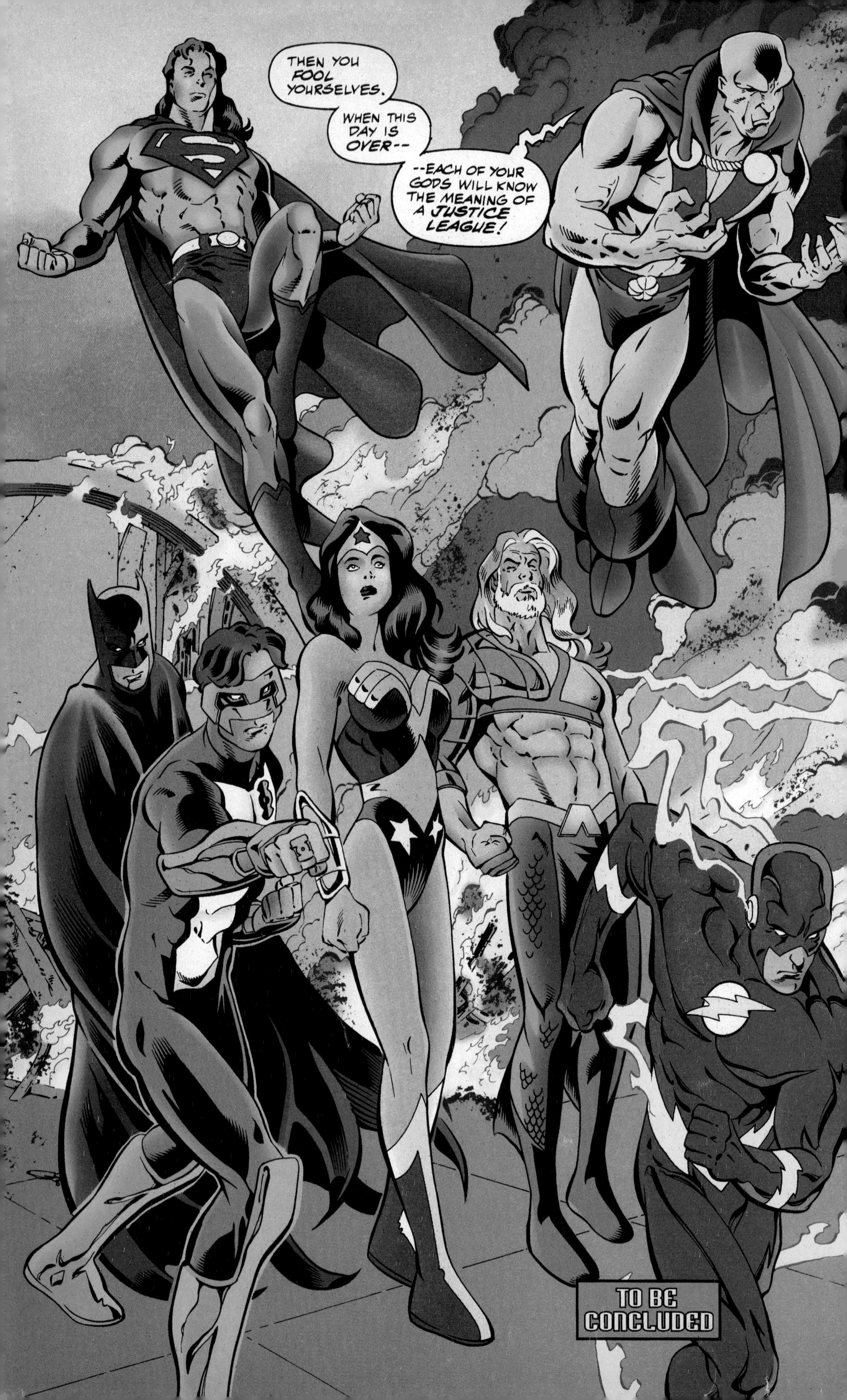
THEN YOU FOOL YOURSELVES.
WHEN THIS DAY IS OVER--
--EACH OF YOUR GODS WILL KNOW THE MEANING OF A JUSTICE LEAGUE!
TO BE CONCLUDED

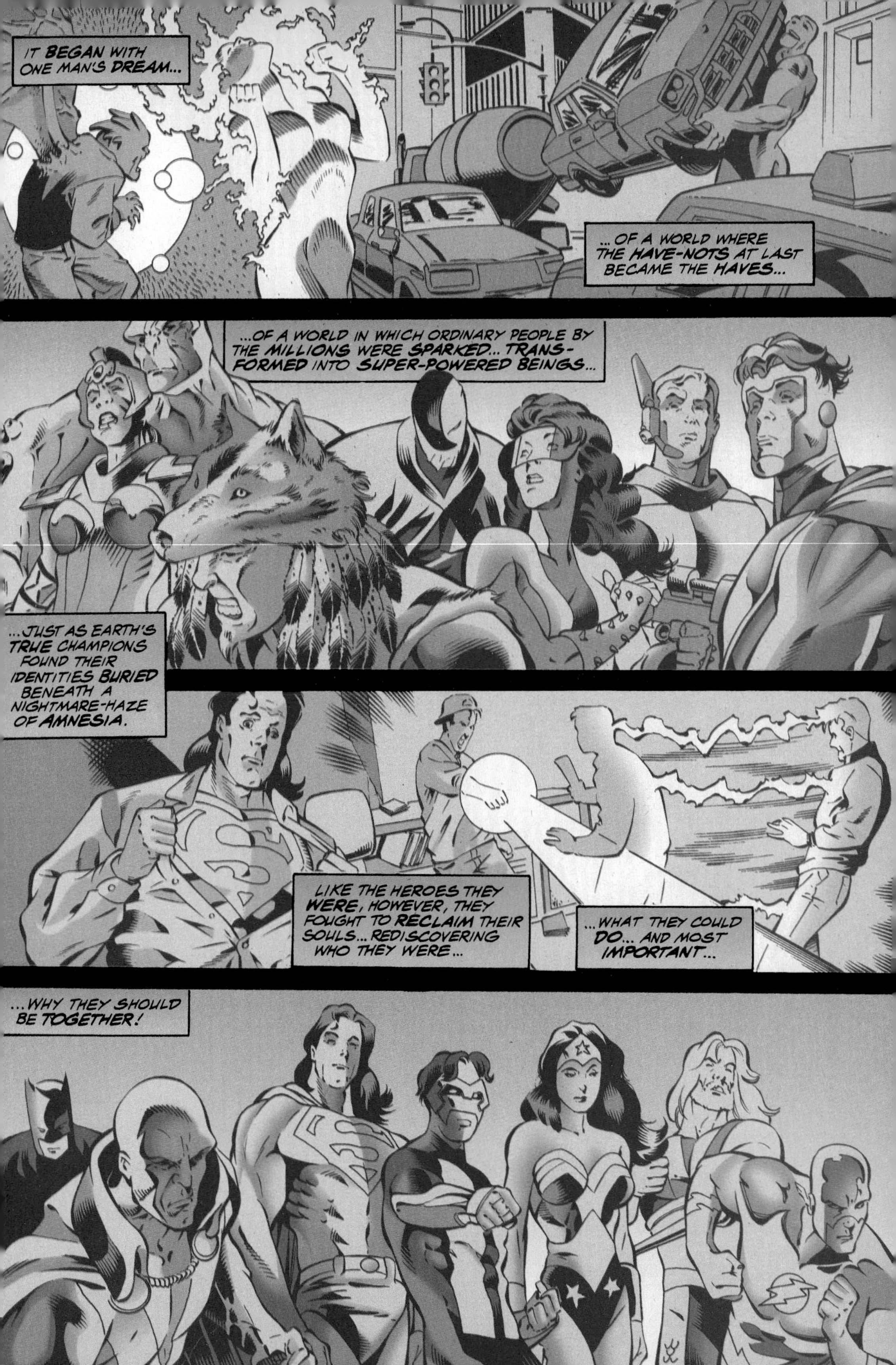

IT BEGAN WITH ONE MAN'S DREAM...
...OF A WORLD WHERE THE HAVE-NOTS AT LAST BECAME THE HAVES...
...OF A WORLD IN WHICH ORDINARY PEOPLE BY THE MILLIONS WERE SPARKED... TRANSFORMED INTO SUPER-POWERED BEINGS...
...JUST AS EARTH'S TRUE CHAMPIONS FOUND THEIR IDENTITIES BURIED BENEATH A NIGHTMARE-HAZE OF AMNESIA.
LIKE THE HEROES THEY WERE, HOWEVER, THEY FOUGHT TO RECLAIM THEIR SOULS...REDISCOVERING WHO THEY WERE...
...WHAT THEY COULD DO... AND MOST IMPORTANT...
...WHY THEY SHOULD BE TOGETHER!

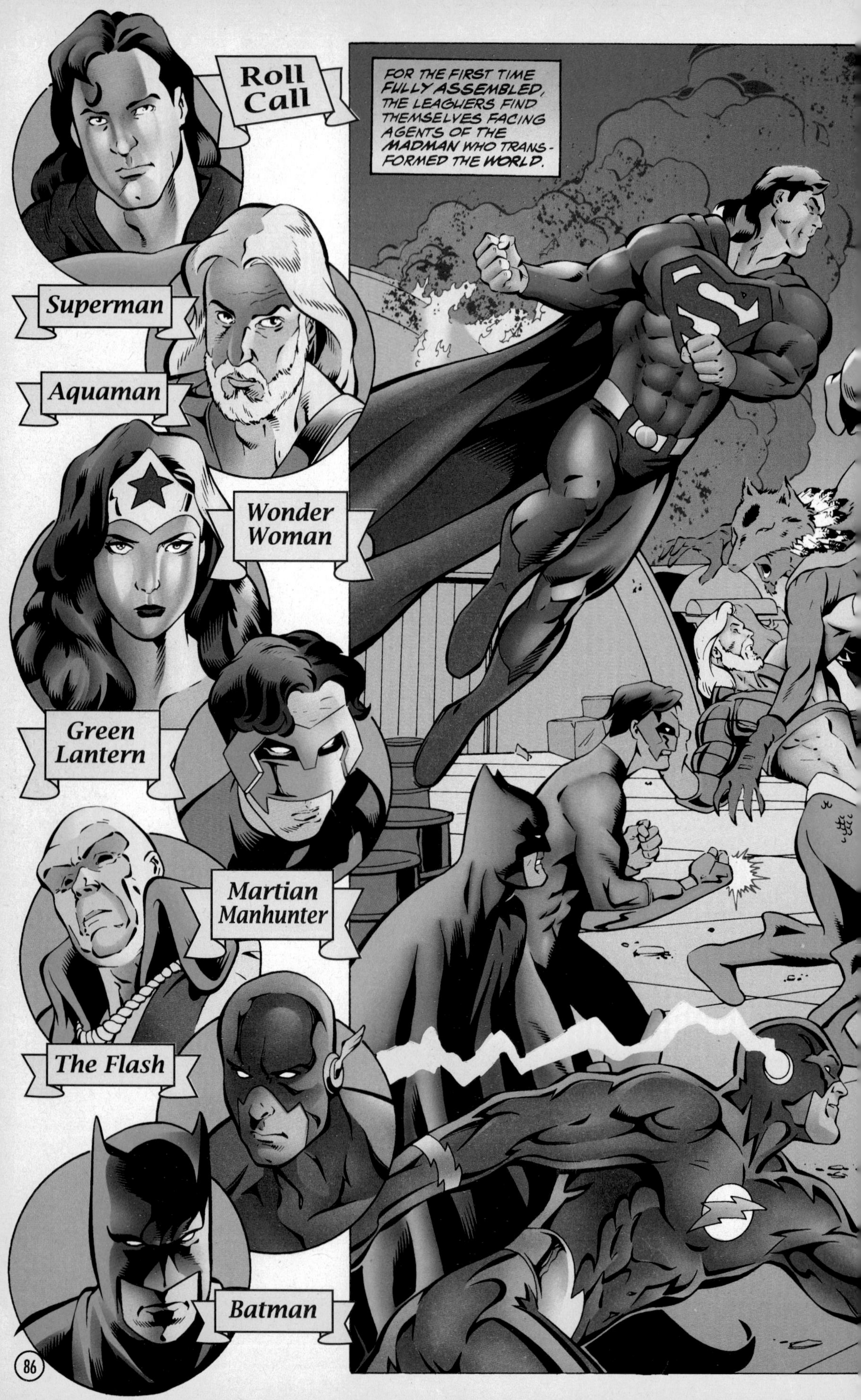

Roll Call
Superman
Aquaman
Wonder Woman
Green Lantern
Martian Manhunter
The Flash
Batman
FOR THE FIRST TIME FULLY ASSEMBLED, THE LEAGUERS FIND THEMSELVES FACING AGENTS OF THE MADMAN WHO TRANSFORMED THE WORLD.

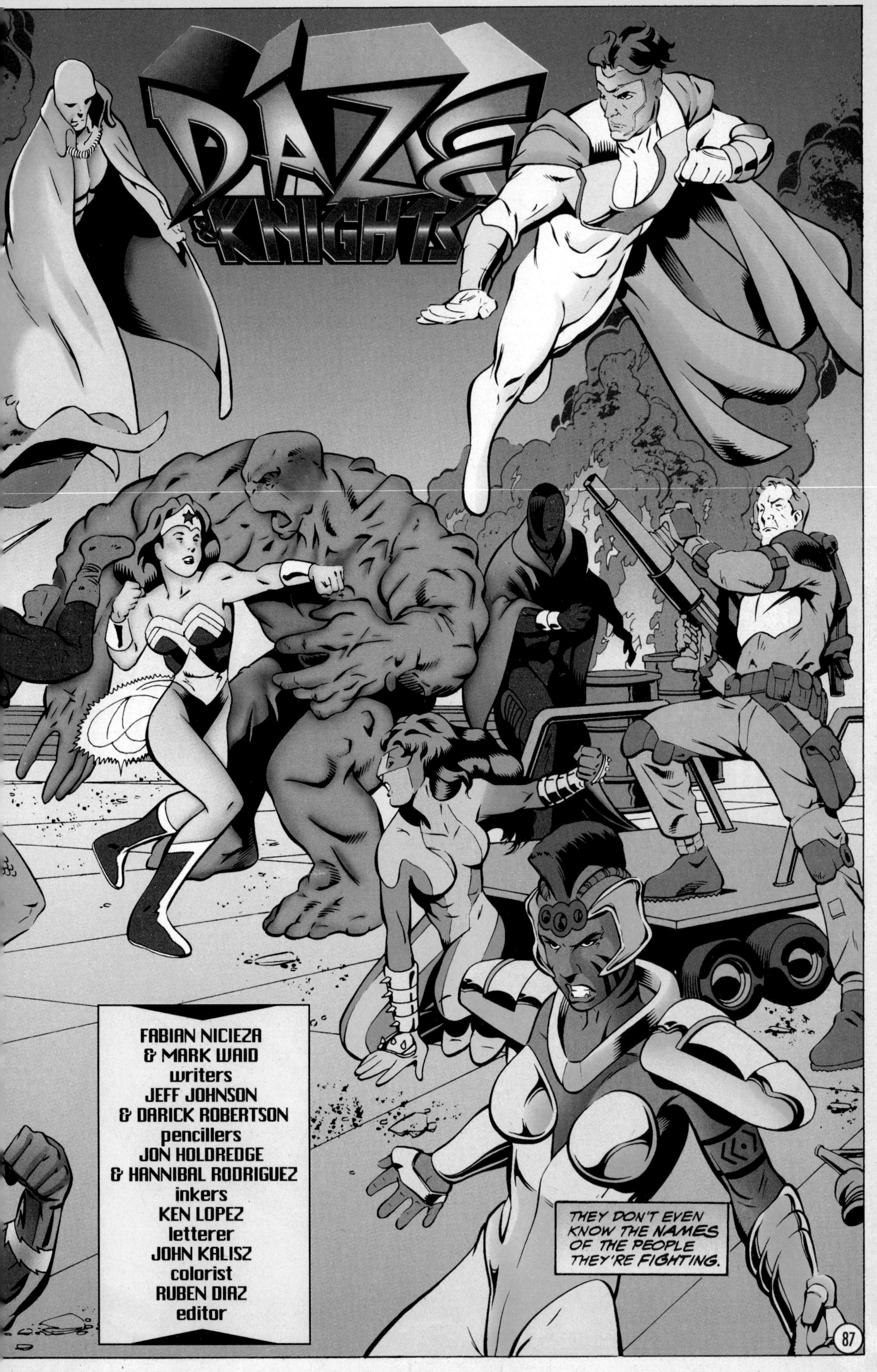
DAZE & KNIGHTS
FABIAN NICIEZA
& MARK WAID
writers
JEFF JOHNSON
& DARICK ROBERTSON
pencillers
JON HOLDREDGE
& HANNIBAL RODRIGUEZ
inkers
KEN LOPEZ
letterer
JOHN KALISZ
colorist
RUBEN DIAZ
editor
THEY DON'T EVEN KNOW THE NAMES OF THE PEOPLE THEY'RE FIGHTING.

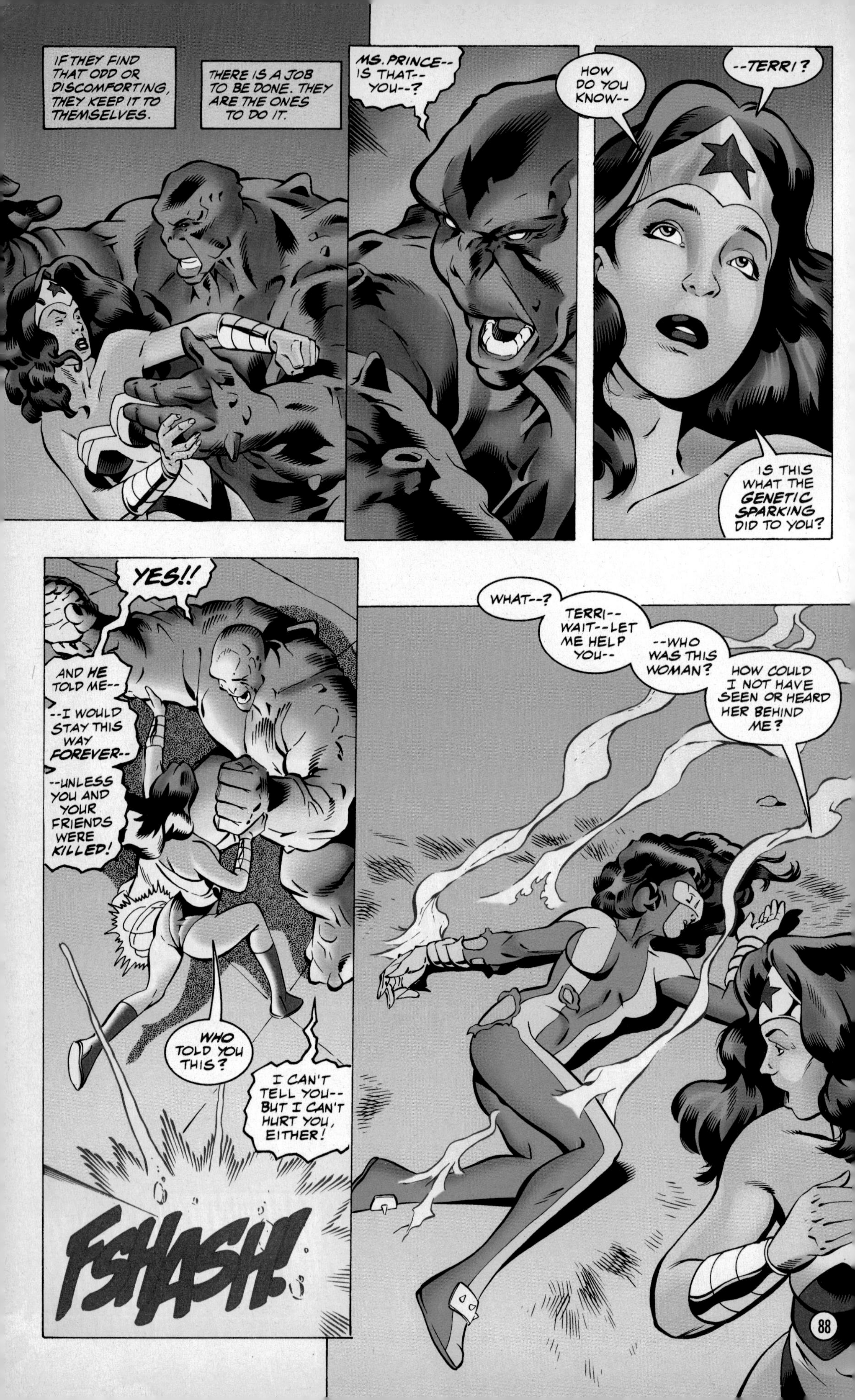
IF THEY FIND THAT ODD OR DISCOMFORTING, THEY KEEP IT TO THEMSELVES.
THERE IS A JOB TO BE DONE. THEY ARE THE ONES TO DO IT.
MS. PRINCE-- IS THAT-- YOU--?
HOW DO YOU KNOW--
--TERRI?
IS THIS WHAT THE GENETIC SPARKING DID TO YOU?
YES!!
AND HE TOLD ME--
--I WOULD STAY THIS WAY FOREVER--
--UNLESS YOU AND YOUR FRIENDS WERE KILLED!
WHO TOLD YOU THIS?
I CAN'T TELL YOU-- BUT I CAN'T HURT YOU, EITHER!
FSHASH!
WHAT--?
TERRI-- WAIT--LET ME HELP YOU--
--WHO WAS THIS WOMAN?
HOW COULD I NOT HAVE SEEN OR HEARD HER BEHIND ME?

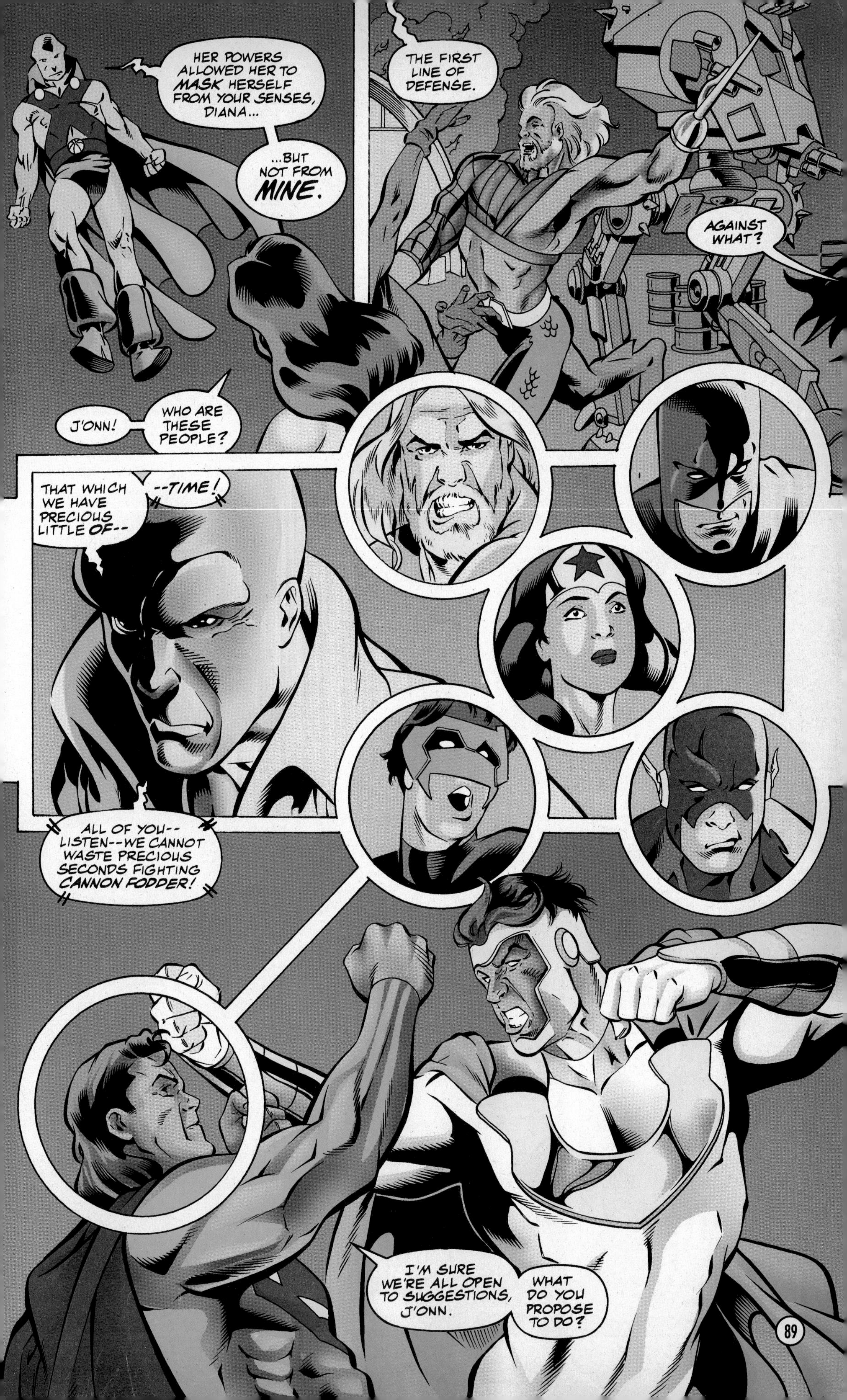

HER POWERS ALLOWED HER TO MASK HERSELF FROM YOUR SENSES, DIANA...
...BUT NOT FROM MINE.
THE FIRST LINE OF DEFENSE.
AGAINST WHAT?
J'ONN!
WHO ARE THESE PEOPLE?
THAT WHICH WE HAVE PRECIOUS LITTLE OF--
--TIME!
ALL OF YOU-- LISTEN--WE CANNOT WASTE PRECIOUS SECONDS FIGHTING CANNON FODDER!
I'M SURE WE'RE ALL OPEN TO SUGGESTIONS, J'ONN.
WHAT DO YOU PROPOSE TO DO?

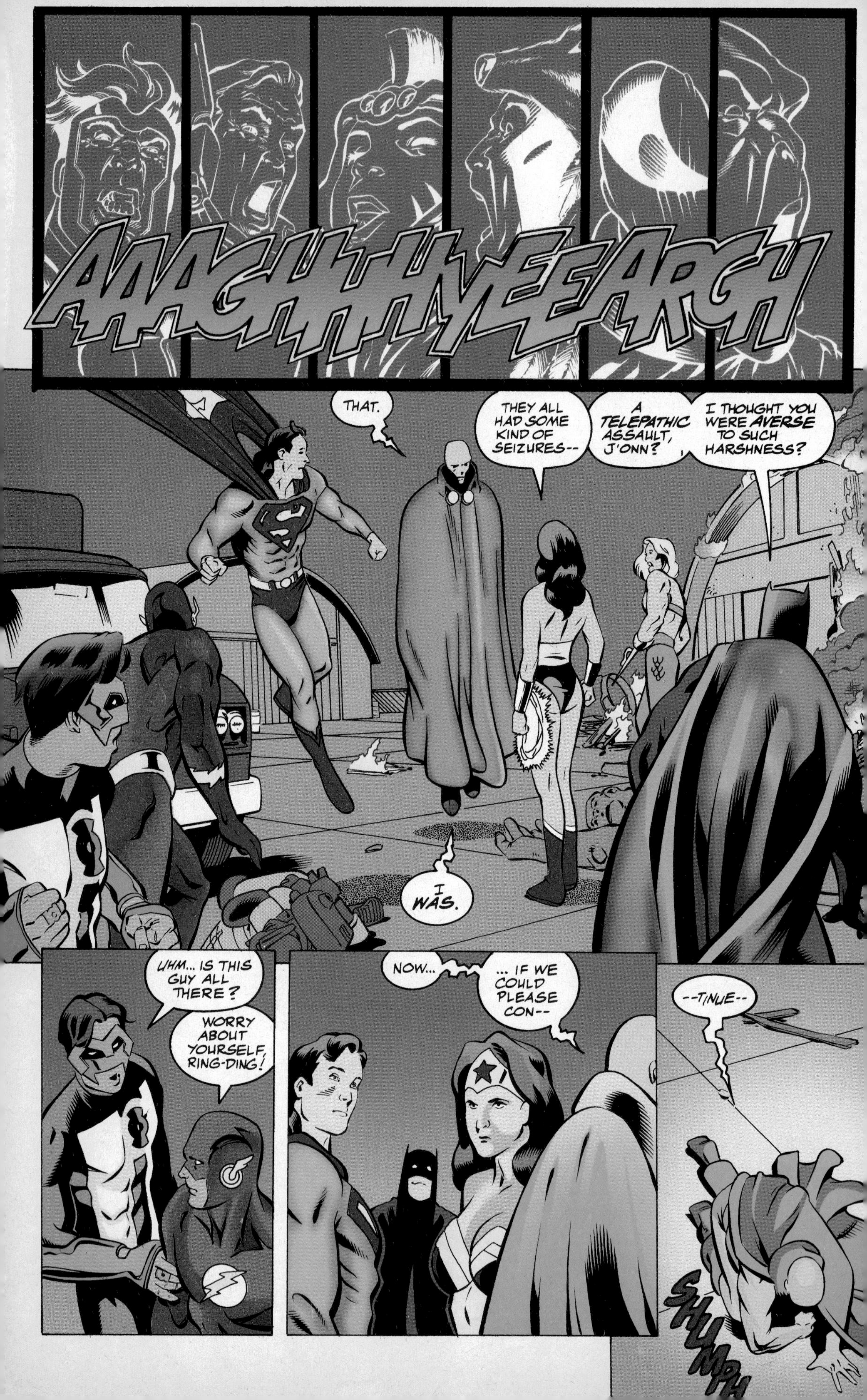
AAAGHHHYEEARGH
THAT.
THEY ALL HAD SOME KIND OF SEIZURES--
A TELEPATHIC ASSAULT, J'ONN?
I THOUGHT YOU WERE AVERSE TO SUCH HARSHNESS?
I WAS.
UHM... IS THIS GUY ALL THERE?
WORRY ABOUT YOURSELF, RING-DING!
NOW...
... IF WE COULD PLEASE CON--
--TINUE--
SHUMPH

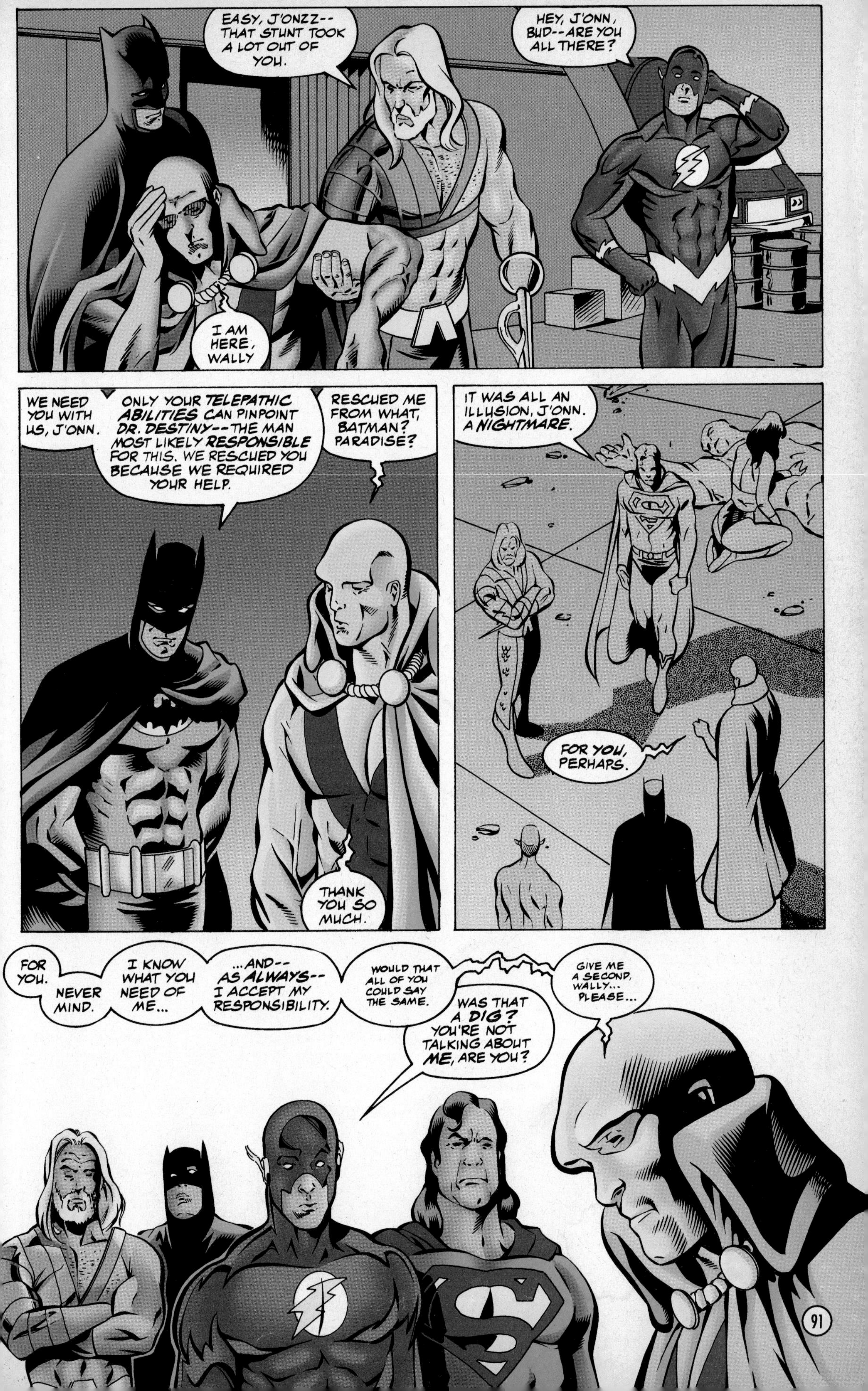

EASY, J'ONZZ-- THAT STUNT TOOK A LOT OUT OF YOU.
HEY, J'ONN, BUD--ARE YOU ALL THERE?
I AM HERE, WALLY
WE NEED YOU WITH US, J'ONN.
ONLY YOUR TELEPATHIC ABILITIES CAN PINPOINT DR. DESTINY--THE MAN MOST LIKELY RESPONSIBLE FOR THIS. WE RESCUED YOU BECAUSE WE REQUIRED YOUR HELP.
RESCUED ME FROM WHAT, BATMAN? PARADISE?
THANK YOU SO MUCH.
IT WAS ALL AN ILLUSION, J'ONN. A NIGHTMARE.
FOR YOU, PERHAPS.
FOR YOU.
NEVER MIND.
I KNOW WHAT YOU NEED OF ME...
...AND-- AS ALWAYS-- I ACCEPT MY RESPONSIBILITY.
WOULD THAT ALL OF YOU COULD SAY THE SAME.
WAS THAT A DIG? YOU'RE NOT TALKING ABOUT ME, ARE YOU?
GIVE ME A SECOND, WALLY... PLEASE...

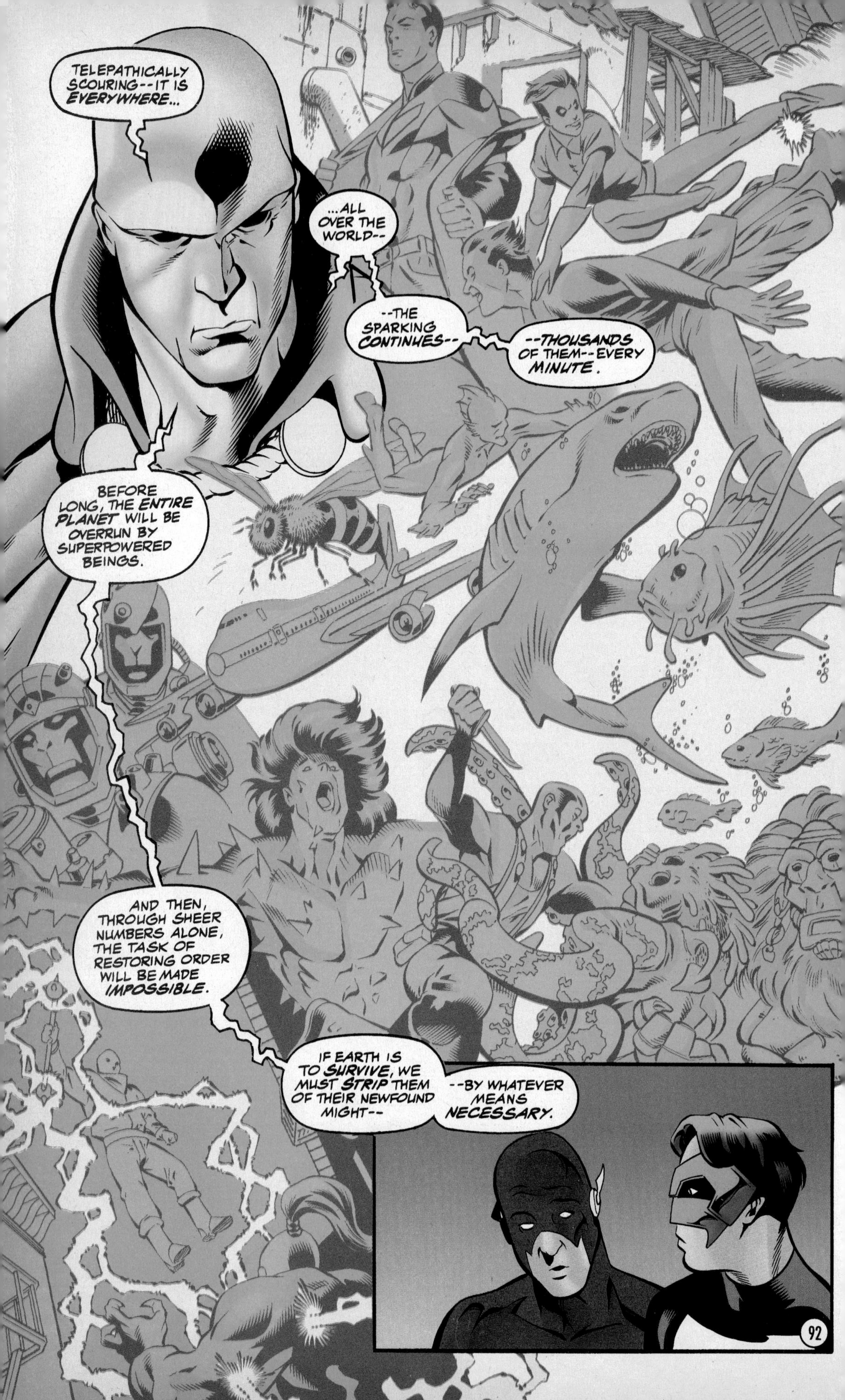
TELEPATHICALLY SCOURING--IT IS EVERYWHERE...
...ALL OVER THE WORLD--
--THE SPARKING CONTINUES--
--THOUSANDS OF THEM--EVERY MINUTE.
BEFORE LONG, THE ENTIRE PLANET WILL BE OVERRUN BY SUPERPOWERED BEINGS.
AND THEN, THROUGH SHEER NUMBERS ALONE, THE TASK OF RESTORING ORDER WILL BE MADE IMPOSSIBLE.
IF EARTH IS TO SURVIVE, WE MUST STRIP THEM OF THEIR NEWFOUND MIGHT--
--BY WHATEVER MEANS NECESSARY.

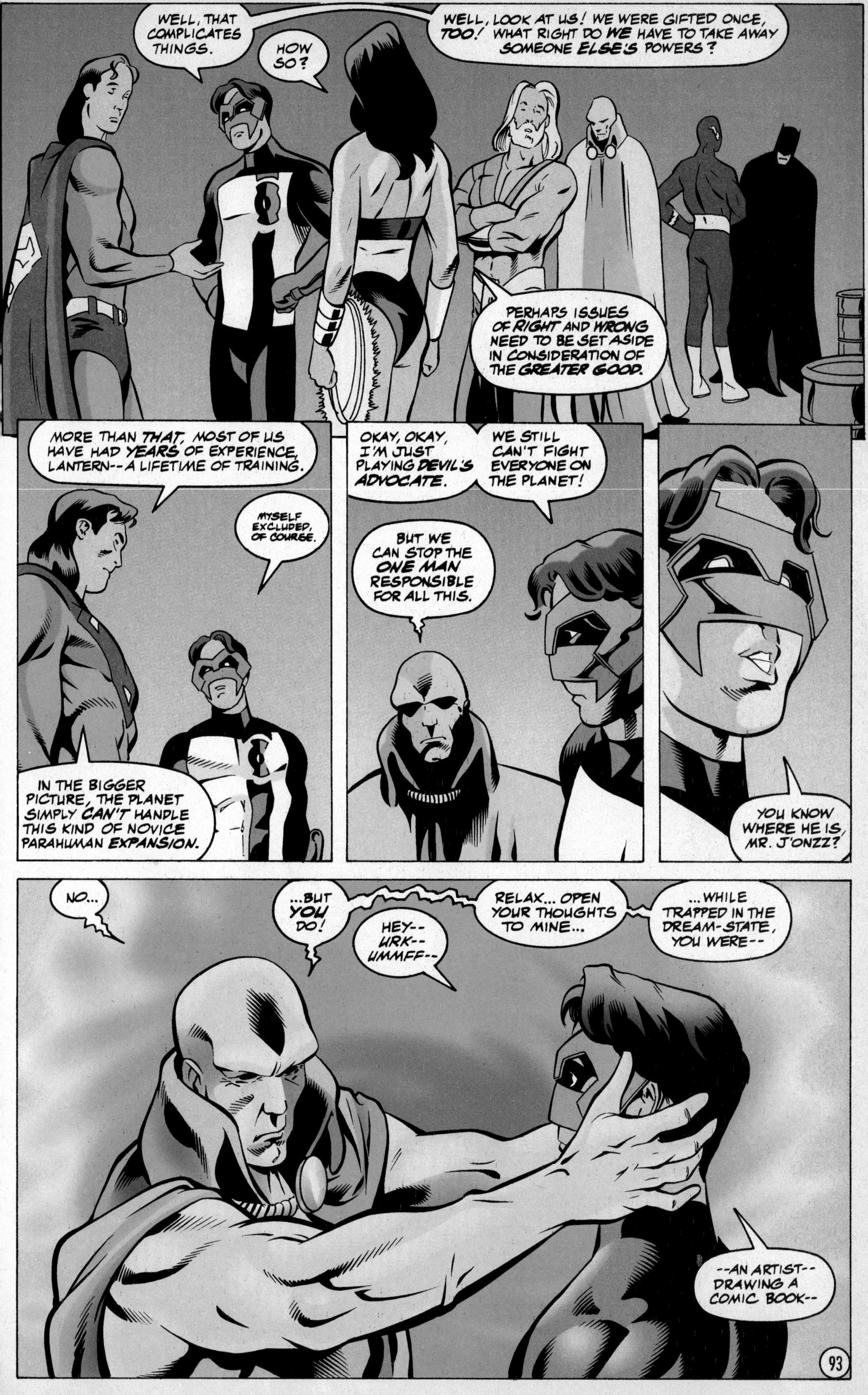
WELL, THAT COMPLICATES THINGS.
HOW SO?
WELL, LOOK AT US! WE WERE GIFTED ONCE, TOO! WHAT RIGHT DO WE HAVE TO TAKE AWAY SOMEONE ELSE'S POWERS?
PERHAPS ISSUES OF RIGHT AND WRONG NEED TO BE SET ASIDE IN CONSIDERATION OF THE GREATER GOOD.
MORE THAN THAT, MOST OF US HAVE HAD YEARS OF EXPERIENCE, LANTERN--A LIFETIME OF TRAINING.
MYSELF EXCLUDED, OF COURSE.
IN THE BIGGER PICTURE, THE PLANET SIMPLY CAN'T HANDLE THIS KIND OF NOVICE PARAHUMAN EXPANSION.
OKAY, OKAY, I'M JUST PLAYING DEVIL'S ADVOCATE.
WE STILL CAN'T FIGHT EVERYONE ON THE PLANET!
BUT WE CAN STOP THE ONE MAN RESPONSIBLE FOR ALL THIS.
YOU KNOW WHERE HE IS, MR. J'ONZZ?
NO...
...BUT YOU DO!
HEY-- URK-- UMMFF--
RELAX... OPEN YOUR THOUGHTS TO MINE...
...WHILE TRAPPED IN THE DREAM-STATE, YOU WERE--
--AN ARTIST-- DRAWING A COMIC BOOK--

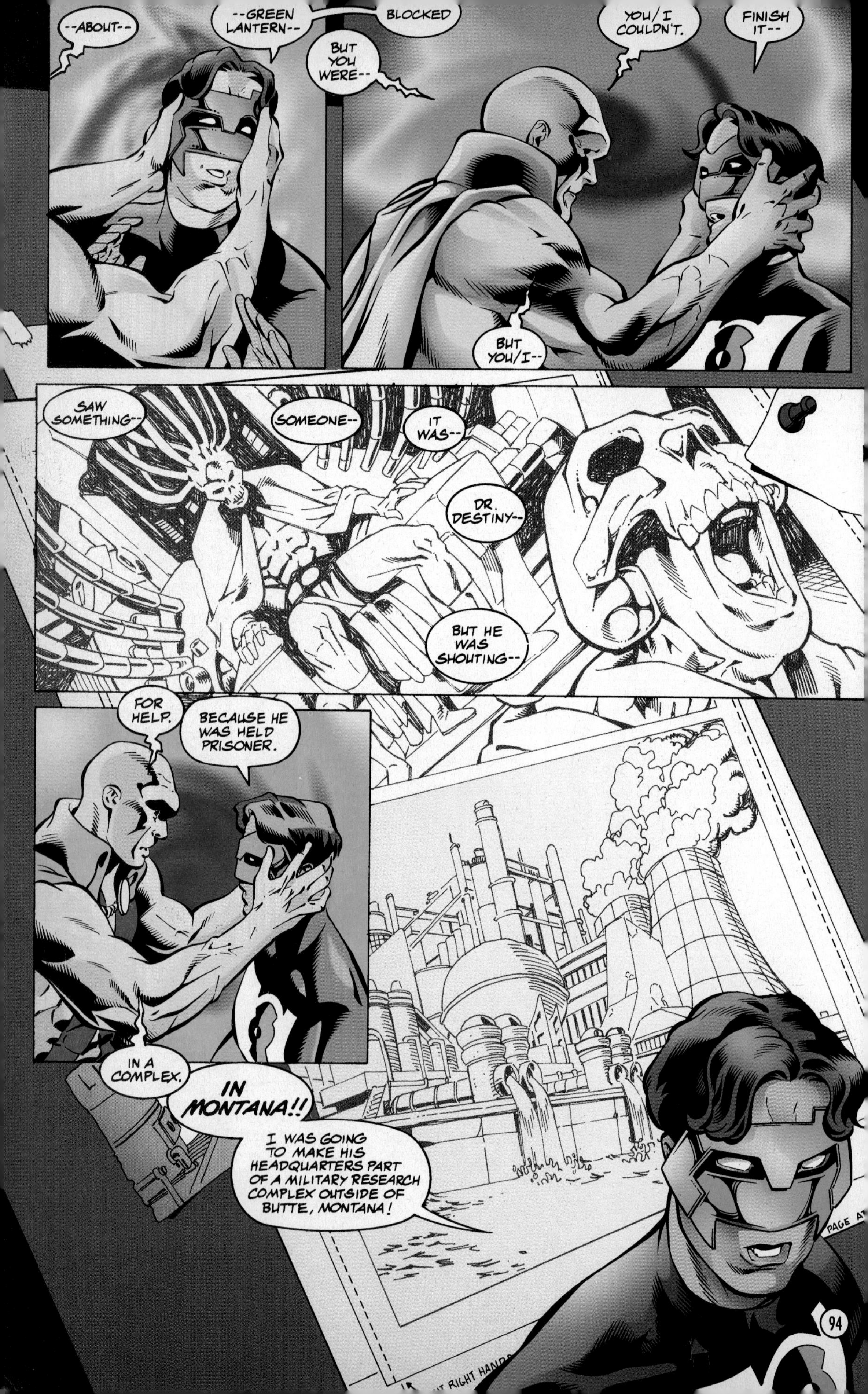
--ABOUT--
--GREEN LANTERN--
BLOCKED
BUT YOU WERE--
YOU/I COULDN'T.
FINISH IT--
BUT YOU/I--
SAW SOMETHING--
SOMEONE--
IT WAS--
DR. DESTINY--
BUT HE WAS SHOUTING--
FOR HELP.
BECAUSE HE WAS HELD PRISONER.
IN A COMPLEX.
IN MONTANA!!
I WAS GOING TO MAKE HIS HEADQUARTERS PART OF A MILITARY RESEARCH COMPLEX OUTSIDE OF BUTTE, MONTANA!

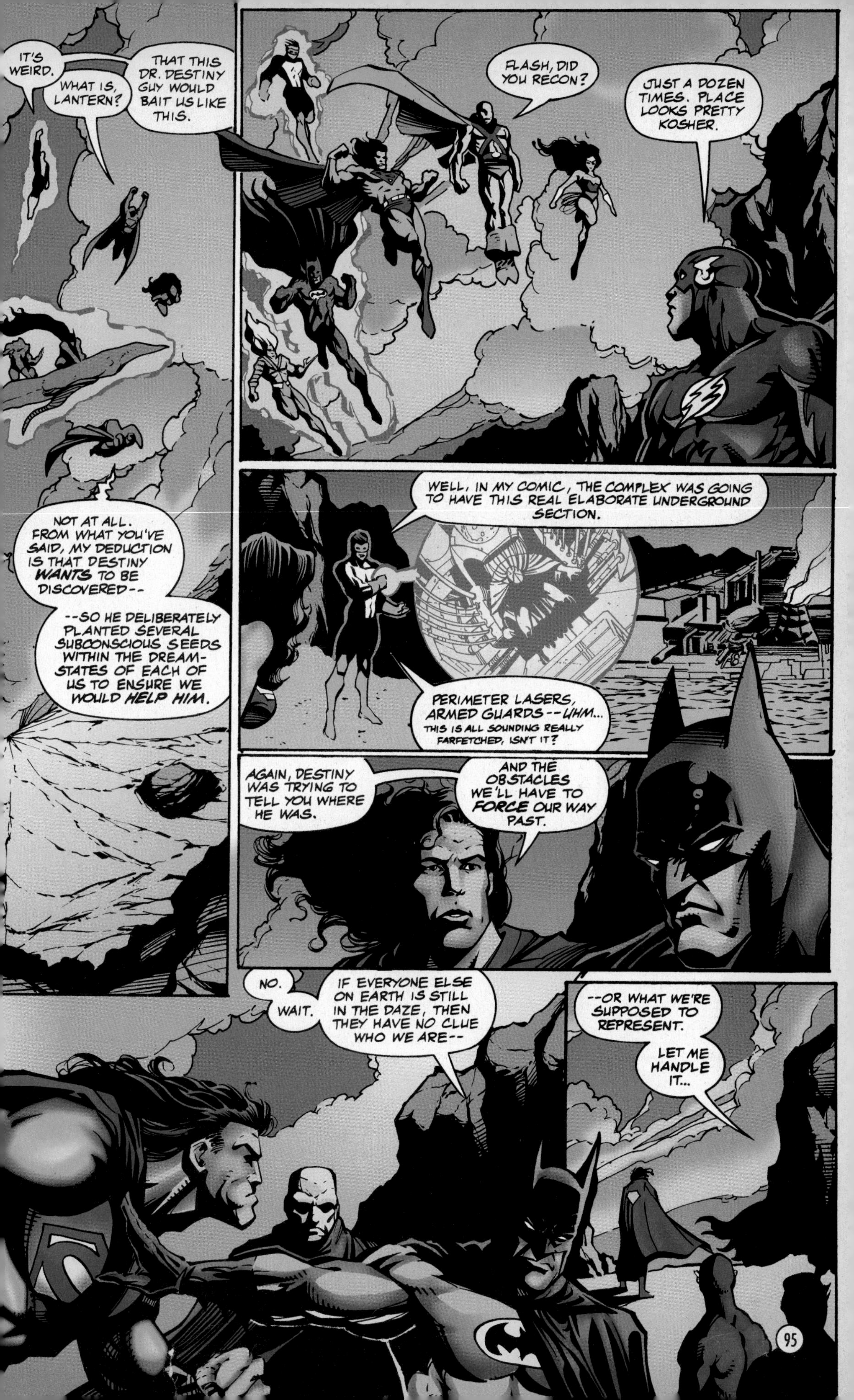
IT'S WEIRD.
WHAT IS, LANTERN?
THAT THIS DR. DESTINY GUY WOULD BAIT US LIKE THIS.
FLASH, DID YOU RECON?
JUST A DOZEN TIMES. PLACE LOOKS PRETTY KOSHER.
NOT AT ALL. FROM WHAT YOU'VE SAID, MY DEDUCTION IS THAT DESTINY WANTS TO BE DISCOVERED--
--SO HE DELIBERATELY PLANTED SEVERAL SUBCONSCIOUS SEEDS WITHIN THE DREAM-STATES OF EACH OF US TO ENSURE WE WOULD HELP HIM.
WELL, IN MY COMIC, THE COMPLEX WAS GOING TO HAVE THIS REAL ELABORATE UNDERGROUND SECTION.
PERIMETER LASERS, ARMED GUARDS--UHM... THIS IS ALL SOUNDING REALLY FARFETCHED, ISN'T IT?
AGAIN, DESTINY WAS TRYING TO TELL YOU WHERE HE WAS.
AND THE OBSTACLES WE'LL HAVE TO FORCE OUR WAY PAST.
NO.
WAIT.
IF EVERYONE ELSE ON EARTH IS STILL IN THE DAZE, THEN THEY HAVE NO CLUE WHO WE ARE--
--OR WHAT WE'RE SUPPOSED TO REPRESENT.
LET ME HANDLE IT...

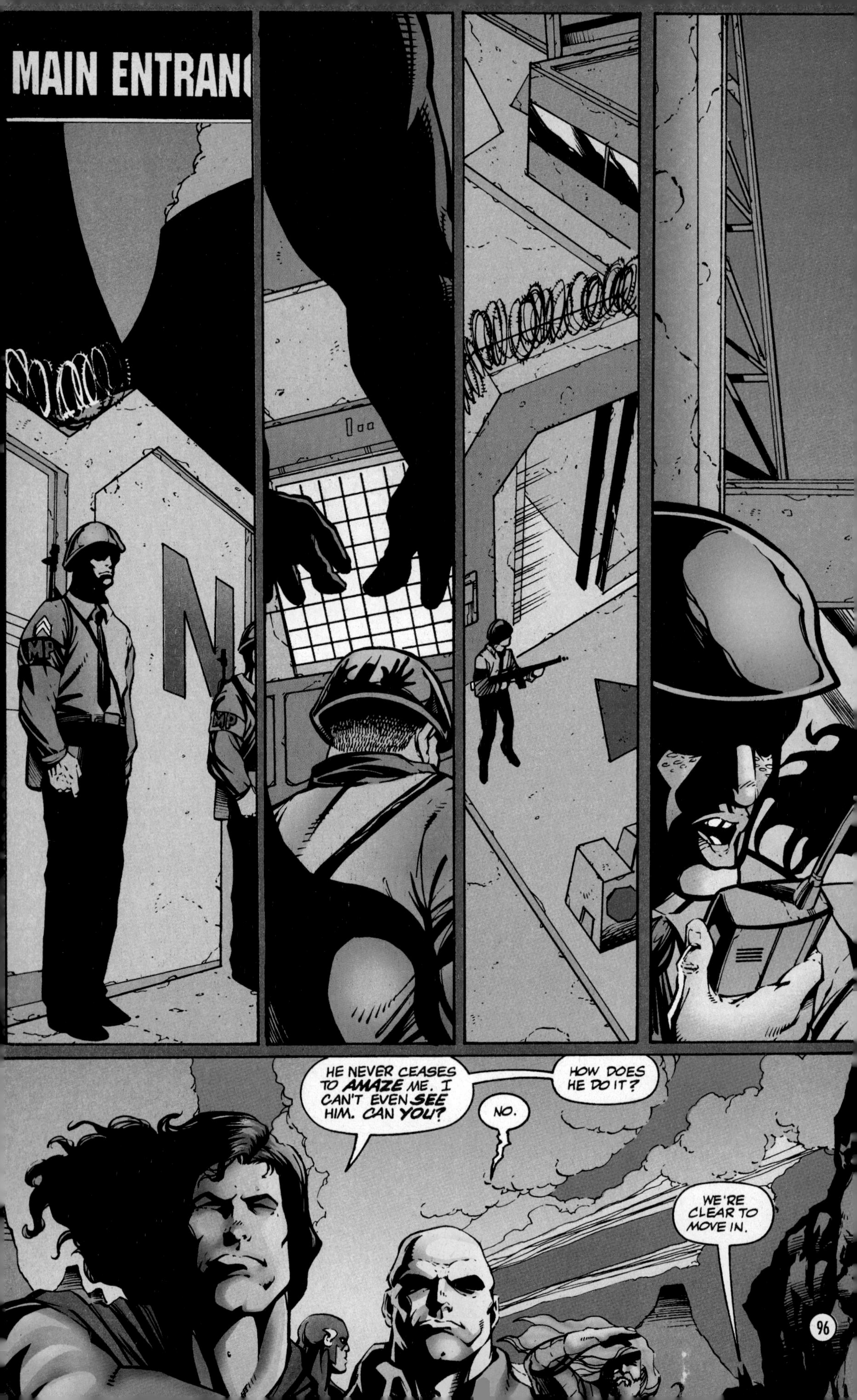
MAIN ENTRANC
MP
MP
HE NEVER CEASES TO AMAZE ME. I CAN'T EVEN SEE HIM. CAN YOU?
HOW DOES HE DO IT?
NO.
WE'RE CLEAR TO MOVE IN.

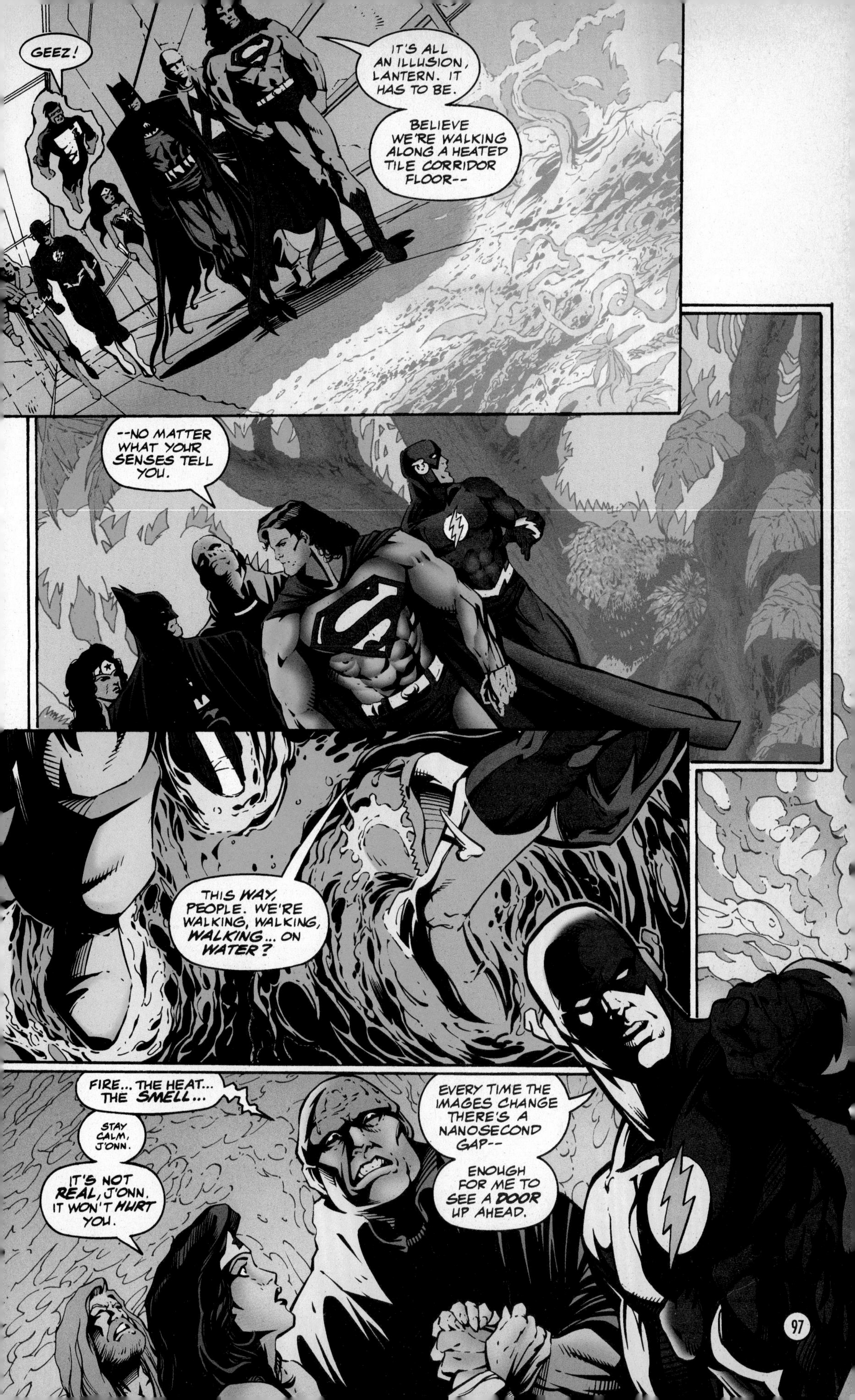
GEEZ!
IT'S ALL AN ILLUSION, LANTERN. IT HAS TO BE.
BELIEVE WE'RE WALKING ALONG A HEATED TILE CORRIDOR FLOOR--
--NO MATTER WHAT YOUR SENSES TELL YOU.
THIS WAY, PEOPLE. WE'RE WALKING, WALKING, WALKING... ON WATER?
FIRE... THE HEAT... THE SMELL...
STAY CALM, J'ONN.
IT'S NOT REAL, J'ONN. IT WON'T HURT YOU.
EVERY TIME THE IMAGES CHANGE THERE'S A NANOSECOND GAP--
ENOUGH FOR ME TO SEE A DOOR UP AHEAD.

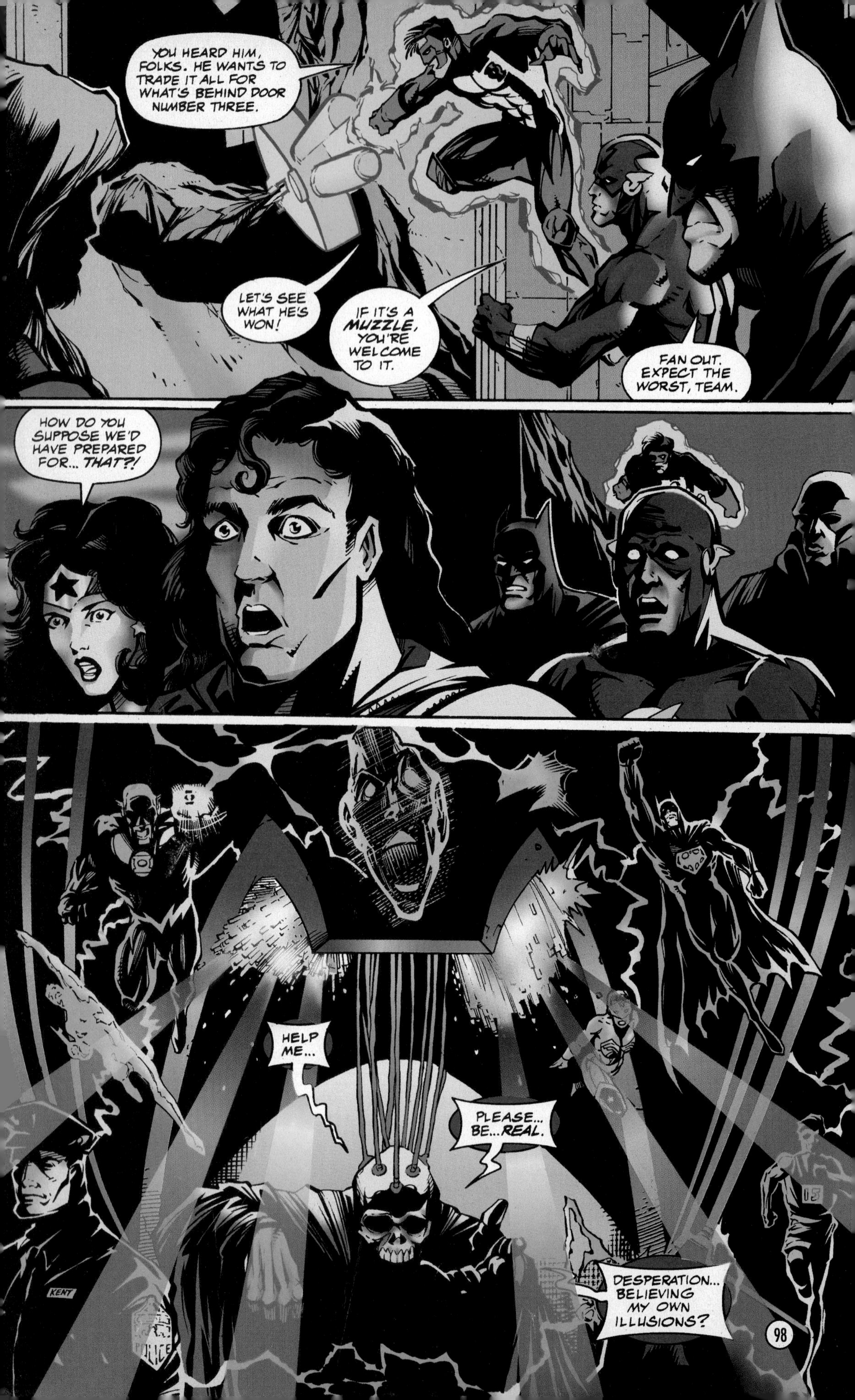
YOU HEARD HIM, FOLKS. HE WANTS TO TRADE IT ALL FOR WHAT'S BEHIND DOOR NUMBER THREE.
LET'S SEE WHAT HE'S WON!
IF IT'S A MUZZLE, YOU'RE WELCOME TO IT.
FAN OUT. EXPECT THE WORST, TEAM.
HOW DO YOU SUPPOSE WE'D HAVE PREPARED FOR... THAT?!
HELP ME...
PLEASE... BE...REAL.
DESPERATION... BELIEVING MY OWN ILLUSIONS?
KENT

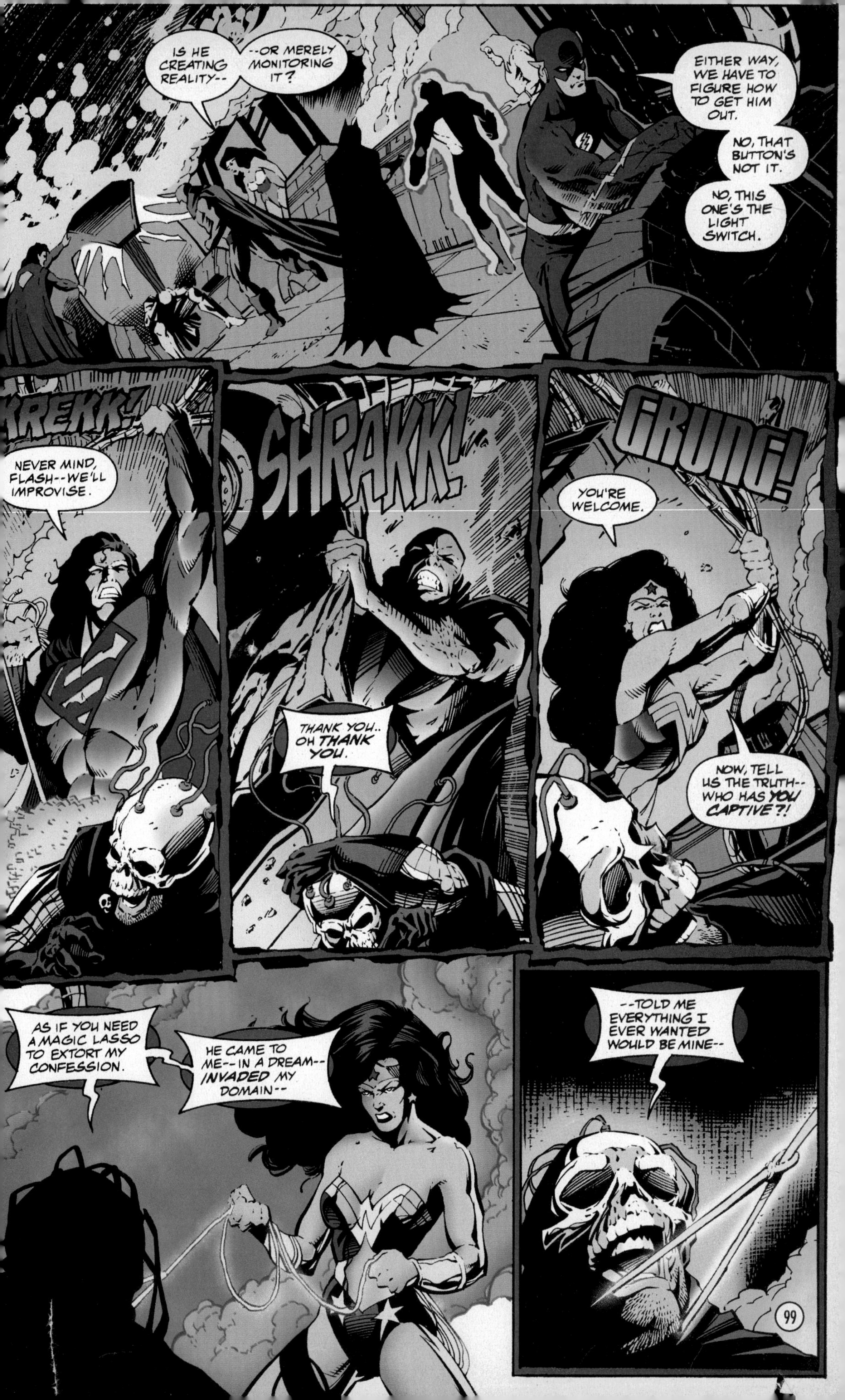
IS HE CREATING REALITY--
--OR MERELY MONITORING IT?
EITHER WAY, WE HAVE TO FIGURE HOW TO GET HIM OUT.
NO, THAT BUTTON'S NOT IT.
NO, THIS ONE'S THE LIGHT SWITCH.
KREKK!
NEVER MIND, FLASH--WE'LL IMPROVISE.
SHRAKK!
THANK YOU.. OH THANK YOU.
GRUNG!
YOU'RE WELCOME.
NOW, TELL US THE TRUTH-- WHO HAS YOU CAPTIVE?!
AS IF YOU NEED A MAGIC LASSO TO EXTORT MY CONFESSION.
HE CAME TO ME--IN A DREAM--INVADED MY DOMAIN--
--TOLD ME EVERYTHING I EVER WANTED WOULD BE MINE--

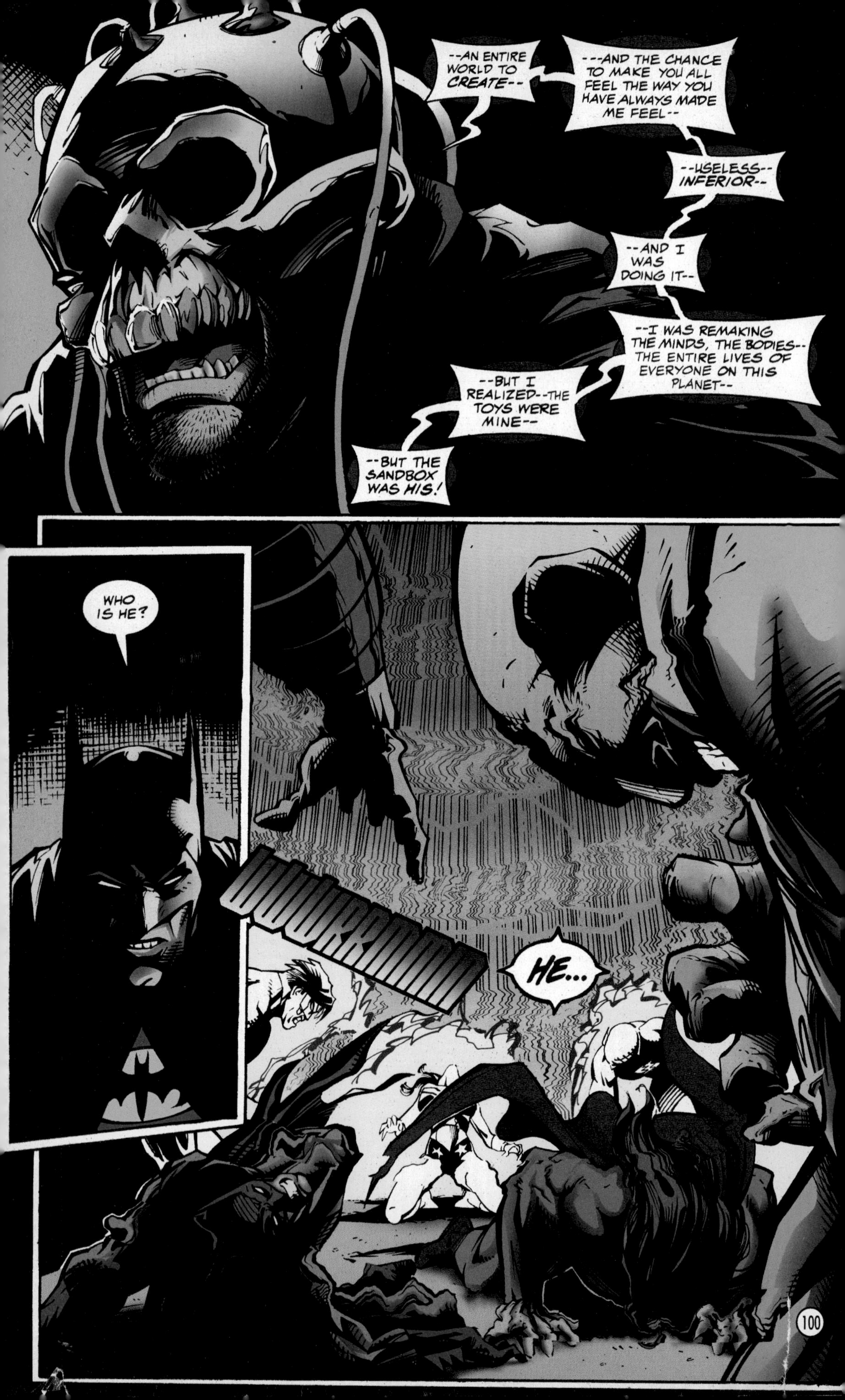
--AN ENTIRE WORLD TO CREATE--
---AND THE CHANCE TO MAKE YOU ALL FEEL THE WAY YOU HAVE ALWAYS MADE ME FEEL--
--USELESS--INFERIOR--
--AND I WAS DOING IT--
--I WAS REMAKING THE MINDS, THE BODIES--THE ENTIRE LIVES OF EVERYONE ON THIS PLANET--
--BUT I REALIZED--THE TOYS WERE MINE--
--BUT THE SANDBOX WAS HIS!
WHO IS HE?
HE...

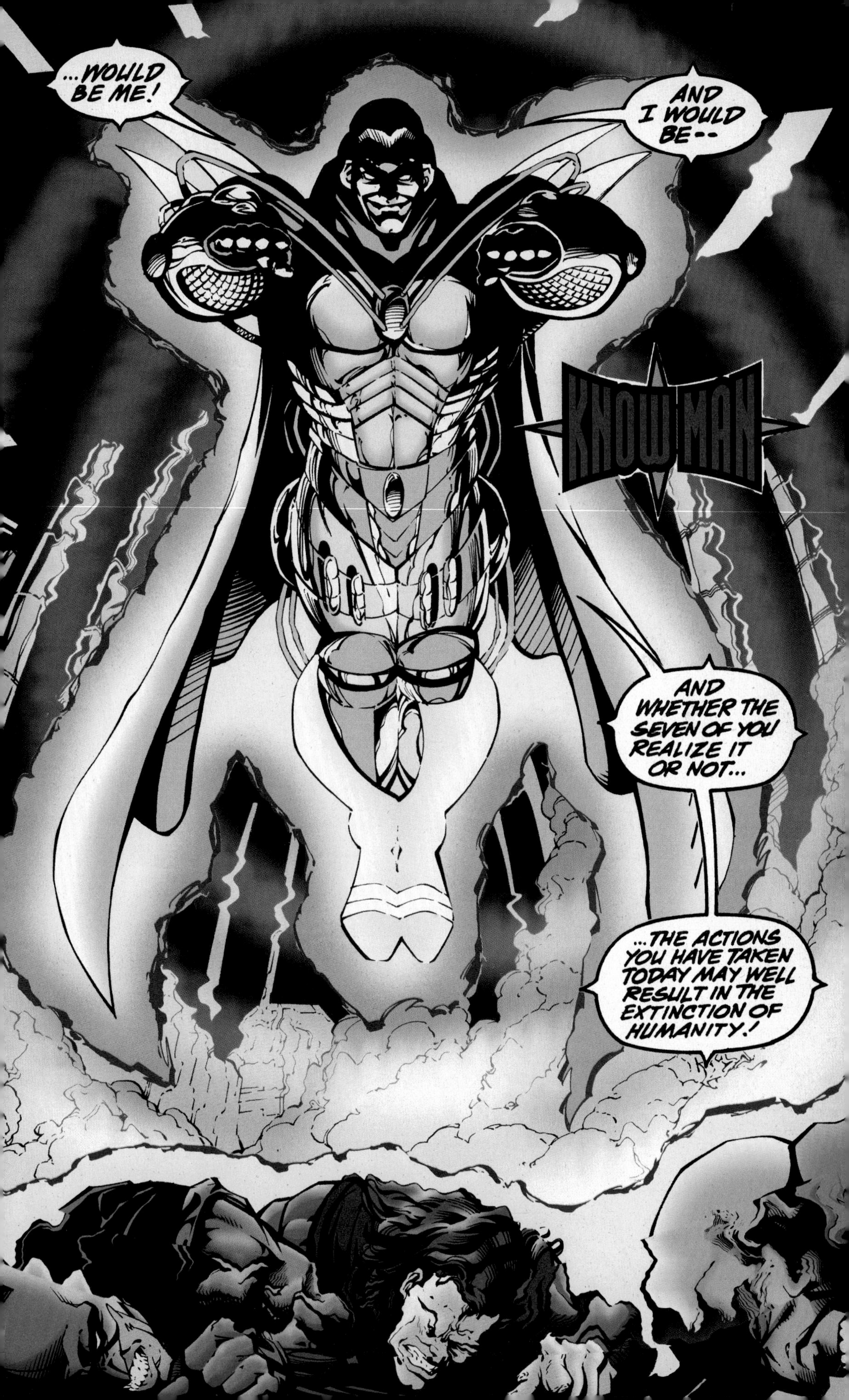
...WOULD BE ME!
AND I WOULD BE--
KNOWMAN
AND WHETHER THE SEVEN OF YOU REALIZE IT OR NOT...
...THE ACTIONS YOU HAVE TAKEN TODAY MAY WELL RESULT IN THE EXTINCTION OF HUMANITY!

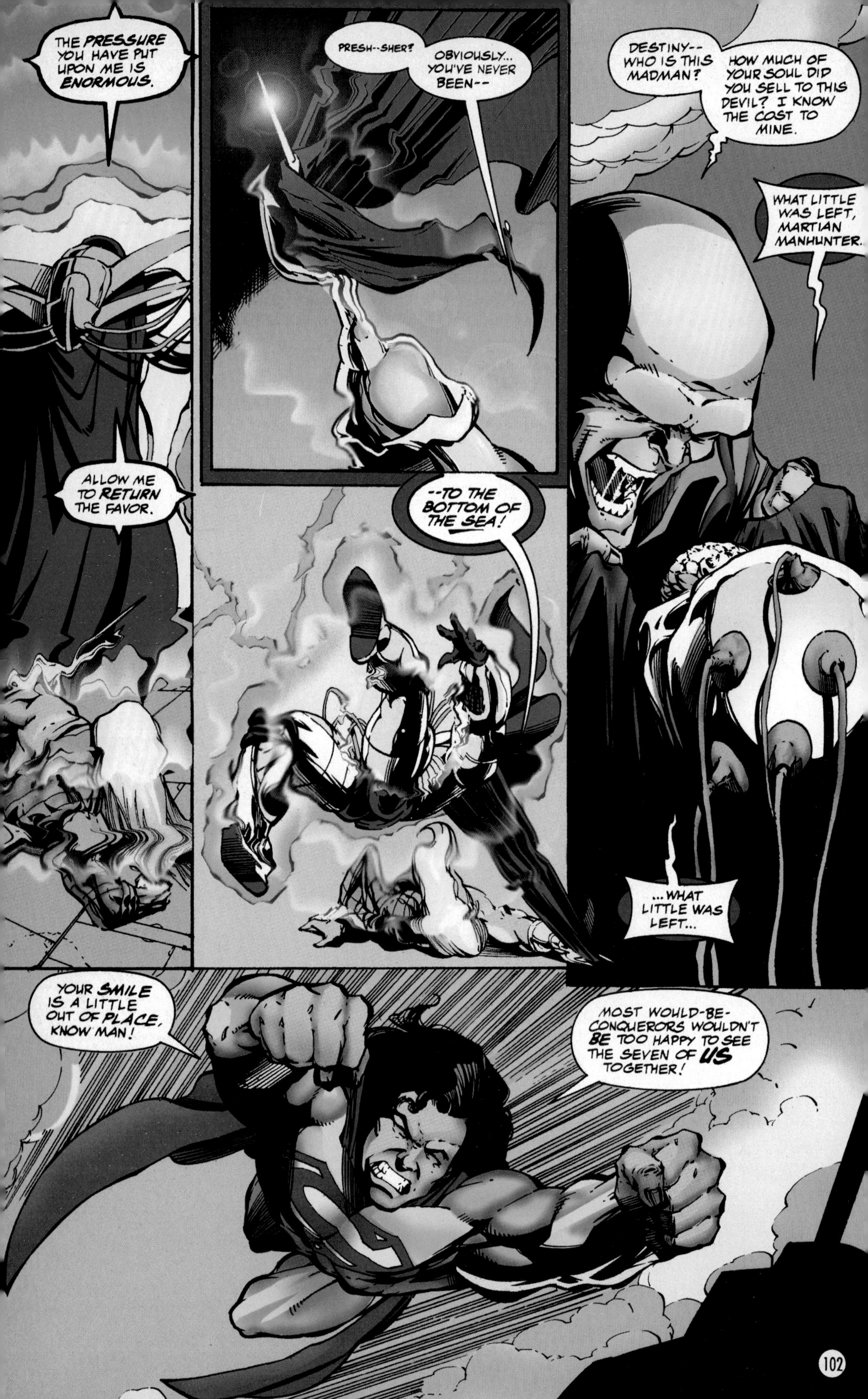

THE PRESSURE YOU HAVE PUT UPON ME IS ENORMOUS.
PRESH--SHER?
OBVIOUSLY... YOU'VE NEVER BEEN--
DESTINY-- WHO IS THIS MADMAN?
HOW MUCH OF YOUR SOUL DID YOU SELL TO THIS DEVIL? I KNOW THE COST TO MINE.
WHAT LITTLE WAS LEFT, MARTIAN MANHUNTER.
ALLOW ME TO RETURN THE FAVOR.
--TO THE BOTTOM OF THE SEA!
...WHAT LITTLE WAS LEFT...
YOUR SMILE IS A LITTLE OUT OF PLACE, KNOW MAN!
MOST WOULD-BE-CONQUERORS WOULDN'T BE TOO HAPPY TO SEE THE SEVEN OF US TOGETHER!

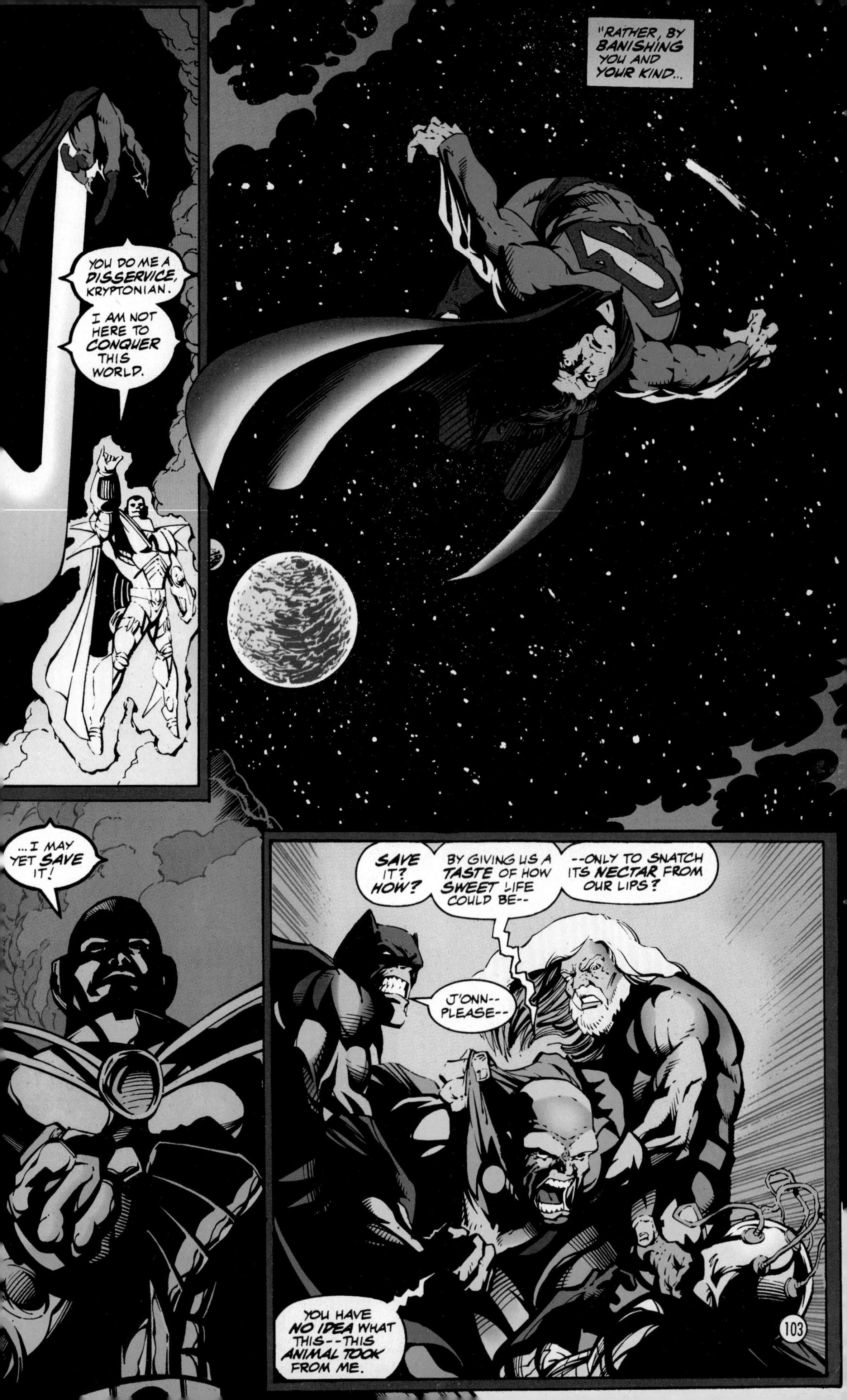
"RATHER, BY BANISHING YOU AND YOUR KIND...
YOU DO ME A DISSERVICE, KRYPTONIAN.
I AM NOT HERE TO CONQUER THIS WORLD.
...I MAY YET SAVE IT!
SAVE IT? HOW?
BY GIVING US A TASTE OF HOW SWEET LIFE COULD BE--
--ONLY TO SNATCH ITS NECTAR FROM OUR LIPS?
J'ONN-- PLEASE--
YOU HAVE NO IDEA WHAT THIS--THIS ANIMAL TOOK FROM ME.

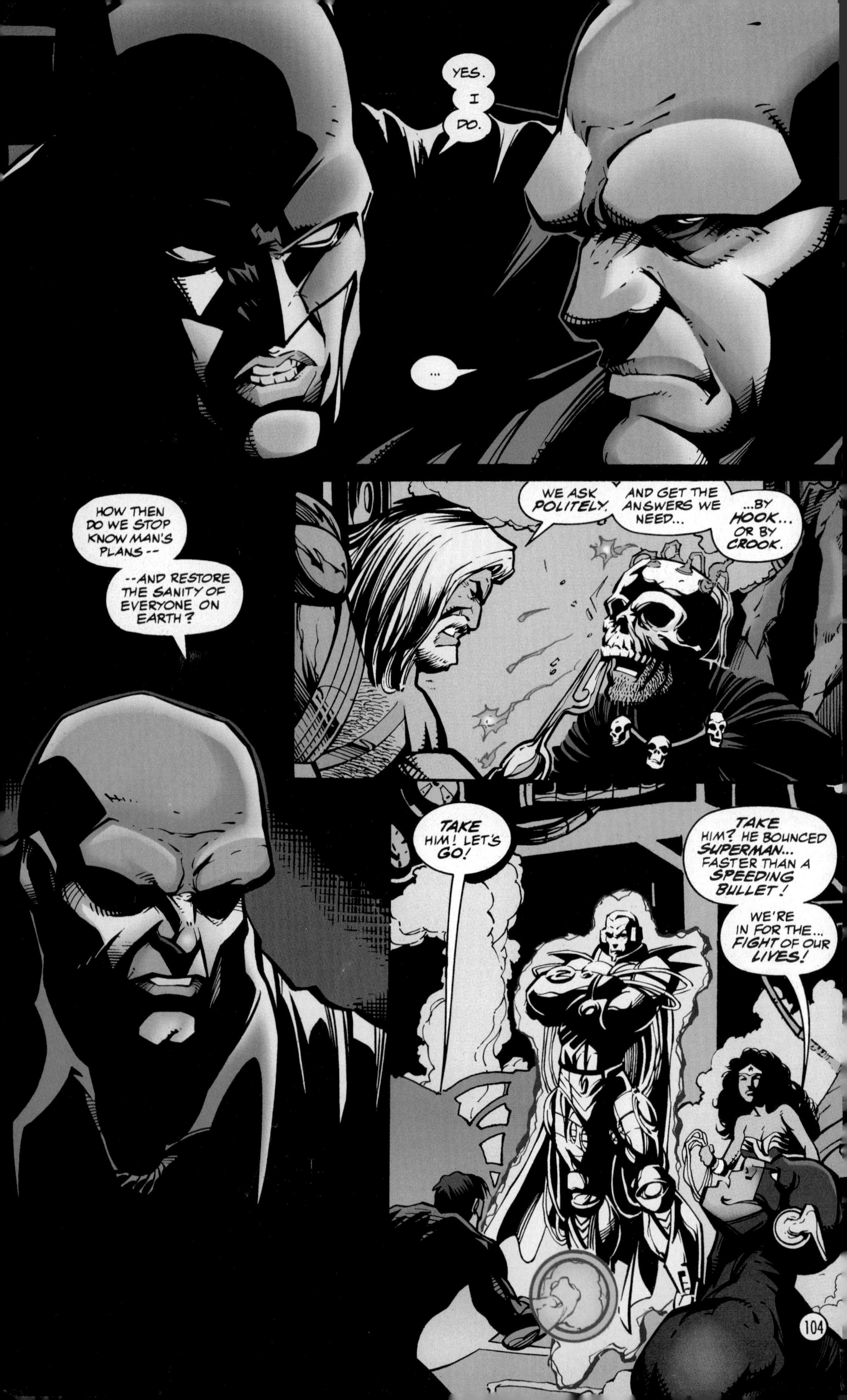
YES. I DO.
...
HOW THEN DO WE STOP KNOW MAN'S PLANS --
-- AND RESTORE THE SANITY OF EVERYONE ON EARTH?
WE ASK POLITELY.
AND GET THE ANSWERS WE NEED...
...BY HOOK... OR BY CROOK.
TAKE HIM! LET'S GO!
TAKE HIM? HE BOUNCED SUPERMAN... FASTER THAN A SPEEDING BULLET!
WE'RE IN FOR THE... FIGHT OF OUR LIVES!

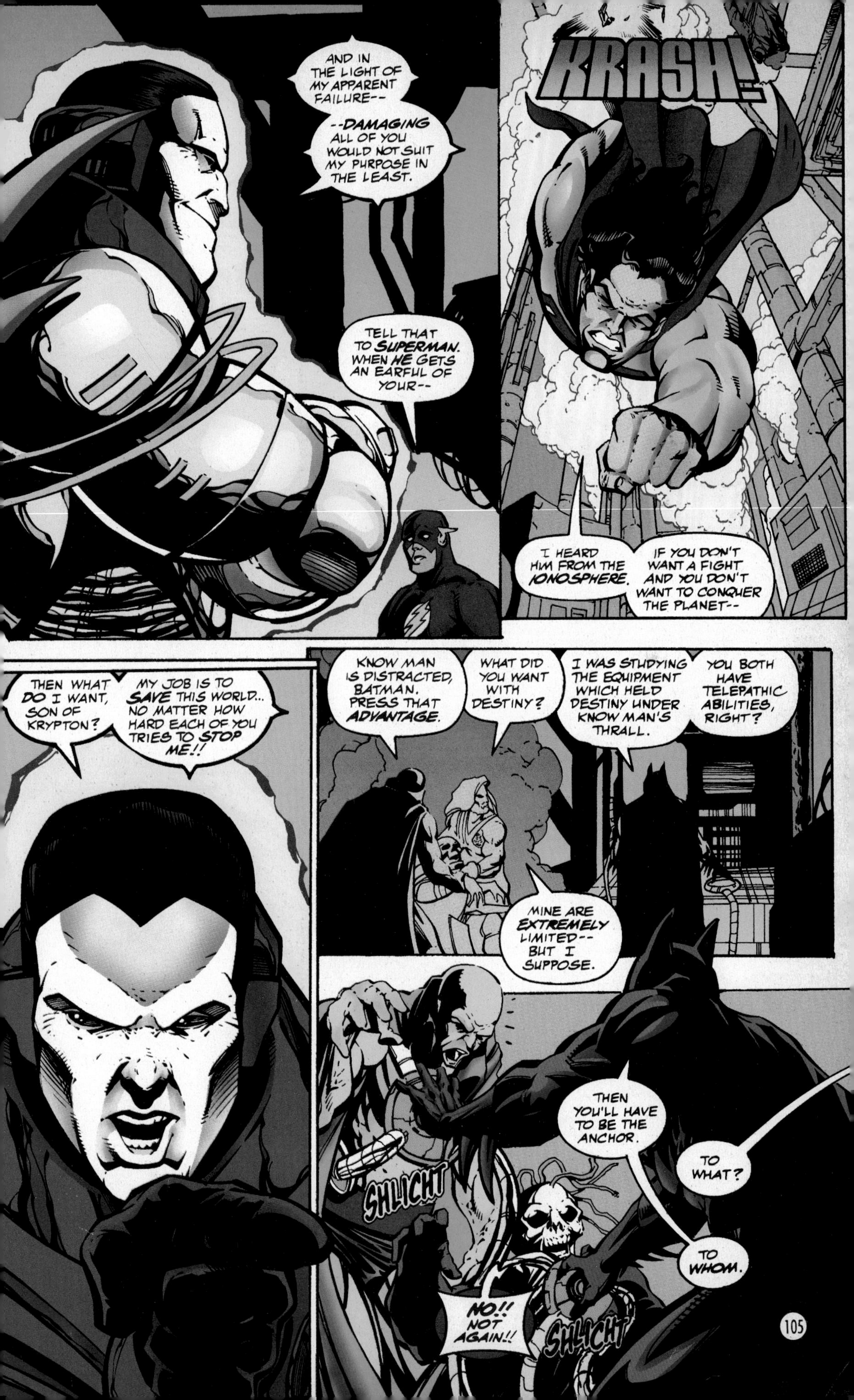
AND IN THE LIGHT OF MY APPARENT FAILURE--
--DAMAGING ALL OF YOU WOULD NOT SUIT MY PURPOSE IN THE LEAST.
TELL THAT TO SUPERMAN. WHEN HE GETS AN EARFUL OF YOUR--
KRASH!
I HEARD HIM FROM THE IONOSPHERE.
IF YOU DON'T WANT A FIGHT AND YOU DON'T WANT TO CONQUER THE PLANET--
THEN WHAT DO I WANT, SON OF KRYPTON?
MY JOB IS TO SAVE THIS WORLD... NO MATTER HOW HARD EACH OF YOU TRIES TO STOP ME!!
KNOW MAN IS DISTRACTED, BATMAN. PRESS THAT ADVANTAGE.
WHAT DID YOU WANT WITH DESTINY?
I WAS STUDYING THE EQUIPMENT WHICH HELD DESTINY UNDER KNOW MAN'S THRALL.
YOU BOTH HAVE TELEPATHIC ABILITIES, RIGHT?
MINE ARE EXTREMELY LIMITED-- BUT I SUPPOSE.
THEN YOU'LL HAVE TO BE THE ANCHOR.
TO WHAT?
SHLICHT
TO WHOM.
NO!! NOT AGAIN!!
SHLICHT

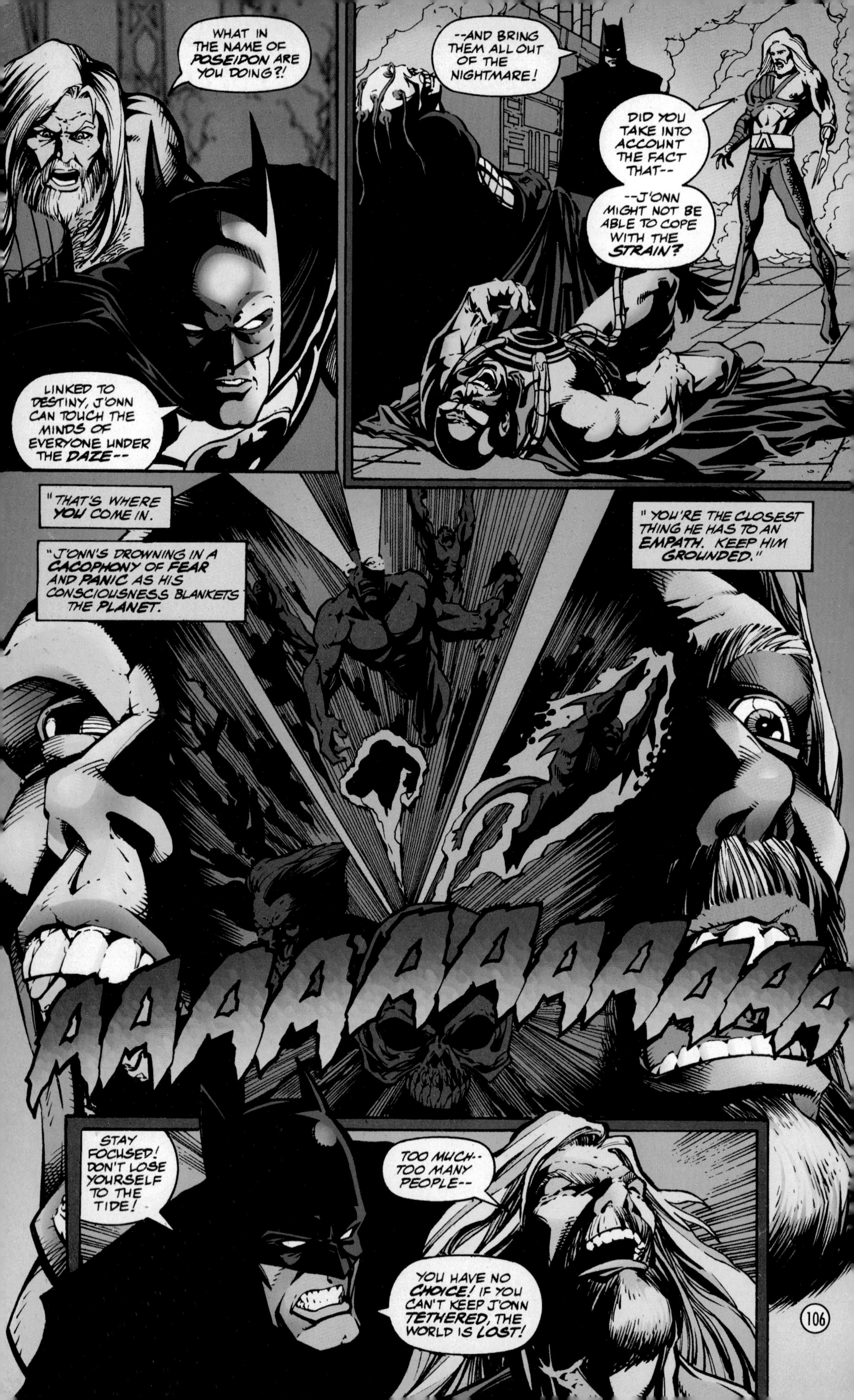

WHAT IN THE NAME OF POSEIDON ARE YOU DOING?!
LINKED TO DESTINY, J'ONN CAN TOUCH THE MINDS OF EVERYONE UNDER THE DAZE--
--AND BRING THEM ALL OUT OF THE NIGHTMARE!
DID YOU TAKE INTO ACCOUNT THE FACT THAT--
--J'ONN MIGHT NOT BE ABLE TO COPE WITH THE STRAIN?
"THAT'S WHERE YOU COME IN.
"J'ONN'S DROWNING IN A CACOPHONY OF FEAR AND PANIC AS HIS CONSCIOUSNESS BLANKETS THE PLANET.
"YOU'RE THE CLOSEST THING HE HAS TO AN EMPATH. KEEP HIM GROUNDED."
AAAAAAAAAAA
STAY FOCUSED! DON'T LOSE YOURSELF TO THE TIDE!
TOO MUCH-- TOO MANY PEOPLE--
YOU HAVE NO CHOICE! IF YOU CAN'T KEEP J'ONN TETHERED, THE WORLD IS LOST!

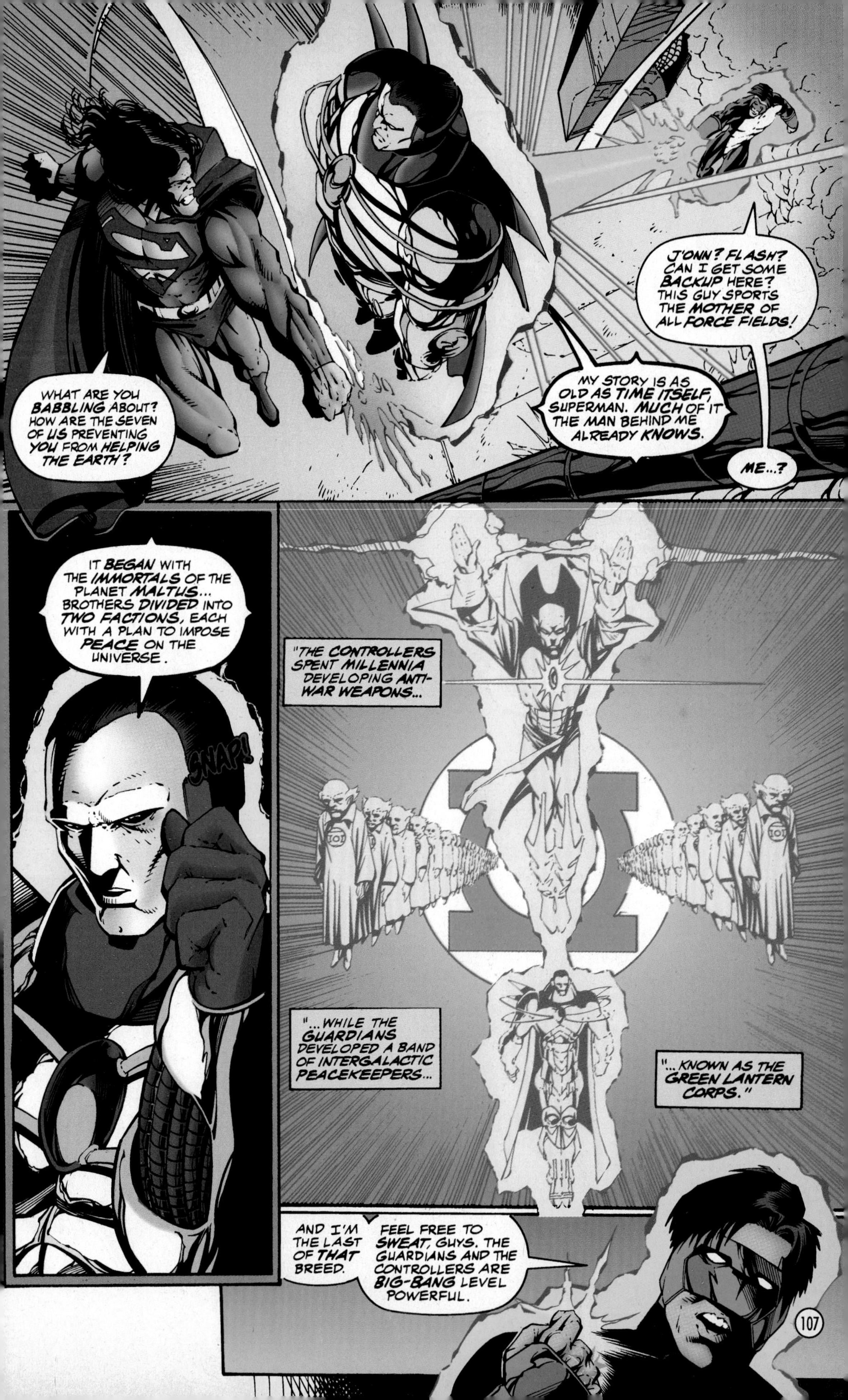
J'ONN? FLASH? CAN I GET SOME BACKUP HERE? THIS GUY SPORTS THE MOTHER OF ALL FORCE FIELDS!
WHAT ARE YOU BABBLING ABOUT? HOW ARE THE SEVEN OF US PREVENTING YOU FROM HELPING THE EARTH?
MY STORY IS AS OLD AS TIME ITSELF, SUPERMAN. MUCH OF IT THE MAN BEHIND ME ALREADY KNOWS.
ME...?
IT BEGAN WITH THE IMMORTALS OF THE PLANET MALTUS... BROTHERS DIVIDED INTO TWO FACTIONS, EACH WITH A PLAN TO IMPOSE PEACE ON THE UNIVERSE.
SNAP!
"THE CONTROLLERS SPENT MILLENNIA DEVELOPING ANTI-WAR WEAPONS...
"...WHILE THE GUARDIANS DEVELOPED A BAND OF INTERGALACTIC PEACEKEEPERS...
"...KNOWN AS THE GREEN LANTERN CORPS."
AND I'M THE LAST OF THAT BREED.
FEEL FREE TO SWEAT, GUYS. THE GUARDIANS AND THE CONTROLLERS ARE BIG-BANG LEVEL POWERFUL.

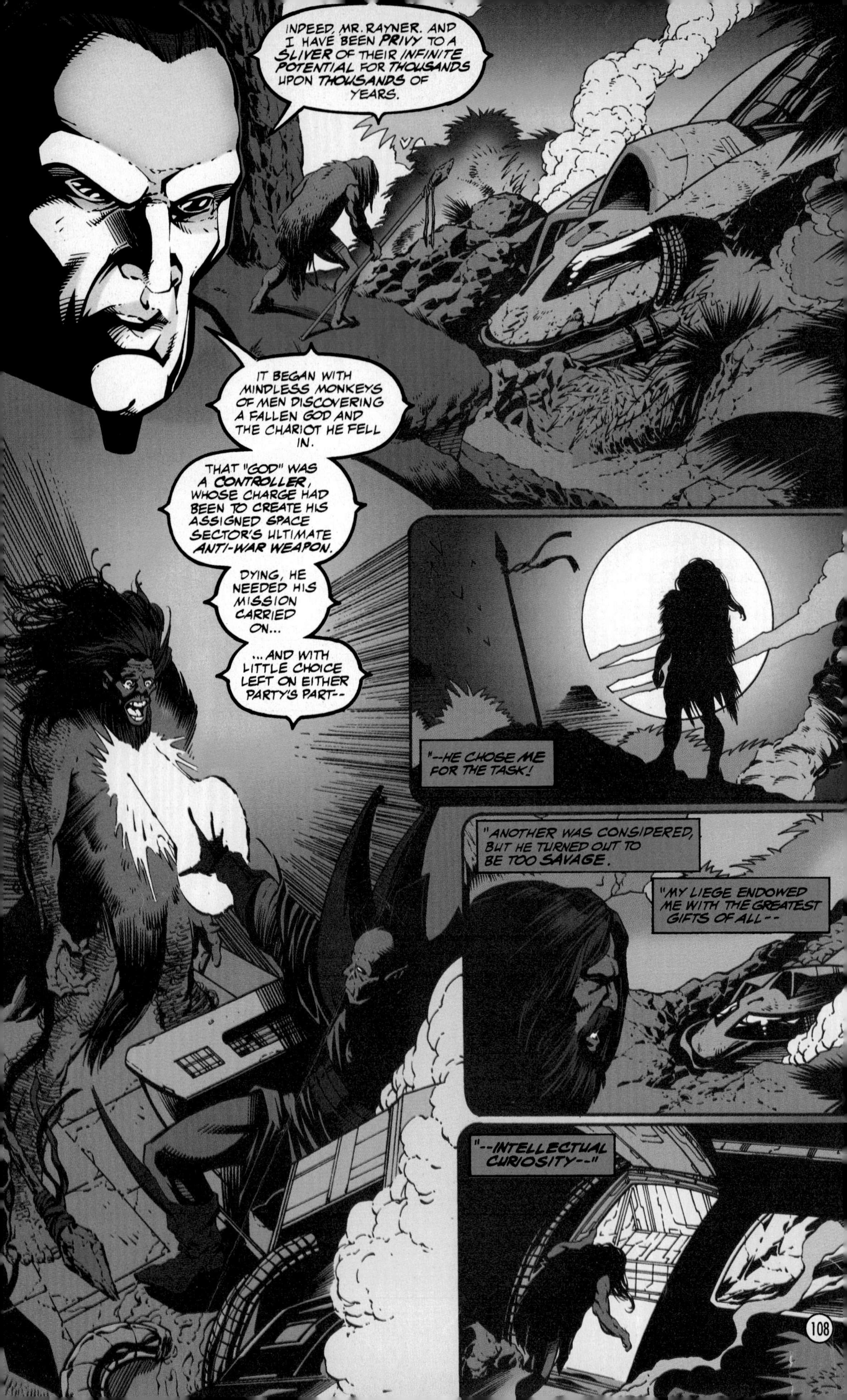
INDEED, MR. RAYNER. AND I HAVE BEEN PRIVY TO A SLIVER OF THEIR INFINITE POTENTIAL FOR THOUSANDS UPON THOUSANDS OF YEARS.
IT BEGAN WITH MINDLESS MONKEYS OF MEN DISCOVERING A FALLEN GOD AND THE CHARIOT HE FELL IN.
THAT "GOD" WAS A CONTROLLER, WHOSE CHARGE HAD BEEN TO CREATE HIS ASSIGNED SPACE SECTOR'S ULTIMATE ANTI-WAR WEAPON.
DYING, HE NEEDED HIS MISSION CARRIED ON...
...AND WITH LITTLE CHOICE LEFT ON EITHER PARTY'S PART--
"--HE CHOSE ME FOR THE TASK!
"ANOTHER WAS CONSIDERED, BUT HE TURNED OUT TO BE TOO SAVAGE.
"MY LIEGE ENDOWED ME WITH THE GREATEST GIFTS OF ALL--
"--INTELLECTUAL CURIOSITY--"

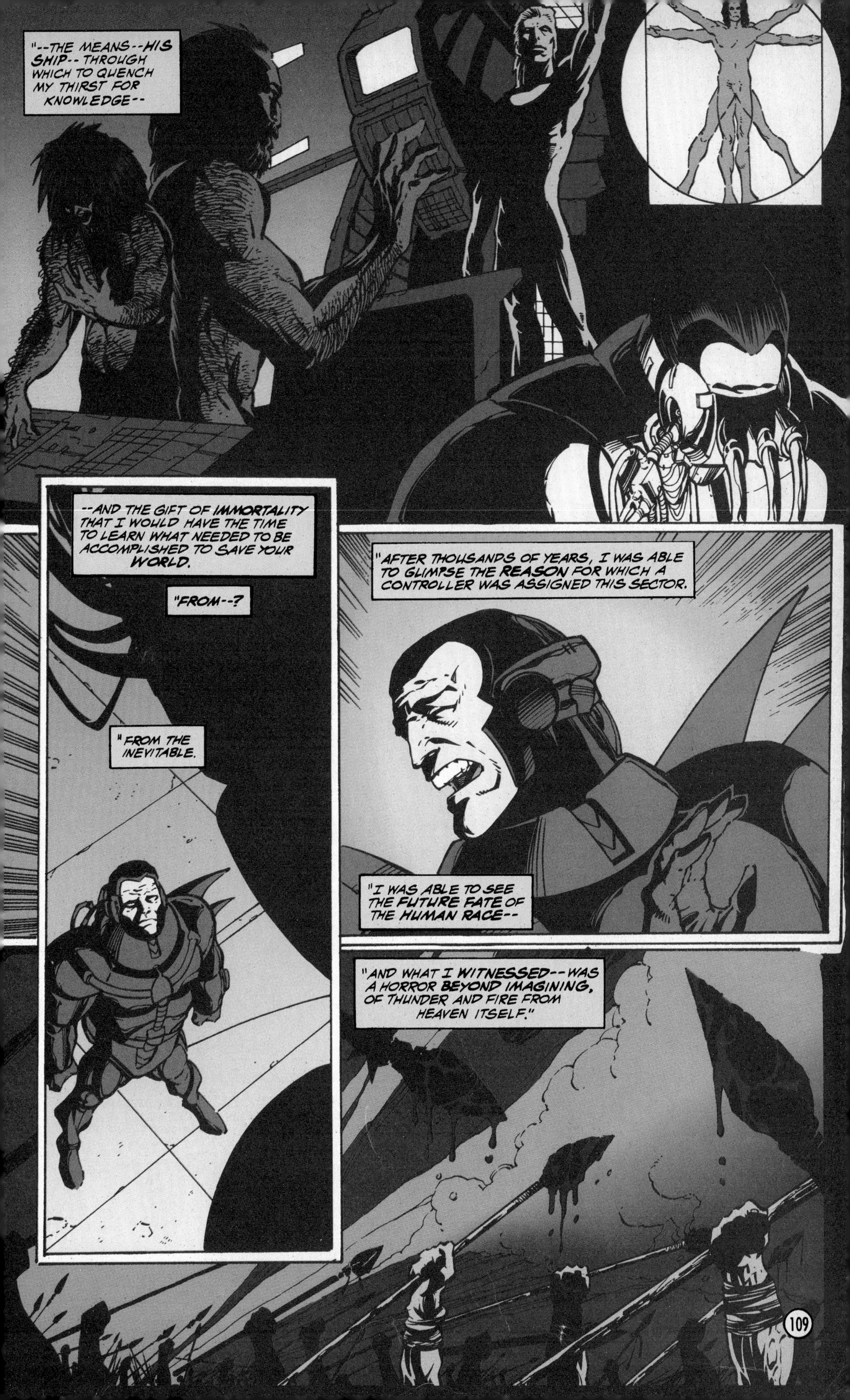
"--THE MEANS--HIS SHIP--THROUGH WHICH TO QUENCH MY THIRST FOR KNOWLEDGE--
--AND THE GIFT OF IMMORTALITY THAT I WOULD HAVE THE TIME TO LEARN WHAT NEEDED TO BE ACCOMPLISHED TO SAVE YOUR WORLD.
"FROM--?
"FROM THE INEVITABLE.
"AFTER THOUSANDS OF YEARS, I WAS ABLE TO GLIMPSE THE REASON FOR WHICH A CONTROLLER WAS ASSIGNED THIS SECTOR.
"I WAS ABLE TO SEE THE FUTURE FATE OF THE HUMAN RACE--
"AND WHAT I WITNESSED--WAS A HORROR BEYOND IMAGINING, OF THUNDER AND FIRE FROM HEAVEN ITSELF."

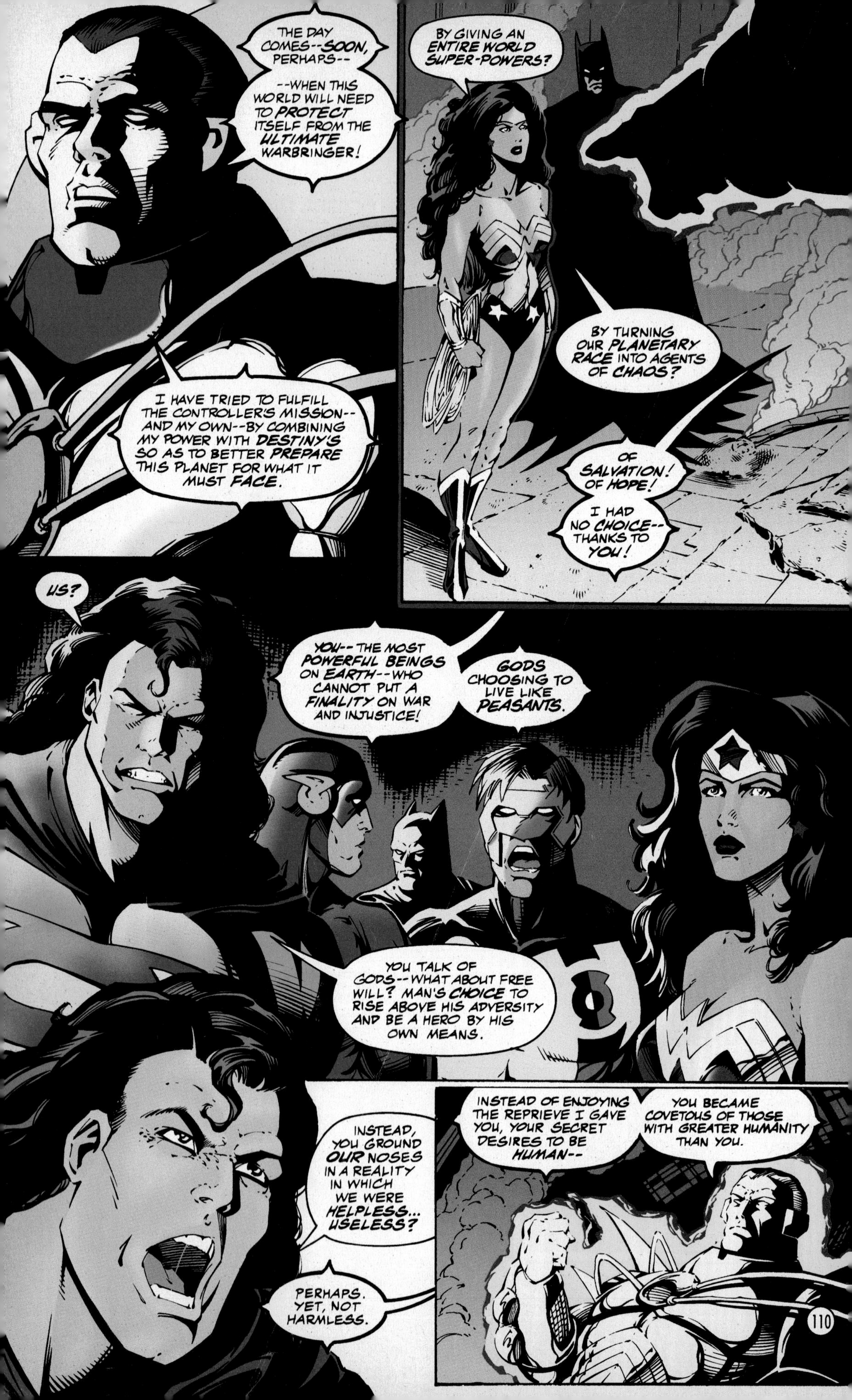
THE DAY COMES--SOON, PERHAPS--
--WHEN THIS WORLD WILL NEED TO PROTECT ITSELF FROM THE ULTIMATE WARBRINGER!
I HAVE TRIED TO FULFILL THE CONTROLLER'S MISSION--AND MY OWN--BY COMBINING MY POWER WITH DESTINY'S SO AS TO BETTER PREPARE THIS PLANET FOR WHAT IT MUST FACE.
BY GIVING AN ENTIRE WORLD SUPER-POWERS?
BY TURNING OUR PLANETARY RACE INTO AGENTS OF CHAOS?
OF SALVATION! OF HOPE!
I HAD NO CHOICE--THANKS TO YOU!
US?
YOU--THE MOST POWERFUL BEINGS ON EARTH--WHO CANNOT PUT A FINALITY ON WAR AND INJUSTICE!
GODS CHOOSING TO LIVE LIKE PEASANTS.
YOU TALK OF GODS--WHAT ABOUT FREE WILL? MAN'S CHOICE TO RISE ABOVE HIS ADVERSITY AND BE A HERO BY HIS OWN MEANS.
INSTEAD, YOU GROUND OUR NOSES IN A REALITY IN WHICH WE WERE HELPLESS... USELESS?
PERHAPS. YET, NOT HARMLESS.
INSTEAD OF ENJOYING THE REPRIEVE I GAVE YOU, YOUR SECRET DESIRES TO BE HUMAN--
YOU BECAME COVETOUS OF THOSE WITH GREATER HUMANITY THAN YOU.
110

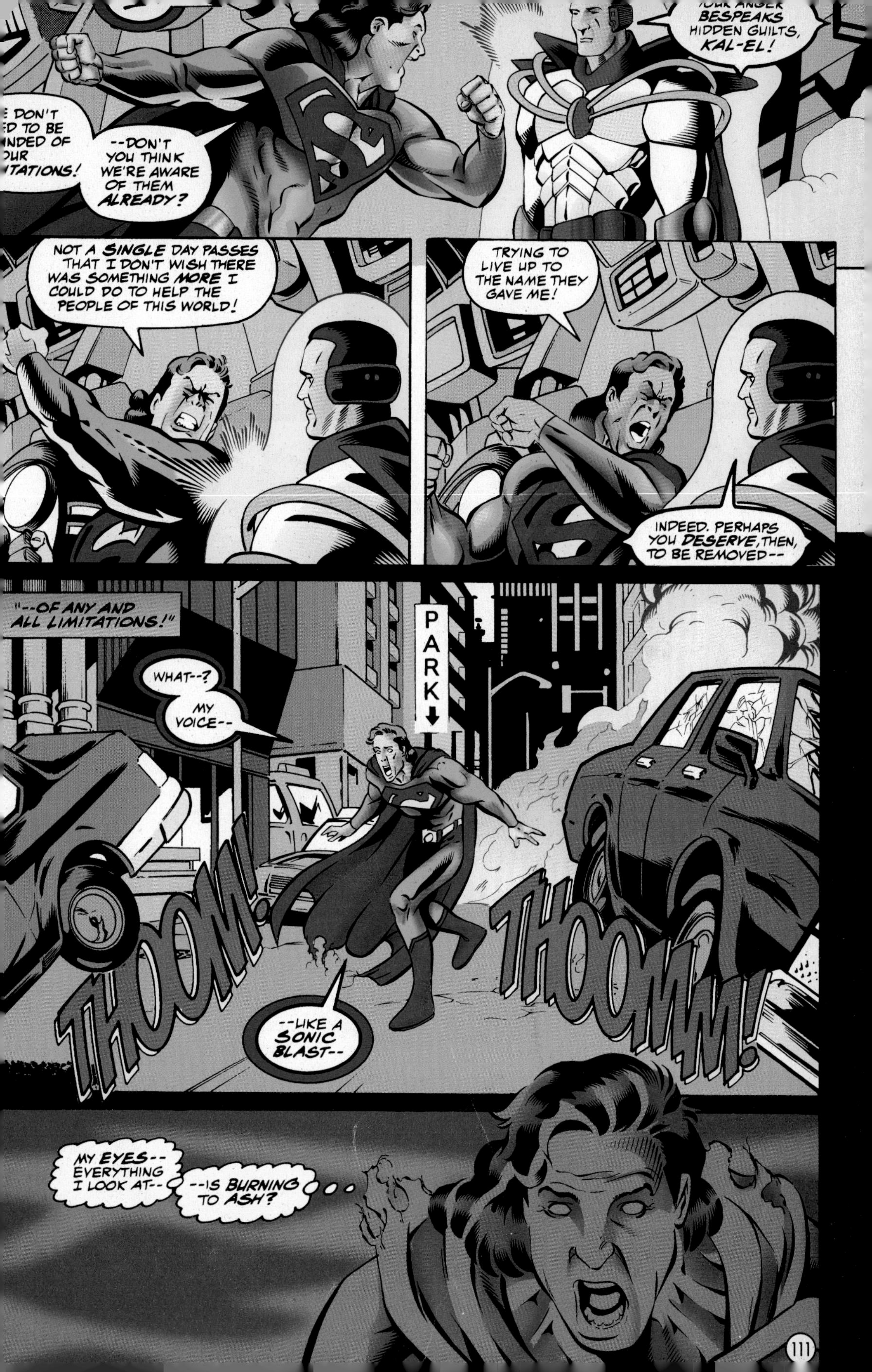

BESPEAKS HIDDEN GUILTS, KAL-EL!
DON'T YOU THINK WE'RE AWARE OF THEM ALREADY?
NOT A SINGLE DAY PASSES THAT I DON'T WISH THERE WAS SOMETHING MORE I COULD DO TO HELP THE PEOPLE OF THIS WORLD!
TRYING TO LIVE UP TO THE NAME THEY GAVE ME!
INDEED. PERHAPS YOU DESERVE, THEN, TO BE REMOVED--
"--OF ANY AND ALL LIMITATIONS!"
PARK
WHAT--? MY VOICE--
THOOM!
THOOMM!
--LIKE A SONIC BLAST--
MY EYES-- EVERYTHING I LOOK AT--
--IS BURNING TO ASH?

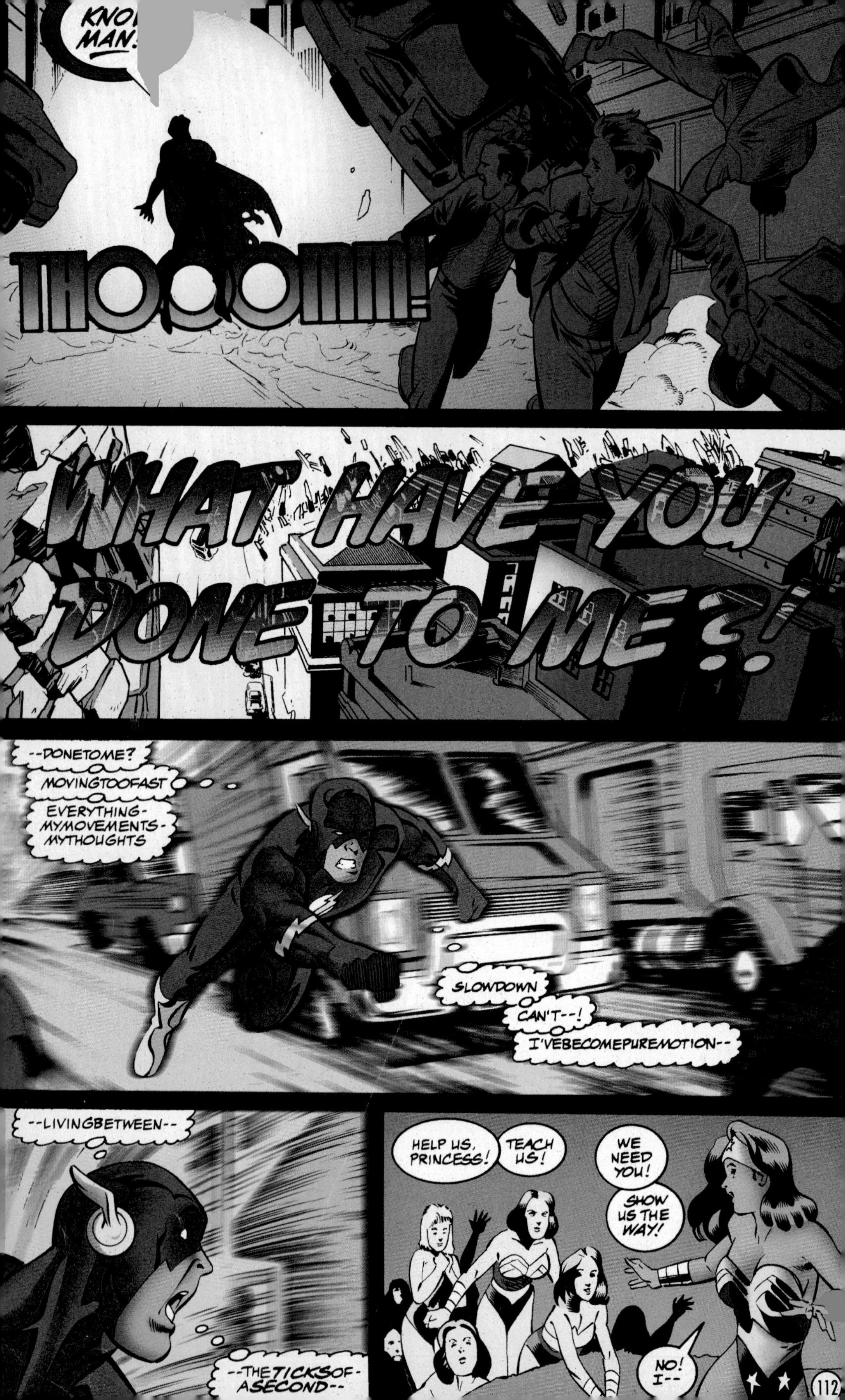
KNO MAN!
THOOOMMM!
WHAT HAVE YOU DONE TO ME?!
--DONETOME?
MOVINGTOOFAST
EVERYTHING-
MYMOVEMENTS-
MYTHOUGHTS
SLOWDOWN
CAN'T--!
I'VEBECOMEPUREMOTION--
--LIVINGBETWEEN--
--THETICKSOF-
ASECOND--
HELP US, PRINCESS!
TEACH US!
WE NEED YOU!
SHOW US THE WAY!
NO! I--

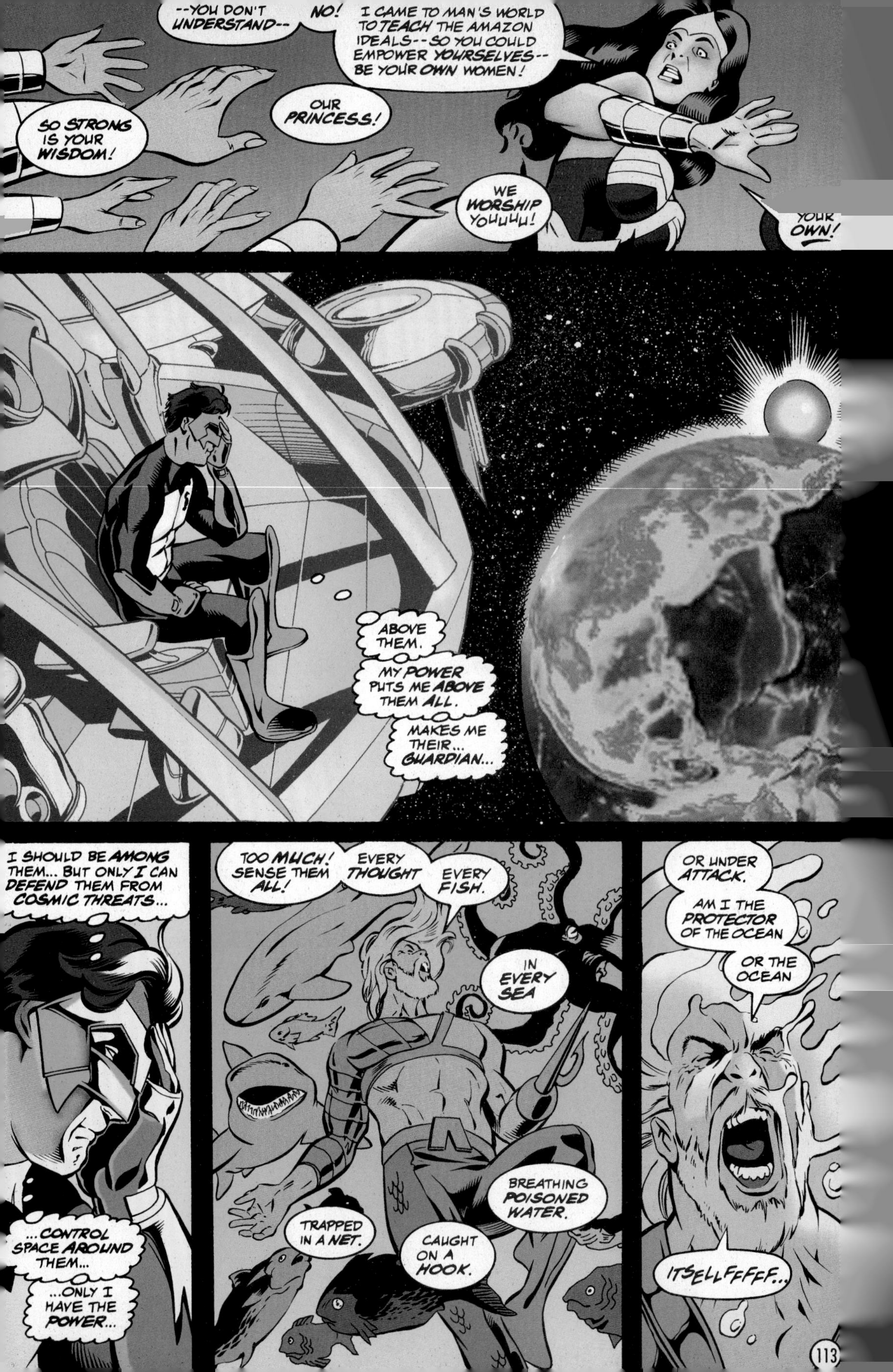
--YOU DON'T UNDERSTAND--
NO!
I CAME TO MAN'S WORLD TO TEACH THE AMAZON IDEALS--SO YOU COULD EMPOWER YOURSELVES--BE YOUR OWN WOMEN!
SO STRONG IS YOUR WISDOM!
OUR PRINCESS!
WE WORSHIP YOUUUUU!
YOUR OWN!
ABOVE THEM.
MY POWER PUTS ME ABOVE THEM ALL.
MAKES ME THEIR... GUARDIAN...
I SHOULD BE AMONG THEM... BUT ONLY I CAN DEFEND THEM FROM COSMIC THREATS...
...CONTROL SPACE AROUND THEM...
...ONLY I HAVE THE POWER...
TOO MUCH! SENSE THEM ALL!
EVERY THOUGHT
EVERY FISH.
IN EVERY SEA
BREATHING POISONED WATER.
TRAPPED IN A NET.
CAUGHT ON A HOOK.
OR UNDER ATTACK.
AM I THE PROTECTOR OF THE OCEAN
OR THE OCEAN
ITSELLFFFFF...

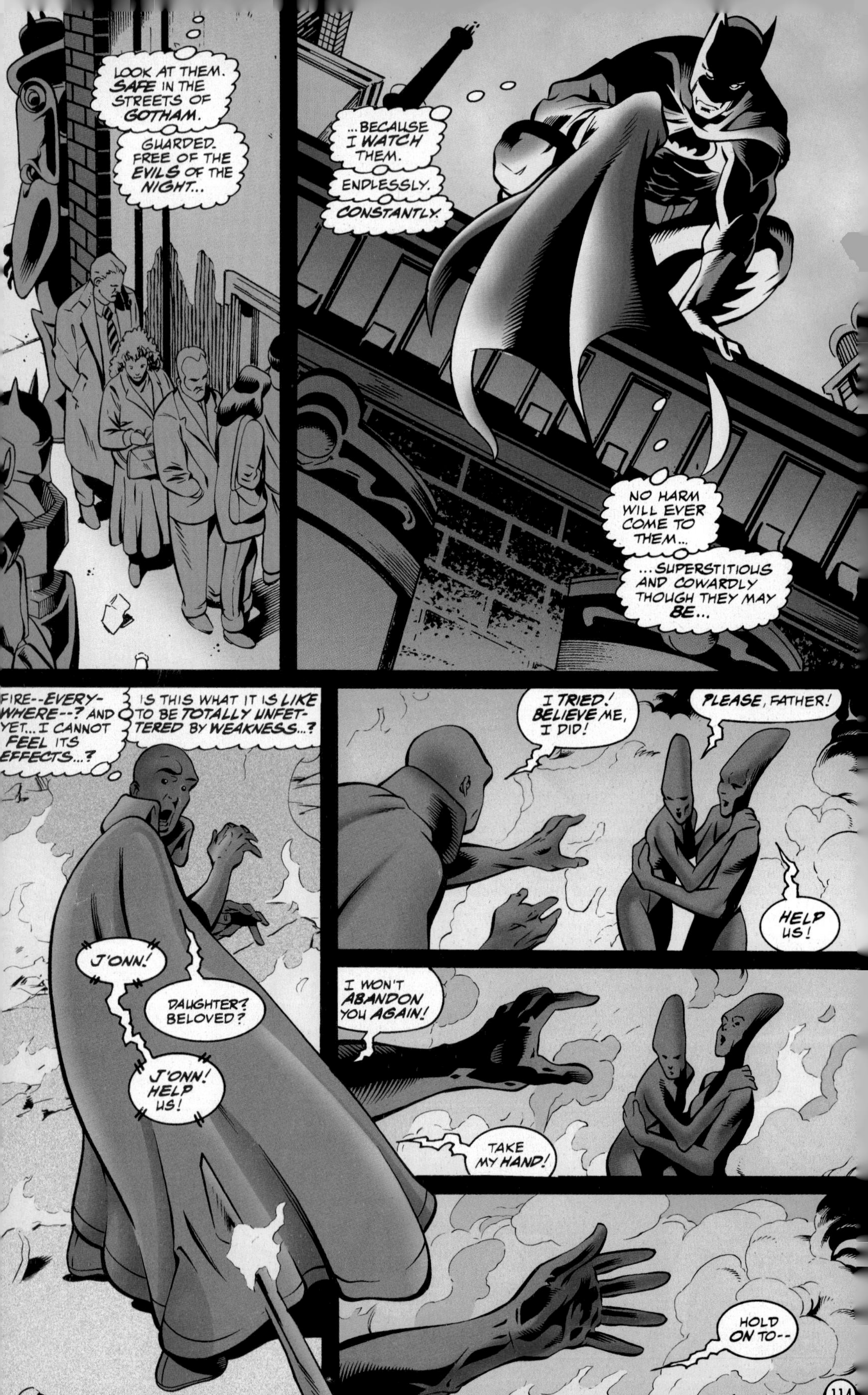
LOOK AT THEM. SAFE IN THE STREETS OF GOTHAM.
GUARDED. FREE OF THE EVILS OF THE NIGHT...
...BECAUSE I WATCH THEM.
ENDLESSLY.
CONSTANTLY.
NO HARM WILL EVER COME TO THEM...
...SUPERSTITIOUS AND COWARDLY THOUGH THEY MAY BE...
FIRE--EVERY-WHERE--? AND YET... I CANNOT FEEL ITS EFFECTS...?
IS THIS WHAT IT IS LIKE TO BE TOTALLY UNFETTERED BY WEAKNESS...?
J'ONN!
DAUGHTER? BELOVED?
J'ONN! HELP US!
I TRIED! BELIEVE ME, I DID!
PLEASE, FATHER!
HELP US!
I WON'T ABANDON YOU AGAIN!
TAKE MY HAND!
HOLD ON TO--

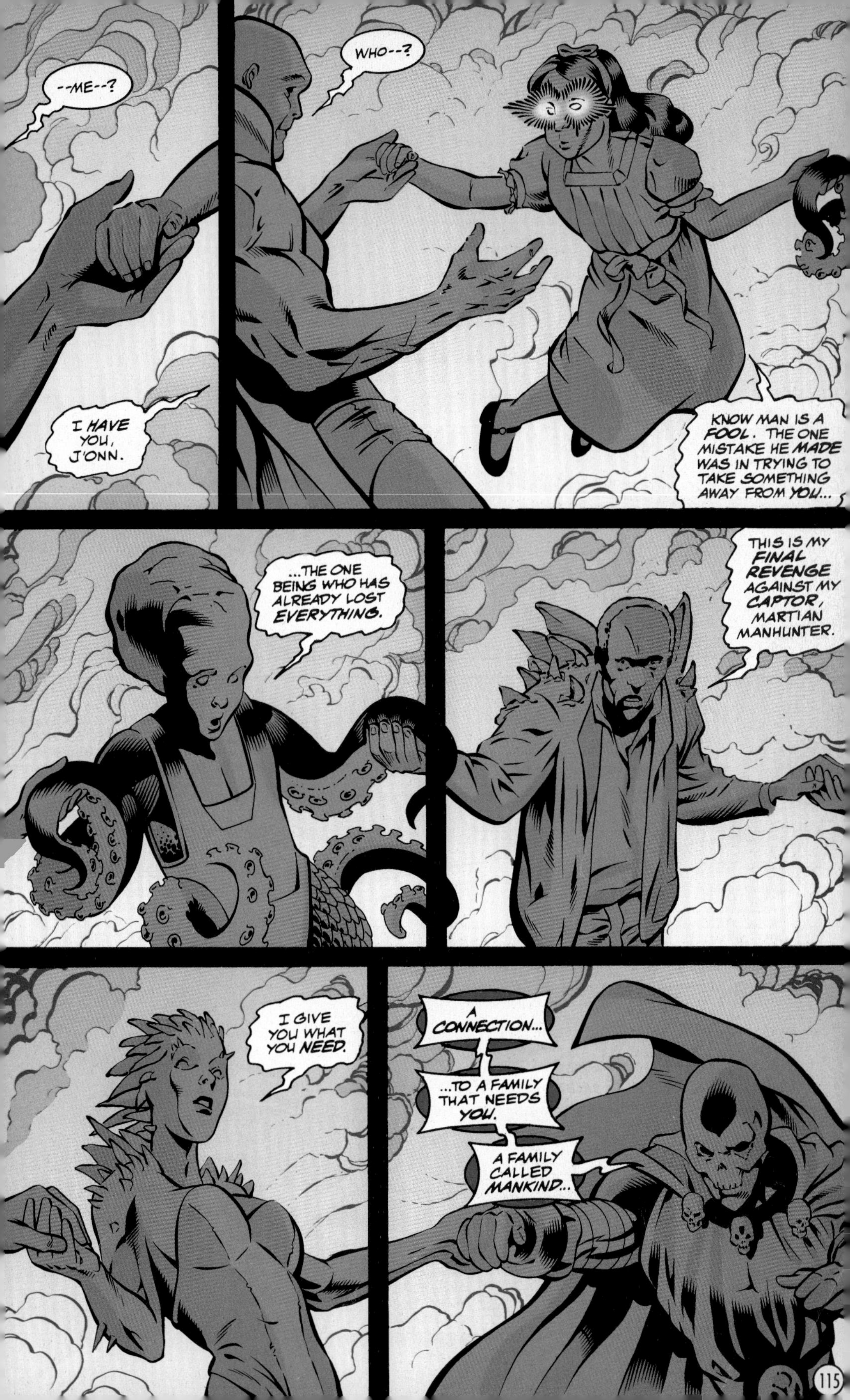
--ME--?
WHO--?
I HAVE YOU, J'ONN.
KNOW MAN IS A FOOL. THE ONE MISTAKE HE MADE WAS IN TRYING TO TAKE SOMETHING AWAY FROM YOU...
...THE ONE BEING WHO HAS ALREADY LOST EVERYTHING.
THIS IS MY FINAL REVENGE AGAINST MY CAPTOR, MARTIAN MANHUNTER.
I GIVE YOU WHAT YOU NEED.
A CONNECTION...
...TO A FAMILY THAT NEEDS YOU.
A FAMILY CALLED MANKIND...

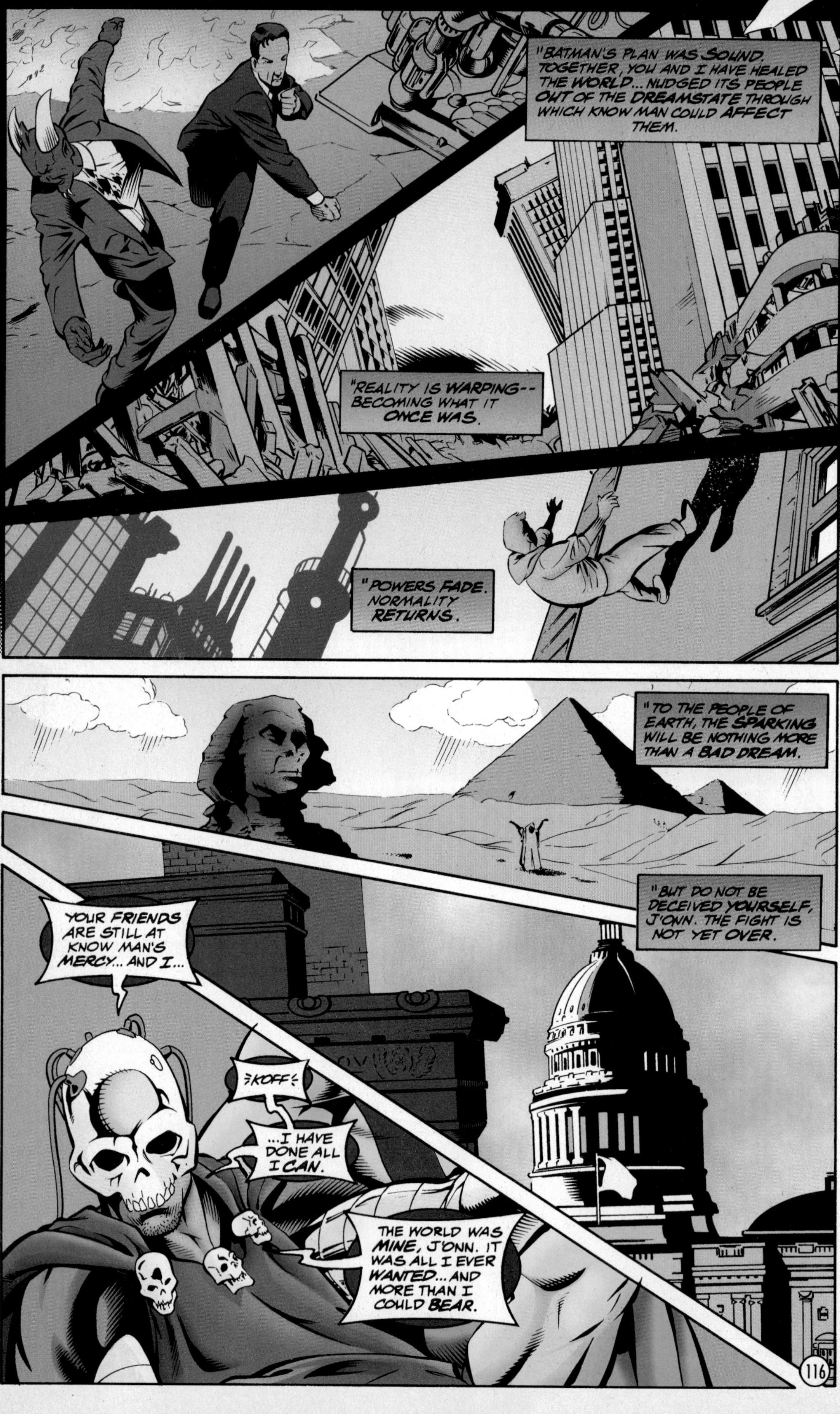

"BATMAN'S PLAN WAS SOUND. TOGETHER, YOU AND I HAVE HEALED THE WORLD... NUDGED ITS PEOPLE OUT OF THE DREAMSTATE THROUGH WHICH KNOW MAN COULD AFFECT THEM.
"REALITY IS WARPING-- BECOMING WHAT IT ONCE WAS.
"POWERS FADE. NORMALITY RETURNS.
"TO THE PEOPLE OF EARTH, THE SPARKING WILL BE NOTHING MORE THAN A BAD DREAM.
"BUT DO NOT BE DECEIVED YOURSELF, J'ONN. THE FIGHT IS NOT YET OVER.
YOUR FRIENDS ARE STILL AT KNOW MAN'S MERCY... AND I...
KOFF
...I HAVE DONE ALL I CAN.
THE WORLD WAS MINE, J'ONN. IT WAS ALL I EVER WANTED... AND MORE THAN I COULD BEAR.

FUNNY.

POWER... IS SUCH... AN ILLUSION...

DIANA...?

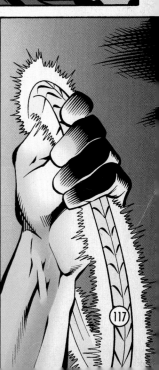

117

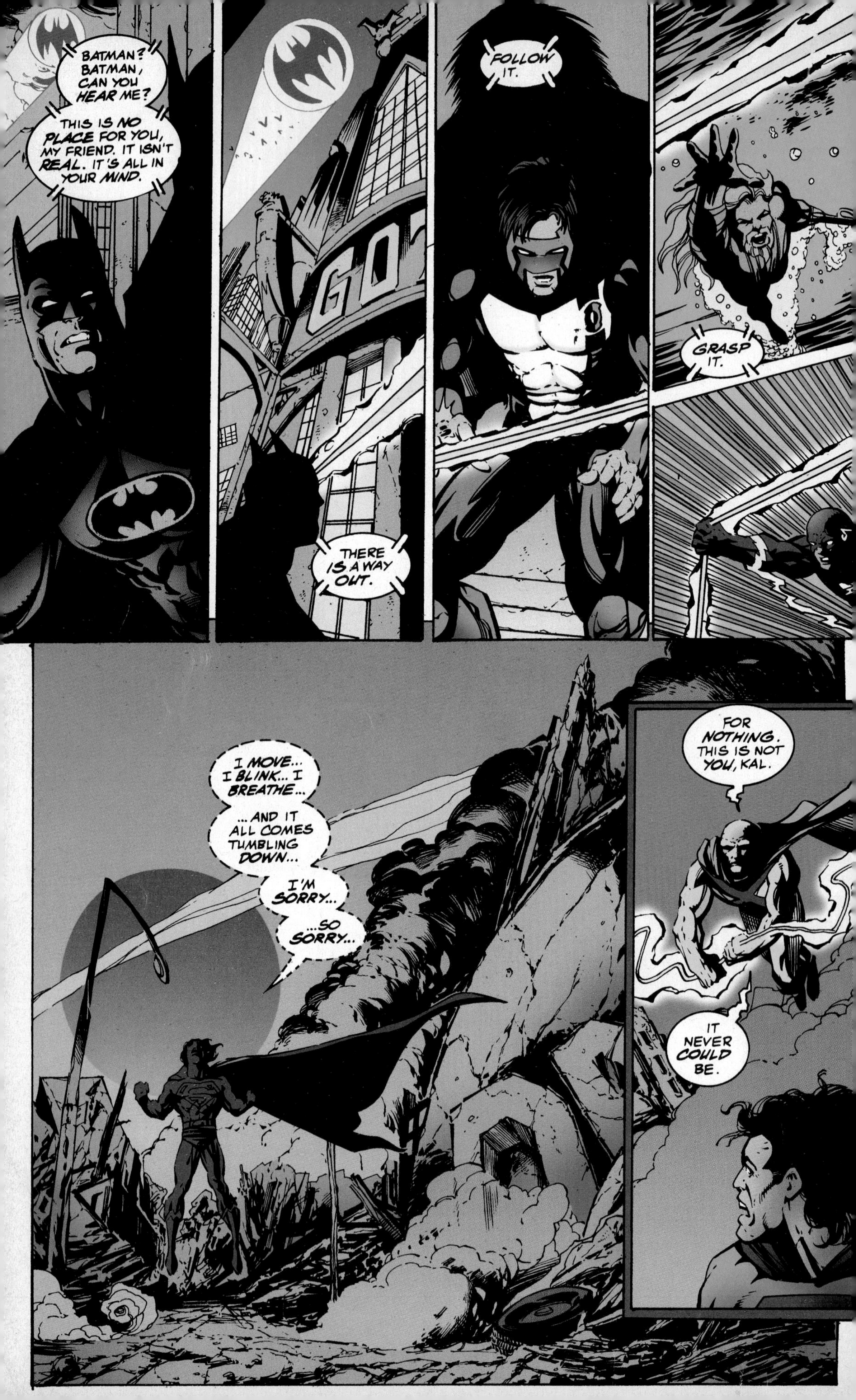
BATMAN? BATMAN, CAN YOU HEAR ME?
THIS IS NO PLACE FOR YOU, MY FRIEND. IT ISN'T REAL. IT'S ALL IN YOUR MIND.
THERE IS A WAY OUT.
FOLLOW IT.
GRASP IT.
I MOVE... I BLINK... I BREATHE...
...AND IT ALL COMES TUMBLING DOWN...
I'M SORRY...
...SO SORRY...
FOR NOTHING. THIS IS NOT YOU, KAL.
IT NEVER COULD BE.

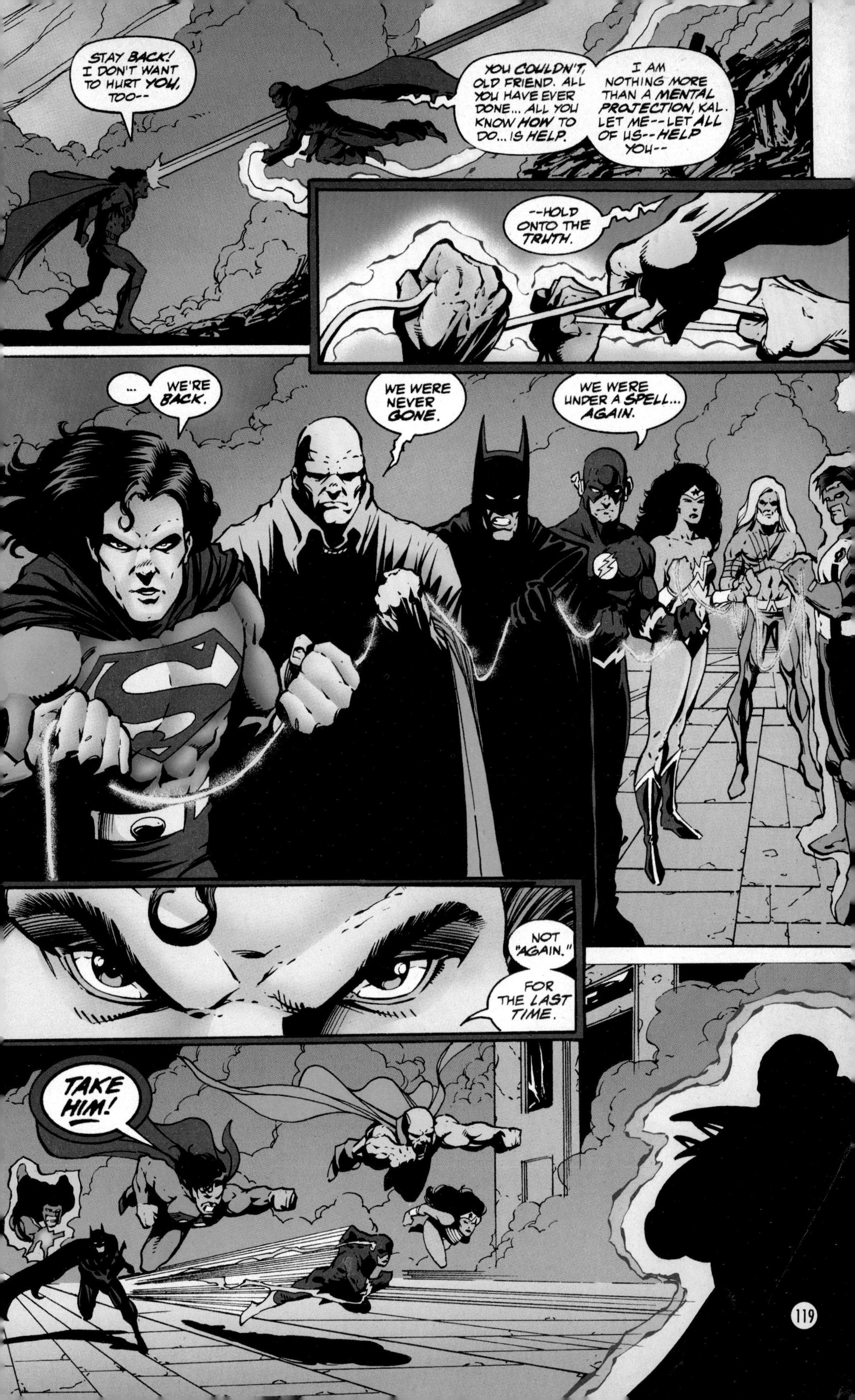
STAY BACK! I DON'T WANT TO HURT YOU, TOO--
YOU COULDN'T, OLD FRIEND. ALL YOU HAVE EVER DONE... ALL YOU KNOW HOW TO DO... IS HELP.
I AM NOTHING MORE THAN A MENTAL PROJECTION, KAL. LET ME--LET ALL OF US--HELP YOU--
--HOLD ONTO THE TRUTH.
...WE'RE BACK.
WE WERE NEVER GONE.
WE WERE UNDER A SPELL... AGAIN.
NOT "AGAIN."
FOR THE LAST TIME.
TAKE HIM!

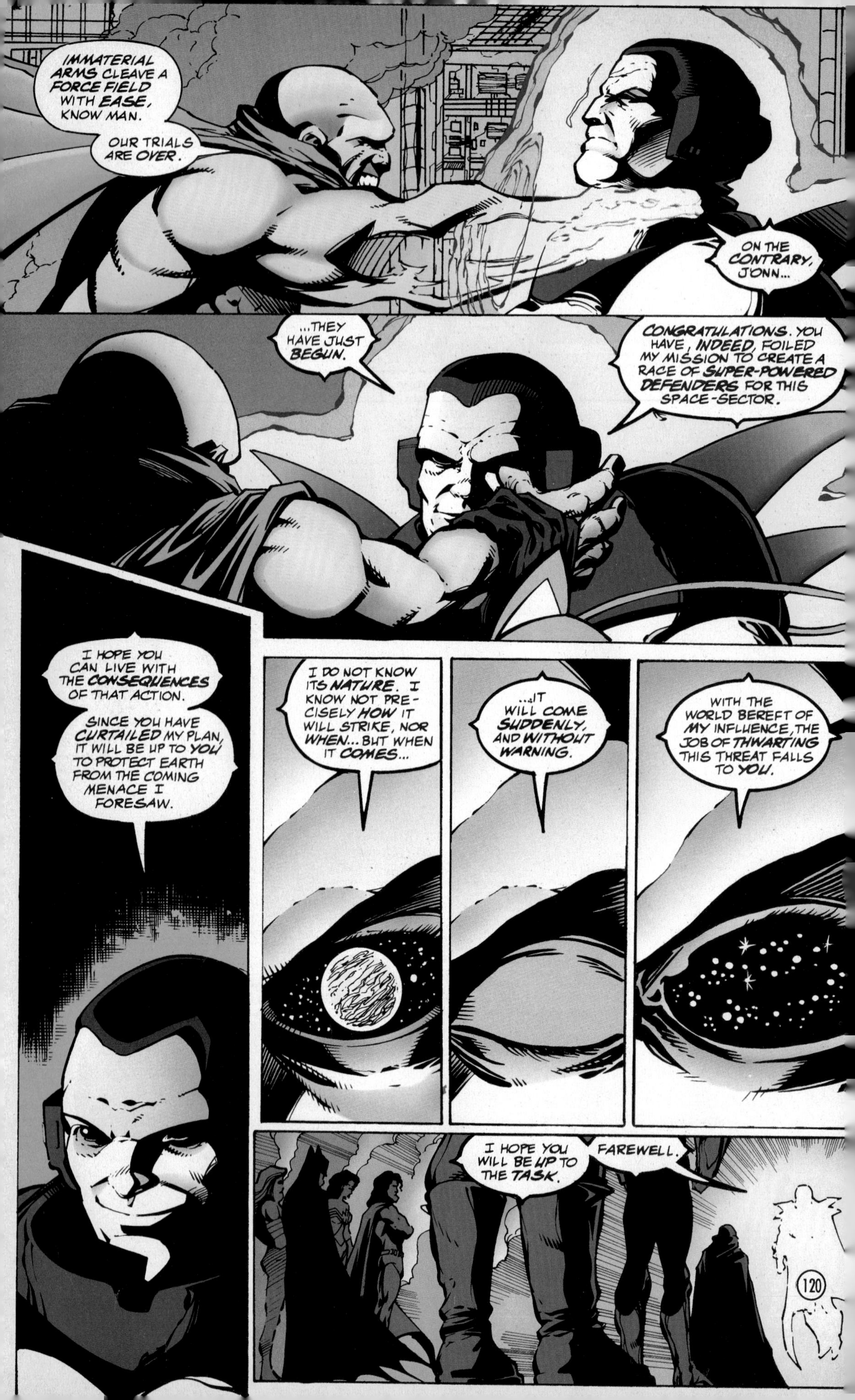
IMMATERIAL ARMS CLEAVE A FORCE FIELD WITH EASE, KNOW MAN.
OUR TRIALS ARE OVER.
ON THE CONTRARY, J'ONN...
...THEY HAVE JUST BEGUN.
CONGRATULATIONS. YOU HAVE, INDEED, FOILED MY MISSION TO CREATE A RACE OF SUPER-POWERED DEFENDERS FOR THIS SPACE-SECTOR.
I HOPE YOU CAN LIVE WITH THE CONSEQUENCES OF THAT ACTION.
SINCE YOU HAVE CURTAILED MY PLAN, IT WILL BE UP TO YOU TO PROTECT EARTH FROM THE COMING MENACE I FORESAW.
I DO NOT KNOW ITS NATURE. I KNOW NOT PRECISELY HOW IT WILL STRIKE, NOR WHEN... BUT WHEN IT COMES...
...IT WILL COME SUDDENLY, AND WITHOUT WARNING.
WITH THE WORLD BEREFT OF MY INFLUENCE, THE JOB OF THWARTING THIS THREAT FALLS TO YOU.
I HOPE YOU WILL BE UP TO THE TASK.
FAREWELL.

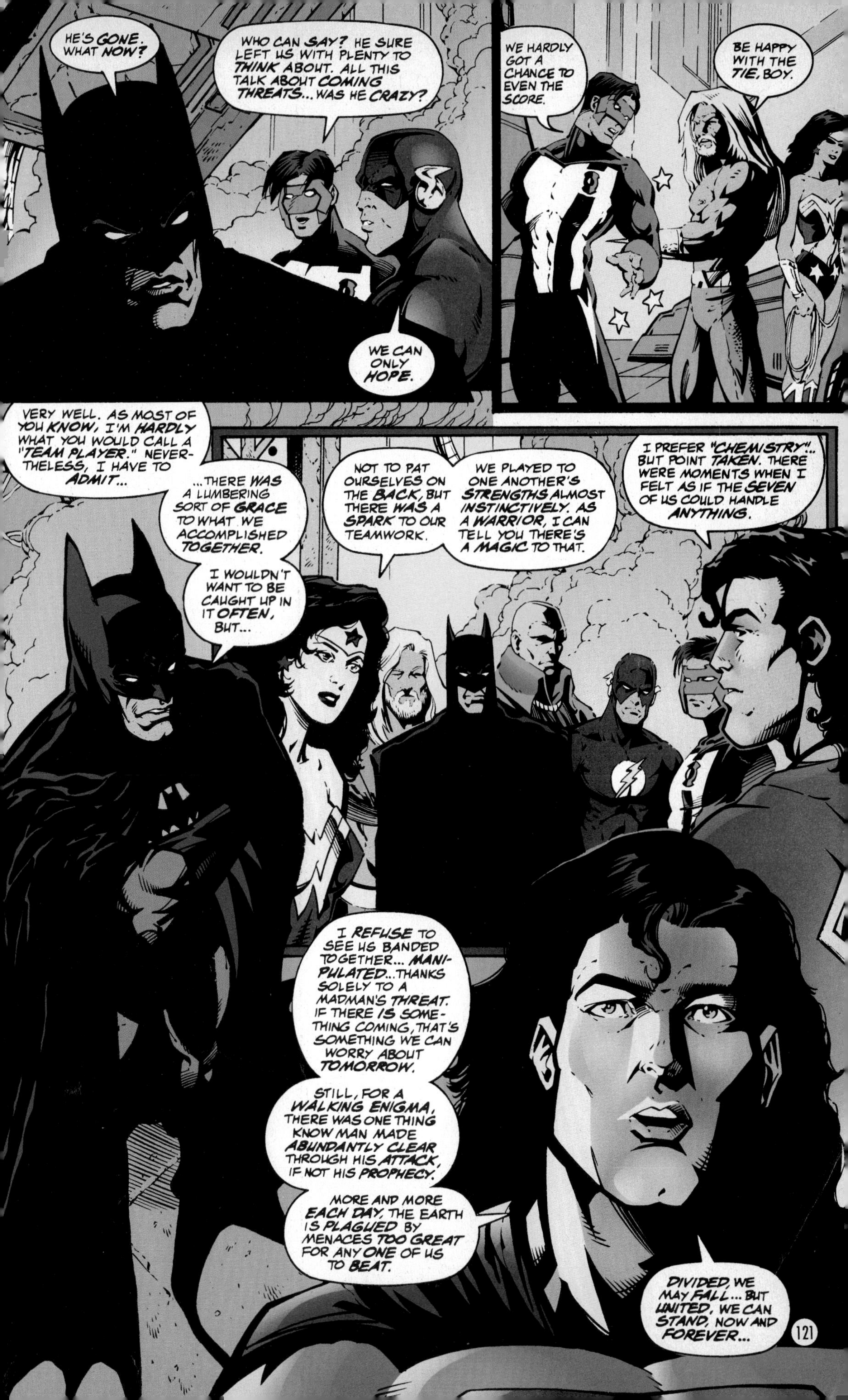
HE'S GONE. WHAT NOW?
WHO CAN SAY? HE SURE LEFT US WITH PLENTY TO THINK ABOUT. ALL THIS TALK ABOUT COMING THREATS... WAS HE CRAZY?
WE CAN ONLY HOPE.
WE HARDLY GOT A CHANCE TO EVEN THE SCORE.
BE HAPPY WITH THE TIE, BOY.
VERY WELL. AS MOST OF YOU KNOW, I'M HARDLY WHAT YOU WOULD CALL A "TEAM PLAYER." NEVERTHELESS, I HAVE TO ADMIT...
...THERE WAS A LUMBERING SORT OF GRACE TO WHAT WE ACCOMPLISHED TOGETHER.
I WOULDN'T WANT TO BE CAUGHT UP IN IT OFTEN, BUT...
NOT TO PAT OURSELVES ON THE BACK, BUT THERE WAS A SPARK TO OUR TEAMWORK.
WE PLAYED TO ONE ANOTHER'S STRENGTHS ALMOST INSTINCTIVELY. AS A WARRIOR, I CAN TELL YOU THERE'S A MAGIC TO THAT.
I PREFER "CHEMISTRY"... BUT POINT TAKEN. THERE WERE MOMENTS WHEN I FELT AS IF THE SEVEN OF US COULD HANDLE ANYTHING.
I REFUSE TO SEE US BANDED TOGETHER... MANIPULATED... THANKS SOLELY TO A MADMAN'S THREAT. IF THERE IS SOMETHING COMING, THAT'S SOMETHING WE CAN WORRY ABOUT TOMORROW.
STILL, FOR A WALKING ENIGMA, THERE WAS ONE THING KNOW MAN MADE ABUNDANTLY CLEAR THROUGH HIS ATTACK, IF NOT HIS PROPHECY.
MORE AND MORE EACH DAY, THE EARTH IS PLAGUED BY MENACES TOO GREAT FOR ANY ONE OF US TO BEAT.
DIVIDED, WE MAY FALL... BUT UNITED, WE CAN STAND, NOW AND FOREVER...

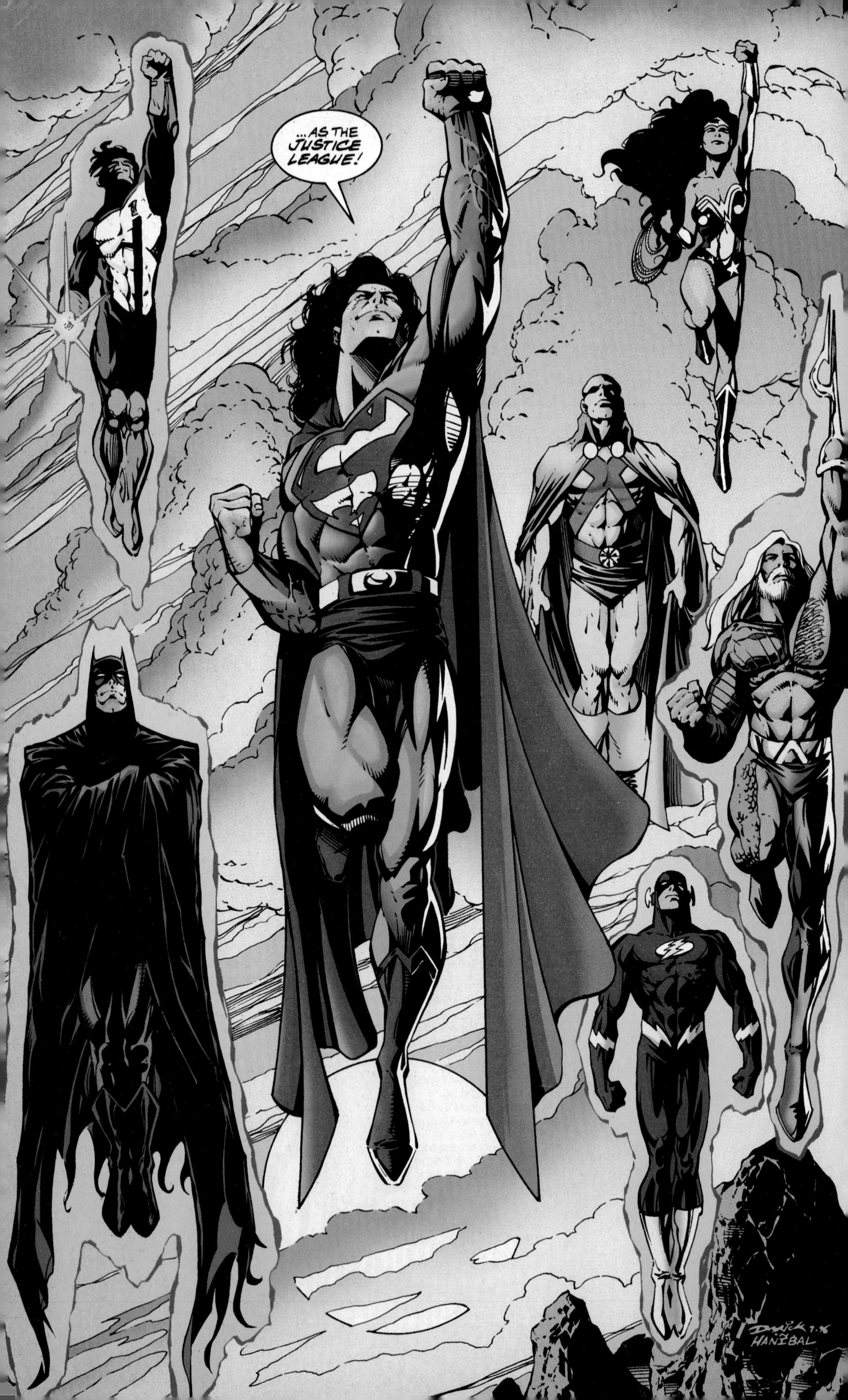
...AS THE JUSTICE LEAGUE!

Superman is the natural leader and the guiding light behind the new Justice League. In spite of his great power, however, he often feels guilty that he may not have as much time to devote to the League as he would like. He worries that it might all fall apart without him but can't help the fact that the demands of his role must take precedence over regular meetings and group bureaucracy. Superman in the Justice League is a slightly troubled individual, putting on a brave front to inspire the others but knowing all the time that he's perhaps bitten off a little more than he can chew. He realizes that he's established something he can't really take as much responsibility for as he might wish, and that becomes a source of mild frustration for him.

SUPERMAN

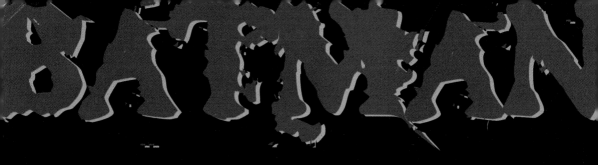

Batman's always been uncomfortable as a team player and regards many of the other super-heroes as amateurs with no training and no real discipline. With their superhuman abilities to protect them, they can afford to wear too-bright costumes and take stupid chances. As far as he's concerned, the last thing he needs is to run around with a bunch of gaudy, devil-may-care ringslingers and super-speedsters, in the midst of whom he's little more than a good target. Swayed by Superman's involvement, however, Batman is a reluctant Justice League member but will only really get involved if the situation absolutely merits it. He's characterized by a supreme confidence in himself and his abilities. There is no problem he cannot solve, and even when he cannot participate in an adventure, he takes the invaluable role of consultant for the League.

As the only woman on the team, Wonder Woman is well aware that she is one of the few super-heroines able to hold her own among the iconic powerhouses who make up the Justice League roster. Nevertheless, deep down she rather enjoys the status of being the only female on the team and showing her superiority over the team members who don't quite have a handle on the warrior spirit she both admires and embodies. Of all her colleagues, she is closest in spirit to Aquaman and gets along surprisingly well with him.

Wally West, unlike his predecessor and mentor, Barry Allen, has worked in team situations for most of his super-hero career. The ups and downs of that career and his years of experience make him one of the most level-headed members of the Justice League. He's the consummate "professional" super-hero, always on hand to keep up morale and raise team spirit. His super-speed gives him the luxury of time—time to talk to the others about problems, time to keep an eye on the group dynamic and ensure that everyone's working together to the best of their abilities. In this sense, he's the natural second-in-command after Superman, but where Superman can't help being a little lofty and remote, the Flash is there with the human touch. He's the fluid medium that binds the team together.

THE FLASH

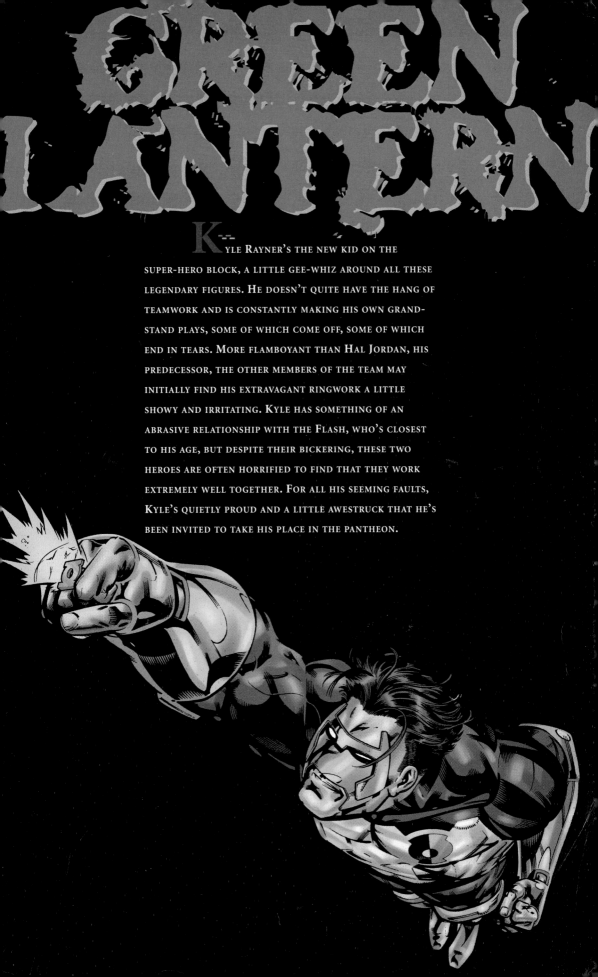

GREEN LANTERN

KYLE RAYNER'S THE NEW KID ON THE SUPER-HERO BLOCK, A LITTLE GEE-WHIZ AROUND ALL THESE LEGENDARY FIGURES. HE DOESN'T QUITE HAVE THE HANG OF TEAMWORK AND IS CONSTANTLY MAKING HIS OWN GRAND-STAND PLAYS, SOME OF WHICH COME OFF, SOME OF WHICH END IN TEARS. MORE FLAMBOYANT THAN HAL JORDAN, HIS PREDECESSOR, THE OTHER MEMBERS OF THE TEAM MAY INITIALLY FIND HIS EXTRAVAGANT RINGWORK A LITTLE SHOWY AND IRRITATING. KYLE HAS SOMETHING OF AN ABRASIVE RELATIONSHIP WITH THE FLASH, WHO'S CLOSEST TO HIS AGE, BUT DESPITE THEIR BICKERING, THESE TWO HEROES ARE OFTEN HORRIFIED TO FIND THAT THEY WORK EXTREMELY WELL TOGETHER. FOR ALL HIS SEEMING FAULTS, KYLE'S QUIETLY PROUD AND A LITTLE AWESTRUCK THAT HE'S BEEN INVITED TO TAKE HIS PLACE IN THE PANTHEON.

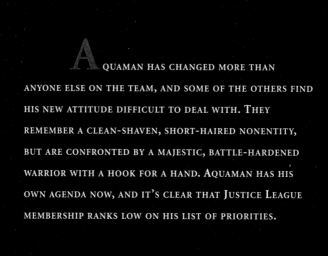

AQUAMAN HAS CHANGED MORE THAN ANYONE ELSE ON THE TEAM, AND SOME OF THE OTHERS FIND HIS NEW ATTITUDE DIFFICULT TO DEAL WITH. THEY REMEMBER A CLEAN-SHAVEN, SHORT-HAIRED NONENTITY, BUT ARE CONFRONTED BY A MAJESTIC, BATTLE-HARDENED WARRIOR WITH A HOOK FOR A HAND. AQUAMAN HAS HIS OWN AGENDA NOW, AND IT'S CLEAR THAT JUSTICE LEAGUE MEMBERSHIP RANKS LOW ON HIS LIST OF PRIORITIES.

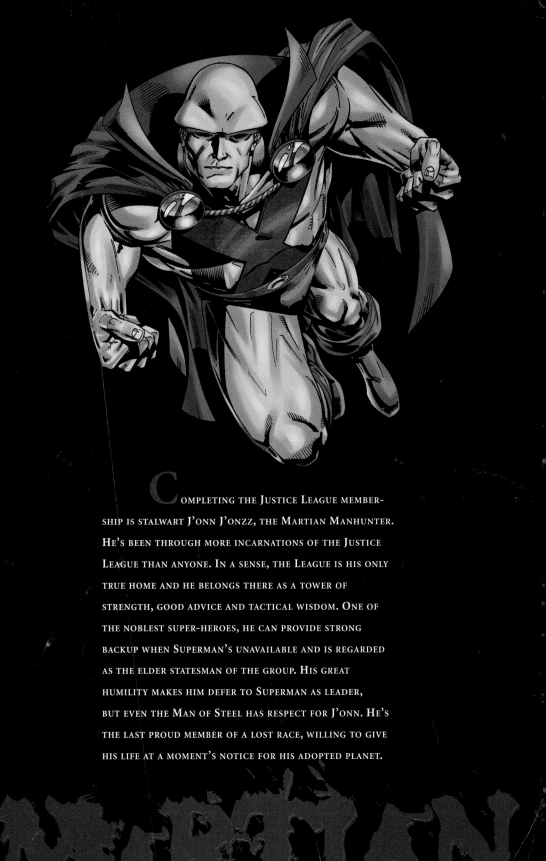

COMPLETING THE JUSTICE LEAGUE MEMBER-
SHIP IS STALWART J'ONN J'ONZZ, THE MARTIAN MANHUNTER.
HE'S BEEN THROUGH MORE INCARNATIONS OF THE JUSTICE
LEAGUE THAN ANYONE. IN A SENSE, THE LEAGUE IS HIS ONLY
TRUE HOME AND HE BELONGS THERE AS A TOWER OF
STRENGTH, GOOD ADVICE AND TACTICAL WISDOM. ONE OF
THE NOBLEST SUPER-HEROES, HE CAN PROVIDE STRONG
BACKUP WHEN SUPERMAN'S UNAVAILABLE AND IS REGARDED
AS THE ELDER STATESMAN OF THE GROUP. HIS GREAT
HUMILITY MAKES HIM DEFER TO SUPERMAN AS LEADER,
BUT EVEN THE MAN OF STEEL HAS RESPECT FOR J'ONN. HE'S
THE LAST PROUD MEMBER OF A LOST RACE, WILLING TO GIVE
HIS LIFE AT A MOMENT'S NOTICE FOR HIS ADOPTED PLANET.

MARTIAN
MANHUNTER

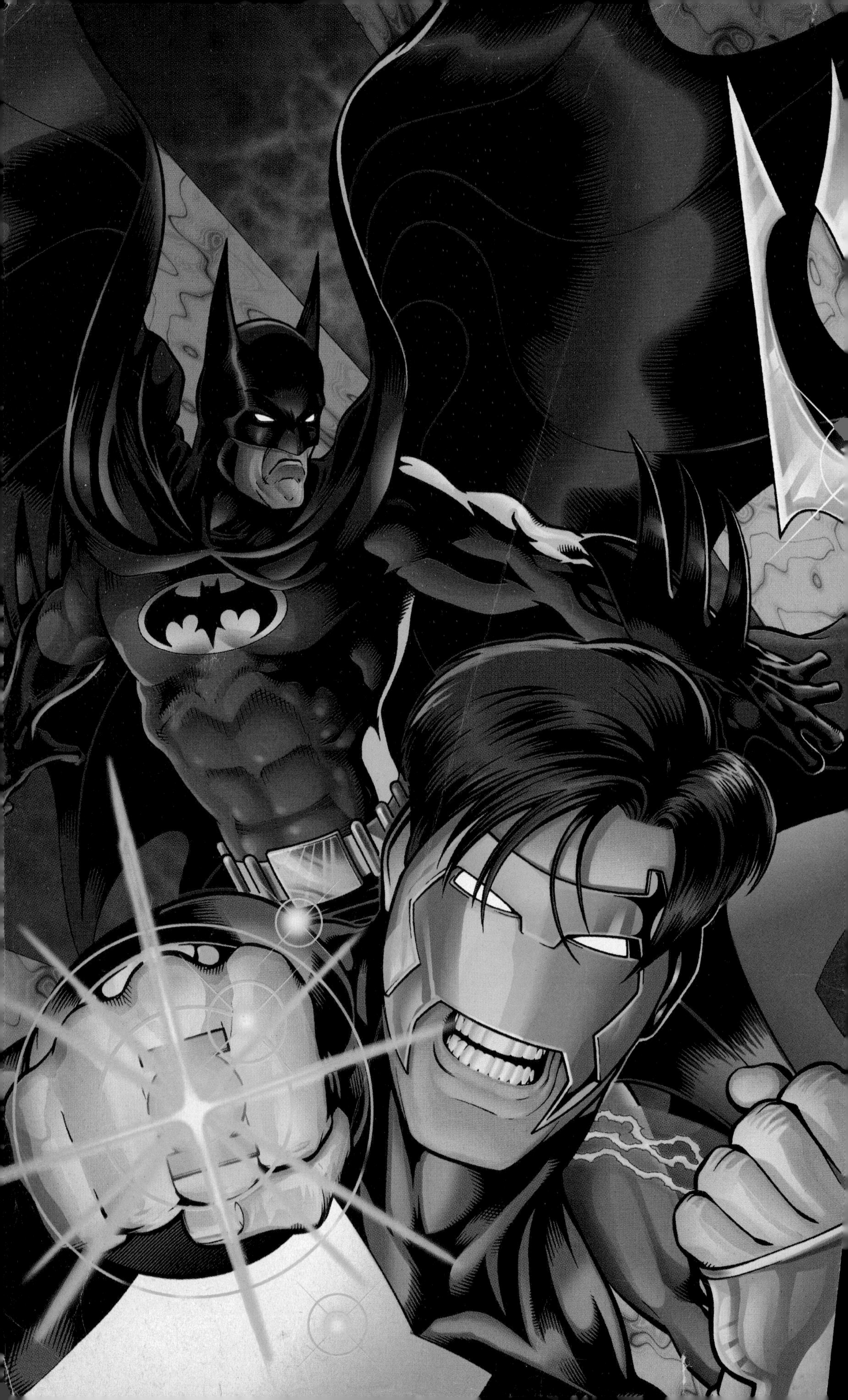

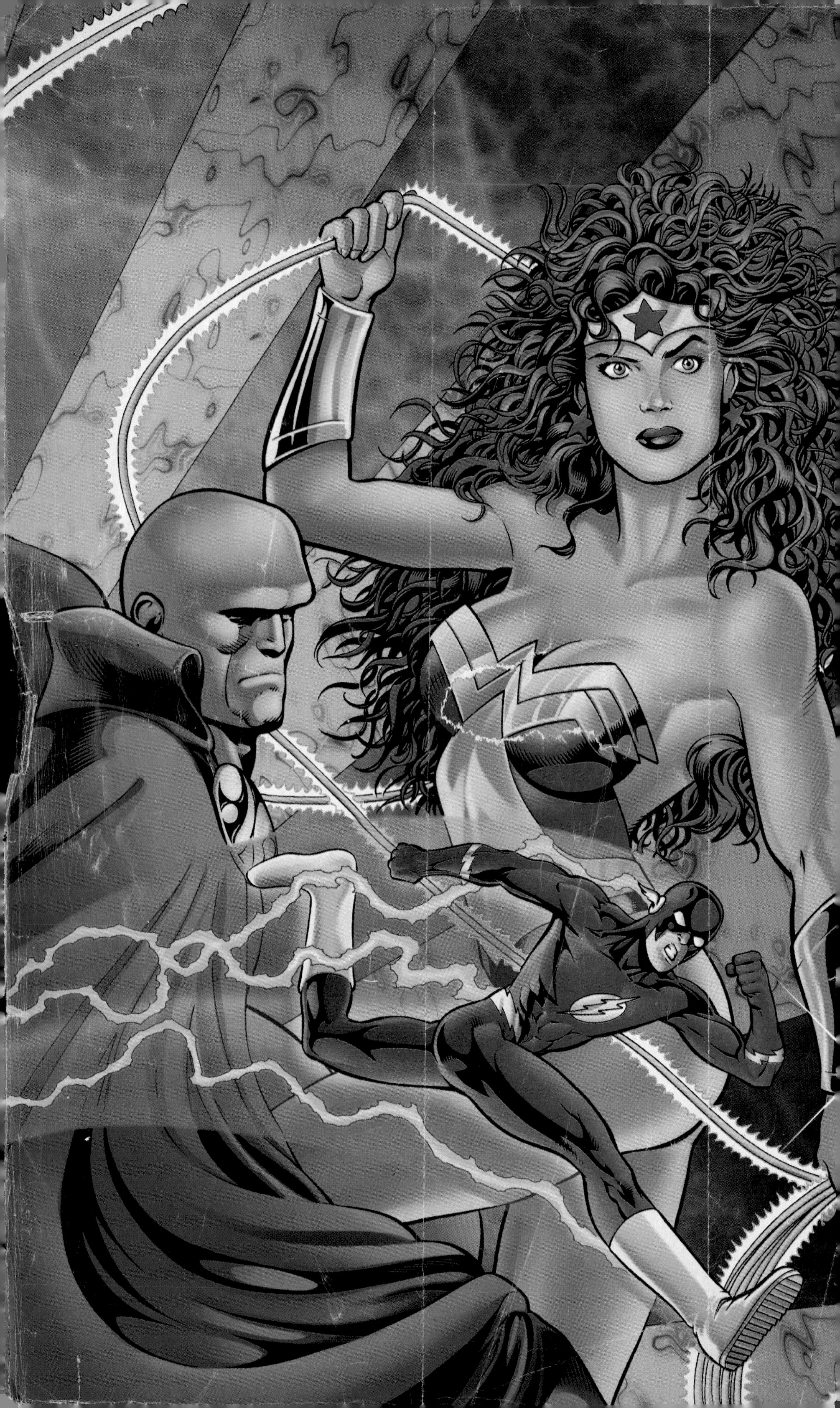

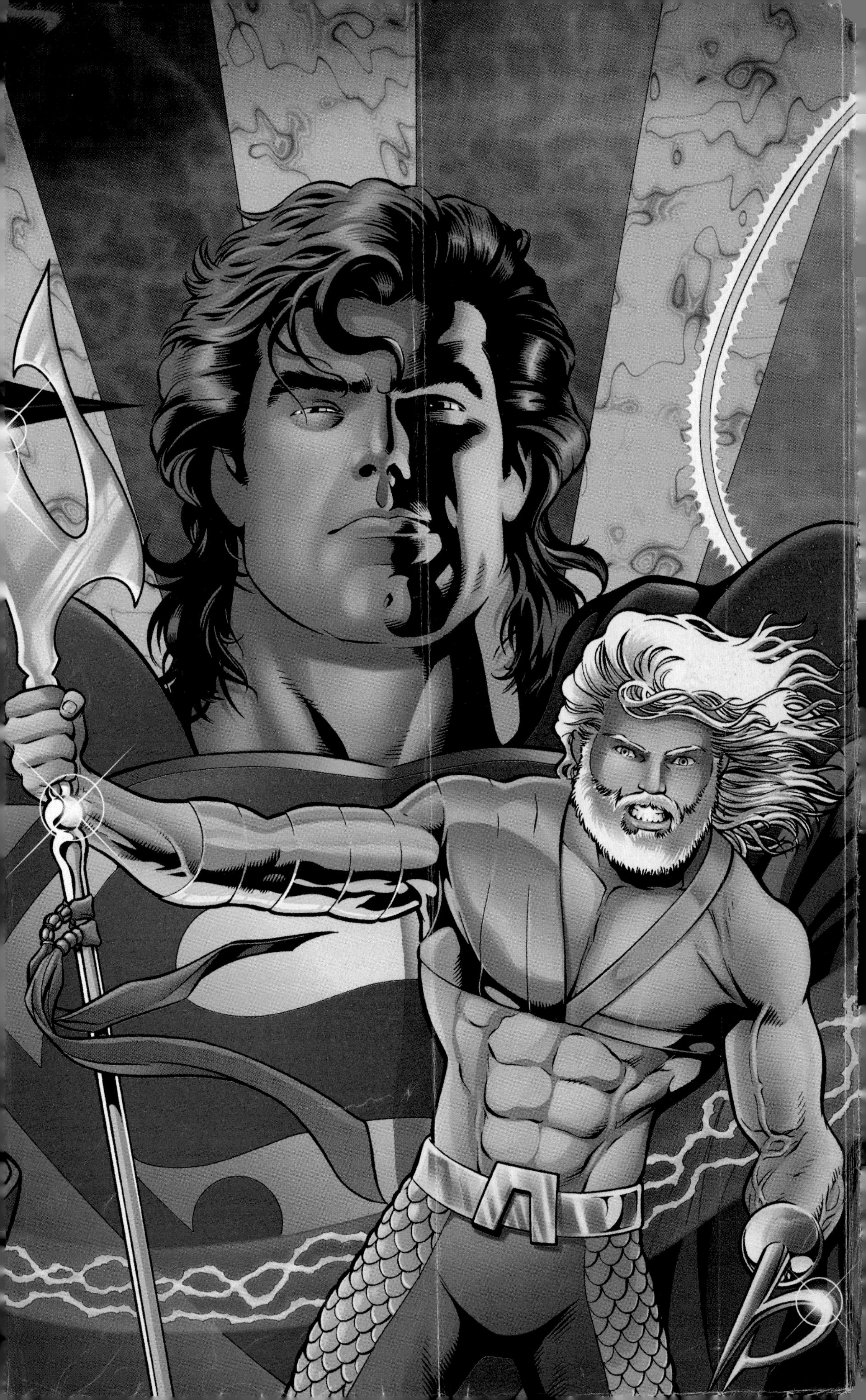

THE STARS OF THE DC UNIVERSE CAN ALSO BE FOUND IN THESE BOOKS:

GRAPHIC NOVELS

DARKSEID VS. GALACTUS: THE HUNGER
John Byrne

ENEMY ACE: WAR IDYLL
George Pratt

GREEN LANTERN: GANTHET'S TALE
Larry Niven/John Byrne

GREEN LANTERN/SILVER SURFER
Ron Marz/Darryl Banks/Terry Austin

JLA/WILDC.A.T.S: CRIME MACHINE
Grant Morrison/Val Semeiks/Kevin Conrad

JUSTICE RIDERS
Chuck Dixon/J.H. Williams/Mick Gray

THE POWER OF SHAZAM!
Jerry Ordway

TITANS: SCISSORS, PAPER, STONE
Adam Warren/Tom Simmons/Joe Rosas

COLLECTIONS

AQUAMAN: TIME & TIDE
Peter David/Kirk Jarvinen/Brad Vancata

THE AMALGAM AGE OF COMICS: THE DC COMICS COLLECTION
Various writers and artists

DC VERSUS MARVEL/MARVEL VERSUS DC
Ron Marz/Peter David/Dan Jurgens/Claudio Castellini/Josef Rubinstein/Paul Neary

THE FLASH: THE RETURN OF BARRY ALLEN
Mark Waid/Greg LaRocque/Roy Richardson

THE GOLDEN AGE
James Robinson/Paul Smith/Richard Ory

THE GREATEST 1950s STORIES EVER TOLD
Various writers and artists

THE GREATEST TEAM-UP STORIES EVER TOLD
Various writers and artists

HAWK & DOVE
Karl & Barbara Kesel/Rob Liefeld

HITMAN
Garth Ennis/John McCrea

IMPULSE: RECKLESS YOUTH
Mark Waid/Humberto Ramos/Wayne Faucher/various

JUSTICE LEAGUE: A MIDSUMMER'S NIGHTMARE
Mark Waid/Fabian Nicieza/Jeff Johnson/Darick Robertson/John Holdredge/Hanibal Rodriguez

JUSTICE LEAGUE: A NEW BEGINNING
Keith Giffen/J. M. DeMatteis/Kevin Maguire

JUSTICE LEAGUE: NEW WORLD ORDER
Grant Morrison/Howard Porter/John Dell

KINGDOM COME
Mark Waid/Alex Ross

LEGENDS: THE COLLECTED EDITION
John Ostrander/Len Wein/John Byrne/Karl Kesel

LOBO'S GREATEST HITS
Various writers and artists

LOBO: THE LAST CZARNIAN
Keith Giffen/Alan Grant/Simon Bisley

LOBO'S BACK'S BACK
Keith Giffen/Alan Grant/Simon Bisley/Christian Alamy

RETURN TO THE AMALGAM AGE OF COMICS: THE DC COMICS COLLECTION
Various writers and artists

THE RAY: IN A BLAZE OF POWER
Jack C. Harris/Joe Quesada/Art Nichols

SOVEREIGN SEVEN
Chris Claremont/Dwayne Turner/Jerome Moore/various

THE SPECTRE: CRIMES AND PUNISHMENTS
John Ostrander/Tom Mandrake

STARMAN: NIGHT AND DAY
James Robinson/Tony Harris/Wade von Grawbadger

STARMAN: SINS OF THE FATHER
James Robinson/Tony Harris/Wade von Grawbadger

WONDER WOMAN: THE CONTEST
William Messner-Loebs/Mike Deodato, Jr.

WONDER WOMAN: THE CHALLENGE OF ARTEMIS
William Messner-Loebs/Mike Deodato, Jr.

WONDER WOMAN: SECOND GENESIS
John Byrne

ZERO HOUR: CRISIS IN TIME
Dan Jurgens/Jerry Ordway

OTHER COLLECTIONS OF INTEREST

CAMELOT 3000
Mike W. Barr/Brian Bolland

RONIN
Frank Miller

WATCHMEN
Alan Moore/Dave Gibbons

ARCHIVE EDITIONS

ALL STAR COMICS ARCHIVES Volume 1
(ALL STAR COMICS 3-6)
Various writers and artists

ALL STAR COMICS ARCHIVES Volume 2
(ALL STAR COMICS 7-10)
Various writers and artists

ALL STAR COMICS ARCHIVES Volume 3
(ALL STAR COMICS 11-14)
Various writers and artists

THE FLASH ARCHIVES Volume 1
(The Scarlet Speedster's adventures from FLASH COMICS 104, SHOWCASE 4, 8, 13, 14, and THE FLASH 105-108)
John Broome/Robert Kanigher/Carmine Infantino/Frank Giacoia/Joe Giella/Joe Kubert

JUSTICE LEAGUE OF AMERICA ARCHIVES Volume 1
(THE BRAVE AND THE BOLD 28-30 and JUSTICE LEAGUE OF AMERICA 1-6)
Gardner Fox/Mike Sekowsky/various

JUSTICE LEAGUE OF AMERICA ARCHIVES Volume 2
(JUSTICE LEAGUE OF AMERICA 7-14)
Gardner Fox/Mike Sekowsky/various

JUSTICE LEAGUE OF AMERICA ARCHIVES Volume 3
(JUSTICE LEAGUE OF AMERICA 15-22)
Gardner Fox/Mike Sekowsky/various

LEGION OF SUPER-HEROES ARCHIVES Volume 1
(The Legion of Super-Heroes' adventures from ADVENTURE COMICS 247, 267, 282, 290, 293, 300-305, ACTION COMICS 267, 276, 287, 289, SUPERBOY 86, 89, 98 and SUPERMAN 147)
Various writers and artists

LEGION OF SUPER-HEROES ARCHIVES Volume 2
(The Legion of Super-Heroes' adventures from ADVENTURE COMICS 306-317 and SUPERMAN'S PAL, JIMMY OLSEN 72)
Various writers and artists

LEGION OF SUPER-HEROES ARCHIVES Volume 3
(The Legion of Super-Heroes' adventures from ADVENTURE COMICS 318-328, SUPERMAN'S PAL, JIMMY OLSEN 76 and SUPERBOY 117)
Various writers and artists

LEGION OF SUPER-HEROES ARCHIVES Volume 4
(The Legion of Super-Heroes' adventures from ADVENTURE COMICS 329-339 and SUPERBOY 124-125)
Various writers and artists

LEGION OF SUPER-HEROES ARCHIVES Volume 5
(The Legion of Super-Heroes' adventures from ADVENTURE COMICS 340-349)
Various writers and artists

LEGION OF SUPER-HEROES ARCHIVES Volume 6
(The Legion of Super-Heroes' adventures from ADVENTURE COMICS 350-358)
Various writers and artists

LEGION OF SUPER-HEROES ARCHIVES Volume 7
(The Legion of Super-Heroes' adventures from ADVENTURE COMICS 359-367 and SUPERMAN'S PAL, JIMMY OLSEN 106)
Various writers and artists

For the nearest comics shop carrying collected editions and monthly titles from DC Comics, call 1-888-COMIC BOOK.

971031